LOSING
PATIENCE

LOSING PATIENCE

The Problems, Alarms and Psychological
Issues of Shaken Baby Syndrome

James Peinkofer, LCSW

New Horizon Press
Far Hills, New Jersey

Requests for permission should be addressed to:
New Horizon Press
P. O. Box 669
Far Hills, NJ 07931

James Peinkofer, LCSW
    Losing Patience:
    The Problems, Alarms and Psychological Issues of Shaken Baby Syndrome

Cover design: Wendy Bass
Interior design: Scribe Inc.

Library of Congress Control Number: 2014930466

ISBN-13 (paperback): 978-0-88282-478-9
ISBN-13 (eBook): 978-0-88282-479-6

New Horizon Press

Manufactured in the U. S. A.

2018   2017   2016   2015   2014   1   2   3   4   5

Dedicated to Norman Guthkelch, MD
In Memory of Alda and Richard Peinkofer

AUTHOR'S NOTE

Though the American Academy of Pediatrics recommends that the term "Abusive Head Trauma" be used to incorporate a wide range of abuse to an infant's head (shaking, impact, etc.), I use the lay term "Shaken Baby Syndrome" for this presentation as it is a concept that is most widely-known, as well as the focus of the mechanism for injury that I present. There has been a significant amount of media attention given to Shaken Baby Syndrome in the past several years and alarmists are sounding the proverbial gong that shaking a baby has no ill effect on a young brain or body, much less being a reason for death. As you will see throughout this book, Shaken Baby Syndrome is real, damaging and potentially lethal.

This book is based on the author's research, personal experiences, interviews and real life experiences. For purposes of simplifying usage, the pronouns his/her and s/he are sometimes used interchangeably. The information contained herein is not meant to be a substitute for evaluation and therapy with mental health professionals.

CONTENTS

Introduction

I will always remember where I was and how I felt when I read my first medical journal article on Shaken Baby Syndrome. I was in the cafeteria of the hospital where I was a pediatric social worker. Our hospital got a few child abuse cases each month, but the hospital on the other side of town seemed to be the primary center for child welfare cases. I had not experienced having a shaken baby within our hospital walls—yet. I had only been in pediatrics for several months. I had pushed for this position, since I had an infant son myself. I wanted to jump into the world of caring for babies—the good and the bad—feet first.

The article "Shaken Baby Syndrome" by Richard Spaide and his team was, for me, a shocking clinical exposé on the dark world into which I was about to launch myself. It was the morning of a bright summer day when I sat in the hospital's cafeteria alone to read the article. Spaide's paper initially discussed the history of the syndrome and then delved into the physiology of the infant brain: its soft, gelatin-like consistency, its nerves and veins loosely attached. The author then described how he believed an actual shaking event occurred.[1] What Spaide detailed sickened me.

I remember pausing to put the pages down on the table in front of me, in order to reflect and to distance myself from the violence. I couldn't believe that such brutality was possible, that it was truly possible for men and women to do such a horrible thing to a tiny human being who was so vulnerable. After I finished reading this article, I read hundreds more in the years ahead. I also experienced real-life events brought on by shaking abuse. I came to see the dark side of caregiving. Over the years, I built emotional armor to wear. The armor was my professional protection for myself, my shield as I looked people in the eye who could be lying to me about shaking their baby.

PART 1

SBS Exposed

CHAPTER 1

What Is Shaken Baby Syndrome?

"A father was arrested and charged Wednesday with reckless homicide in the July shaking death of his infant daughter," the *South Bend Tribune* reported. "Steve Edward Gill, 21, was arrested after an Elkhart County Circuit Court grand jury returned an indictment late Tuesday, according to the Elkhart County prosecutor's office...His daughter, Patience Gill..., died July 30 at Memorial Hospital in South Bend at the age of seven weeks, according to the death notice published at the time...The grand jury met all day Tuesday and heard testimony from many witnesses before returning the indictment."[1]

It was a perfect storm that came together in July 2000 at the Gill home: A young father, who fit the profile of a caregiver most at risk to use shaking as a method of controlling an out-of-control situation. An infant, whose own victimology placed her in harm's way, through no fault of her own. Patience was communicating a need. At seven weeks of age, she was on the cusp of using crying as her primary method of that communication. But her father didn't speak the same language. He couldn't tell what she wanted and became more and more frustrated by her screams, which would escalate, as would his anxiety. He had no one to turn to in order to give him support or a break from the constant crying. He may have used one or two methods to attempt to soothe his daughter, but they failed. He didn't want to fail. He wanted to be viewed as a father who could handle any situation. He was the one left to take care of her. Leaving the house for a half-hour wasn't an option. What would people think if he did that? He'd be a failure as a caregiver, as a father. Instead, he took his daughter into his hands to control the situation, to make the crying stop.

Final Diagnosis of Patience Gill

1. Craniocerebral trauma:
   a. Left cheek contusions
   b. Subscalpular contusions, posterior (occipital) and left parietal skull
   c. No skull or facial bone fractures
   d. Diffuse subdural hemorrhage
   e. Scattered subarachnoid hemorrhages
   f. Marked cerebral edema
   g. Bilateral optic nerve hemorrhages
   h. Diffuse axonal injury
   i. Retinal hemorrhages
   j. Deep posterior neck hemorrhage, small
2. No other injuries identified.

Cause of Death:

Craniocerebral trauma

Manner of Death:

Homicide

Every year, thousands of infants and children are shaken by parents and caregivers. The exact numbers are unknown, as there is no database of Shaken Baby Syndrome (SBS) cases, but cases are estimated to fall between 1,000 and 1,500 cases in the U.S. alone. Since many cases are missed diagnoses or are less traumatic, the actual numbers are most likely in the thousands. The missed cases may be ones that are not ruled as abusive or a child was shaken but not hospitalized, etc. So the estimated number is just a best guess. In 2003, Heather T. Keenan and her associates calculated that approximately three hundered children in the U.S. *died* from being shaken, which correlates with previous estimates of SBS deaths.

How can a child be injured so seriously by being shaken? A baby's head is larger than an adult's. It takes up approximately 25 percent of an infant's body weight. The head also tends to be floppy, since a baby does not initially have strong neck muscles. These muscles develop and strengthen over time. A large, floppy head makes the forces of shaking severe. It also affects the forces of impact (if impact occurs after shaking).

The damage of shaking occurs within the fragile organs of a child. Shaking tears apart an infant's developing brain, which is soft and rapidly growing. Across the brain, the connective bridging veins are loosely attached, so when a whipping motion occurs during shaking, the resultant combination is very destructive and potentially lethal for an infant or child. Another injury that occurs from violent shaking is retinal hemorrhage. The eye nestles as a globe within the socket and shaking causes a pulling at the back of the eye, which is where the retina is. This extreme pulling causes tiny hemorrhages throughout the entire retina. These widespread hemorrhages cannot be seen with the naked eye; a trained ophthalmologist is needed for an examination. The physiology of the brain and eye will be explained in greater detail in the next chapter.

Who is shaken? Sixty percent of the victims are male. It is presumed that the reason for this is the perpetrator believes a male child should not cry—even though the child is simply communicating a need. Crying is the number one trigger to initiate a shaking event. For toddlers, the trigger is typically a behavioral one, such as toilet training or temper tantrums. The average age of victims is six months. In the victimology chapter, I will explain the reasons why certain children are targeted to be shaken.

In terms of injury from shaking, only 20 percent come out of the shaking with a "positive" outcome. Approximately 60 percent have lifelong physical consequences—blindness, mental retardation, paralysis and permanent disability. There is a 20 to 25 percent death rate. Male perpetrators have been found to be more lethal shakers.

Besides intracranial bleeding and retinal hemorrhages, shaking an infant or young child can cause cerebral edema, body fractures and other injuries. Research has not shown how severe the shaking must be to cause these injuries, so in prevention efforts, parents are cautioned to not shake babies *at all*. Perpetrator accounts and comparison studies to accidental injuries put the common injuries found in SBS in the violent to severe shaking arena. Light tossing, play, sudden movements, jostling and light shaking (captured in abuse videos) have been shown not to cause the high-level injuries diagnosed by clinicians.

Child abuse statistics for many parts of the world, including the United States, are indicative of worldwide trends. One study that captured what SBS is all about and that signalled the seriousness of the condition was a recent one from 2013. Thomas Niederkrotenthaler and his group found that shaking injuries were much more severe and more lethal than accidental head injuries. Using the new Centers for Disease Control and Prevention definition for abusive head trauma (AHT), they searched a children's hospital inpatient database and found the national rates for AHT were 39.8 per 100,000 population for children less than one year old and 6.8 per 100,000 population for children one year old. They reported the demographics of AHT as being: more often less than one year of age, male, enrolled in Medicaid, hospitalized longer, died during hospitalization, seen at children's hospitals and hospitals outside the Northeast.

The researchers recommended targeting socioeconomically disadvantaged families with children less than a year old who live in the South, Midwest and West for prevention purposes. The authors proposed that a more concentrated study of hospitals and hospital regions would be significant in reporting AHT injury.

Why do parents and caregivers shake children? There are multiple reasons, but ultimately it comes down to control as well as a lack thereof. It is a double-edged sword—a crying child who can't be soothed effectively and an out-of-control parent or caregiver. It is a punishment inflicted on someone who is completely vulnerable. Some individuals just don't care for infants and children and they are placed in a situation where they are alone with one without support. That can become very dangerous.

In taking the steps to charge and bring a perpetrator of SBS to court, there first needs to be a medical diagnosis. This can be a problem because doctors can come up with wrong diagnoses. Dr. Carol Jenny looked at missed diagnoses of SBS in the 1990s and found that ER and doctor's office visits missed signs that a baby had been shaken 30 percent of the time, especially if an infant had a moderate shaking event and was not in dire need of medical attention, but rather was fussy, irritable, vomiting, etc. These symptoms can be confused with a virus or other ailment, especially without the use of a CT scan to rule out head injury. Subsequent shakings in the home may cause more dramatic injuries because the abuser may dangerously assume that the baby wasn't really harmed by the initial shaking and he or she wasn't blamed for the abuse, so the baby is shaken again and the shaking is usually harder.

SBS is a tragedy that can be prevented. There are a plenty of ways to soothe a crying infant, just as there are signs of potential danger that parents can perceive when leaving their child with a caregiver. The chapters that follow will not only describe the history and physiology of SBS, but also how we are all affected legally, socially and emotionally by this deadly form of child abuse.

Elijah Fisher

My name is Emily Bodily and I am the Parent Spokesperson for the National Center on Shaken Baby Syndrome. My son was shaken in 1998 and, after putting up a valiant fight for four days, my precious son, Elijah, lost the fight and passed away.

The story begins when my son Elijah was sixteen months old and went for a visit with his biological father, Jason, for the weekend of December 19. My nightmare began with a phone call from Jason on the morning of Monday, December 21. He told me Elijah had fallen off the bed and stopped breathing, and the paramedics wanted to know which hospital to take Elijah to.

I went to the hospital and eventually was told my son had been shaken and would most likely not live. I have found this is the way most parents are thrown into the SBS abyss. Elijah struggled for four days, putting up a fight that looked promising to the outside world; however, in my heart, as his mother, I knew he was losing the fight and I was losing all strength to go on day after day and watching his little body only struggle more and more. On December 24, 1998, I told the doctors to take my son off life support and I knew he would not be able to take one single breath for himself.

I believe to this day that Jason loved Elijah, but what I did not and still don't understand is how he could have gotten so angry with such a precious little boy and use so much force on him. Jason told investigators he could not stop Elijah from crying and that became overwhelming and frustrating to him so he shook him.

In 1998, and currently, the National Center on Shaken Baby Syndrome tracks cases of SBS victims, especially local ones. When my child's case occurred, they came to offer support at the hearings and eventually asked if I would be interested in making a documentary that would be used to help educate parents and caregivers on the dangers of Shaken Baby Syndrome. We started filming the documentary in 1999, while the court hearings for Jason were still proceeding. I felt that the film was a way I could help the community and the world understand what happens with SBS victims, family members and so many more who are thrown into a world they knew nothing about and have no desire to learn about. The debut of Elijah's Story was in September of 2000 at the National Conference on Shaken Baby Syndrome. It was at that time I found that this video was going to be a very effective tool to use in the fight for shaken baby victims and families everywhere.

Whether your child survived this awful abuse or passed away, we as parents and family members go down paths that we never want to wish upon anyone. If your child did not survive, you are in mourning of all the wonderful things you will miss through the years. You have to somehow stay strong for the many trial dates you have and come up with the money to pay all different kinds of expenses for the funeral cost and medical bills. If your child survived, you will need to learn many medical procedures and keep a record of all medical issues going on with your child. You will more than likely become his personal nurse and have your days filled with doctor appointments. You will also mourn for the child you have lost, but rejoice in the smallest accomplishments.

If you are a parent or other family member reading this, I am not going to be able to tell you how you should feel or what to expect around any corner you may turn, because each victim, whether they survive or not, is different, and each family member or friend who must go through this deals with something different each time.

In my particular case, Elijah's father, Jason, ended up pleading guilty to a first-degree murder charge and was sentenced to twenty-five years to life in Utah State Prison. In his plea agreement he will be required to serve a minimum of twelve years. It is a sad thing to have to say, considering the other sentences that I have heard of, that I feel fortunate to have him in there for that length of time.

One of the things that has helped me get through this hell is that I had to come to grips regarding my anger towards Jason. I was not okay for many years, hating Jason the way I did. However, now coming up on the sixth anniversary of Elijah's death and expecting my first child since then, I now can say I don't hate Jason; I am very angry with Jason because in a matter of minutes he took so much away from me. But what is very important, which it took me at least two years after my son's death to realize, was that I am okay with being angry. I do not let it rule my life nor do I ever want to forget it all or "just get over it."

I invite you to explore our website, www.dontshake.org. You will find two other letters, one from a grandparent who is raising her granddaughter and one from a mother whose child was shaken by a daycare provider. I hope that each of these letters will help comfort you and give you some inspiration.

Nothing can change what has happened to you and it will take a long time to sort out your feelings about it all and find a way to move on in a positive way. My hope for any parent or family member experiencing this is that the anger will not rule your life. I have been able to find some positive ways to deal with my situation and anger by helping other parents and talking publicly about my personal experience.

—Emily Bodily

SBS CASE HOT SPOTS IN THE UNITED STATES

In November 2013, the Medill Justice Project published their study of U.S. counties that had the highest rates of shaken baby syndrome cases. These include: Douglas, Nebraska; Richmond, Georgia; Sarpy, Nebraska; Summit, Ohio and Weber, Utah. These counties were adjusted for population and found to have significantly higher rates than other U.S. counties. When looking at a statewide level, Nebraska ranked number one with the most SBS cases per 100,000 people, followed by Utah, Oklahoma, Wisconsin and Ohio.

Why do these particular counties in the U.S. have higher incidence rates than others? This is an unanswered question, but the report proposes that either some counties are better at identifying SBS cases and charging perpetrators or alternatively that there is a high number of caregivers who are violently shaking infants in those areas.

SBS AROUND THE WORLD

Over the past eleven years, the National Center on Shaken Baby Syndrome has hosted biannual conferences in countries including Australia, Japan, Canada, Scotland and France. Twenty years ago, SBS was recognized primarily in the U.S., Canada, Australia and the UK. Since then, recognition that shaking is used as a means of discipline has grown in terms of awareness in many more countries. There has been an increasing number of prevention initiatives around the world.

In 1999, the World Health Organization (WHO) estimated that 40 million children were subject to abuse and neglect. WHO does not separate SBS into its own entity; thus, countries are left to address or ignore shaking children as a problem. Recently, India has started to address SBS as a matter of concern. In a 2013 article, SH Subba and his associates rang the alarm bell of child abuse: "…The culture of corporal punishment is still viewed as normal and, when that crosses the line and becomes child battery, is not watched closely by any agency."

Child abuse is a rare occurrence in Sweden due to the ban on corporal punishment since the 1970s. A national survey of parents from 2011 found that 3 percent of the parents beat their children during the previous year, nine out of ten parents expressed negativity about corporal punishment of children and no parent of a child below one year of age claims to have shaken his or her child. In recent years, there were several cases where infants have been severely injured after being shaken by their parents, but this has led to special efforts being made to inform parents of the serious consequences shaking can have on children.

In 2001, the Canadian government developed a joint statement on SBS and proposed a population-based surveillance to establish the incidence of SBS and address risk factors for shaking. They also recommended prevention strategies for the general community, as well as those who are most vulnerable (this includes child development information, parenting programs and anger management).

Japan's incidence of SBS was recently highlighted in a journal article by K. Mori and his team. They found that Japan's most recent SBS trends had similar characteristics to their Western counterparts in terms of age of incidence, perpetrator (an increasing number of fathers) and birth defects as a trigger for SBS.

As the concept of Shaken Baby Syndrome continues to spread across the globe, hopefully prevention strategies will increase as well. Such programs need to be supported on a government level in order for increased awareness to be instilled in the general populace.

CHAPTER 2

The History of SBS

Many believe that shaking as a form of child abuse began in the 1970s, as the term is frequently referenced as having been "coined" during this era. However, shaking and the confessions of caregivers who performed this abuse began much earlier. Their accounts are key to understanding that shaking an infant or young child can be deadly. The media did not make shaking a household name until the 1950s, when the daughter of a Connecticut state senator confessed to shaking three infants to death and injuring many more. Let's look at some earlier stories.

The first reference to an abusive shaking that made headlines occurred in Kansas City, Missouri, in 1905. John David Stewart came home after work one evening and accused his wife of keeping their ten-month-old daughter quiet during the day and allowing her to cry at night. He was tired of it, so he "shook her hard and slammed her on the bed," and told his wife to take care of her. She later died. Stewart was arrested, convicted of fourth degree manslaughter and given a two-year prison sentence.[1]

The next account of a shaking incident occurred in Oneonta, New York, in 1937. Young Thomas Hinkley, Jr., age fifteen months, was shaken to death by Clyde Proctor, an unemployed truck driver who lived with the boy's mother. Proctor originally stated that the boy had fallen from a highchair (one of the first noted perpetrator excuses for an injury), which was accepted as fact by the Otsego County coroner. But further investigation by the District Attorney and Chief of Police found discrepancies in Proctor's story. Proctor stated that he witnessed the boy fall from the highchair as he looked through a window from the yard and that Mrs. Hinkley was out of the room for a moment, when, in fact, she was in town during the time of the "accident." Investigators brought these inconsistencies to Proctor's attention, and he ultimately confessed to shaking the boy, because the child had bitten him on the hand. Proctor was then arrested. He later pled guilty to first-degree manslaughter and was sentenced to ten years in prison.[2]

In 1938, James McCoy violently shook his five-month-old son, George, which landed the infant in the hospital in "poor condition with a broken neck." This was before CT scans and MRIs existed. A fractured neck was an assumption of the medical providers, as studies on the physiology of young children were in the early stages in those days.[3]

Shaken Baby Syndrome wasn't the original name of this form of child abuse that would kill 25 percent of its victims and leave another 60 percent with lifelong disabilities. In 1971, Dr. Norman Guthkelch, a British pediatric neurosurgeon, postulated that a number of infants and children that he operated on who had bleeding on the brain might have been shaken. It was customary in Britain to say, "Give him a good shake," so Guthkelch wondered if such a mechanism could be the cause of brain bleed, or *subdural hematomas*, to put it clinically. In his paper, "Infantile Subdural Hematoma and Its Relationship to Whiplash Injuries," Guthkelch laid out his hypothesis cleanly.[4]

He reflected on his visit to an American neurosurgeon, Ayub Ommaya, who was studying the effects of rapid acceleration and deceleration whiplash injuries in car accidents for the auto safety industry. Ommaya anesthetized rhesus monkeys and placed the primates in a contoured chair on moving sleds, securing them with a strap. He also cut a section off their skulls, placed see-through windows in their places and used film to capture images of the brain as the sleds raced forward on a twenty-foot long track at a high speed and suddenly braked to simulate a car crash. He was able to see on film the damage on a monkey's brain— how the blood vessels would pull and snap in response to the high velocity movement and seep out to fill a section of the brain with blood. This study resulted in the article "Whiplash Injury and Brain Damage: An Experimental Study" being published in the prestigious publication *Journal of the American Medical Association* (JAMA).[5]

The experiments, supported in part by the U.S. Navy, led Ommaya to conclude that whiplash, resulting from shaking, can cause cerebral concussions and brain injury, including bleeding on the surface of the brains of these monkeys who had been used in scientific research.

Guthkelch also made his own simple experiment by filling a flask with a solution of paraffin wax and coconut flakes. He shook the flask and noted that the coconut swirled about. When he struck it against a hard table, he then noted that the coconut didn't move. He also recounted a story from a fellow neurosurgeon who told him of a time that he developed a subdural hematoma from being on a bobsled ride at a local carnival. Finally, Guthkelch spoke with a social worker at his hospital who told him tales of parents coming into the emergency room with spite in their voices about their young children whom they brought in. He knew about the dark side of parenting, but hadn't put the pieces of shaking as a mechanism together. His article on the subject received modest, lukewarm attention in the medical field. It was another syndrome that wasn't named or given notoriety until a different clinician picked up the ball and ran with it—into the record books.

John Caffey, MD, was a successful radiologist in Pittsburgh, Pennsylvania in the 1940s. His contribution to the world of child welfare began when he wrote a journal article about long-bone fractures in young children. Caffey reviewed the cases of many children that he saw and described the unusual findings of periosteal reactions in arms and legs coupled with subdural hematomas ("Multiple Fractures in Long Bones of Infants Suffering from Chronic Subdural Hematoma").[6] As for the manner in which these injuries occurred, Caffey opened the proverbial abuse box in his article, only to shut it quickly. He implied that in some cases of long-bone injuries in children, parents possibly could be the culprits. He did not explicitly blame this condition on the shaking and twisting of young bones, he only hinted at it. The issue was revisited twenty years later when Henry Kempe's "The Battered Child" was published in the pages of *JAMA*.[7]

Dr. Caffey attempted to create his own child abuse coinage with the publication of his article "Parent-Infant Traumatic Stress Syndrome," or PITS for short.[8] The year after Guthkelch's article on shaking was published, Caffey finally received recognition. He incorporated Guthkelch's treatise and created his own—"On the Theory and Practice of Shaking Infants," which was published in *The American Journal of Diseases in Children* in 1972.[9] Caffey offered keen insight into a dangerous form of child abuse that had never been described in such detail before. It was an "ah ha" moment in the field of pediatrics and clinicians could put a name to a condition they had seen for years and to the act that caused the condition. Two years later, Caffey wrote a "Part II" follow-up to his whiplash shaking article.[10] Here he chronicled the deadly spree of violence that a baby nurse from New Haven, Connecticut had unleashed on her tiny victims in the 1940s and 50s. Her name? Virginia Belle Jaspers. She had confessed to killing infants by shaking them to death. Caffey thus sealed his name as the creator of what would be called Shaken Baby Syndrome (or SBS). This recognition lasted another forty years, until credit returned to Dr. Guthkelch as the first clinician to describe the syndrome as it is known today.

Virginia Jaspers was the daughter of a successful Connecticut state senator. She had aspirations to work with children in the homes of new parents in and around New Haven beginning in the early 1940s. Though qualified to do so, having recently completed high school and attending a basic pediatric nursing program at a nearby nunnery, she had a physical presence that caused people to be taken aback. Jaspers stood six feet tall and weighed two hundred and twenty pounds. She was extremely talkative and overcompensated for her appearance by being excessively pleasant to her clients. She became well-respected in her chosen field; her name was even added to the list that local pediatricians kept to recommend baby nurses to new parents. It was during these years of caregiving that her lethal side came out. The first baby she shook to death was three-week-old Cynthia Hubbard. Alone with the baby, who was crying excessively, Jaspers became highly volatile. Cynthia's parents never knew what killed their infant, but her death certificate listed her cause of death as "congenital malformation," like something let loose inside the girl and she died.[11]

Jaspers's temper continued to get the best of her. She shook and killed Jennifer Malkan in 1950 and then Abbe Kapsinow six years later. The nurse also inflicted injuries on twelve other infants and children during her tenure as a caregiver. She slapped babies, shook them and broke bones. This was her modus operandi for handling crying, bottle refusal and other normal behaviors of the young.

Though suspicions about Jaspers surfaced over the years, there were only two action-takers. One was Marvin Schaeffer, the father of three-month-old Bruce, whose leg was broken by Jaspers while Marvin and his wife were out at a party. He convinced one area pediatrician, Robert Salinger, to strike Jaspers from his list of preferred nurses and asked him for help in getting justice for his son. But it wasn't until 1956, when the nurse caused the death of twelve-day-old Abbe Kapsinow, that Dr. Salinger and others went to authorities with their concerns and let them know they didn't believe it to be accidental.

When Virginia Jaspers was finally interviewed about the deaths, she broke down and confessed. This was vital to our understanding of perpetrators and Shaken Baby Syndrome today, because Jaspers was one of the first in history to confess to shaking an infant to death. No one guided her or suggested to her that shaking was a lethal form of abuse—she said this herself. The act of violently shaking tiny infants will not only do irreparable harm, but can kill them as well. This was her tactic to put infants under her control when they became out of control. One boy was "lucky." He was shaken but lived through it. Yet he was left permanently handicapped from the act. As Jaspers confessed and as word got out, people all across the U.S. were shocked about the "Killer Baby Nurse from New Haven." She fits today's criteria of a serial killer but didn't shoot, stab or poison adults; instead, she brutally shook babies and they died.

Jaspers was sentenced to ten to twenty years in prison for manslaughter but only served a few short years in jail. She was never allowed to care for children again and later led a quiet life.

Once Guthkelch and Caffey opened the door to shaking as a mechanism for abuse, others followed. Over the years, thousands of journal articles, research papers and presentations have been featured in the pages of respected medical periodicals. Yet there have been unscrupulous authors as well—those who have set out to dispute the very nature of SBS and have sought to deny its existence. Because of these individuals, many court cases have been lost and perpetrators set free. This is the dark side of the clinical aspect of SBS.

CHAPTER 3

Effects on Young Brains

Emily Grace

I am the mother of an angel in heaven named Emily Grace. Emily was born September 6, 2009. She was a perfectly healthy, beautiful baby girl. Her father lived with us at the time. On the morning of November 17, 2009, I got up and got ready for work. I kissed my baby girl, told her that I loved her, then looked at her father and told him if he had any problems to call me and I would come home immediately. He said, "It's okay, I got it." I went to work and just two hours into my shift he calls and is frantic, saying Emily had a seizure and stopped breathing and is on her way to the hospital. Immediately I rushed home to pick him up and get to the hospital. Once we got there we were taken into a waiting room and asked for consent to do a spinal tap because Emily's white blood cell count was high. They did the procedure and told me she had been placed on a ventilator and they were airlifting her to another hospital that was better equipped to take care of her. I rode in the helicopter with her to Sutton Children's Hospital in Shreveport, Louisiana.

Once we got there, Emily was taken to the ICU and evaluated. A pediatric specialist came in and questioned me about what I knew and her health history, etc. At the time we still didn't know what was going on, so they went with the first diagnosis of hypothermic sepsis. Once they got her stabilized, they did a CT scan that showed brain swelling and blood around the brain. None of their findings were ever discussed with me until the day she died. They immediately started her on a different type of IV fluid to help with the swelling. That night she wasn't showing any signs of distress, but we couldn't touch her because they didn't want her overstimulated.

The next day her condition was about the same, so her dad and I went home so I could get clean clothes. My mom stayed with Emily. We were headed back to the hospital when my mom called saying Emily was breathing a little bit. We finally got back to Emily's room and they were doing tests on her again (checking her eyes, taking a full body CT scan, etc.). Nothing really changed that day. We still couldn't touch her because her brain swelling wasn't going down. The next morning I was told they were going to be doing tests on her brain to see if there was any activity, because the CT scans showed severe brain damage. They also told me if she was to survive she would be severely handicapped with little to no quality of life. On that night a neurosurgeon came in and told me she was brain dead, but I begged for a second opinion.

The next morning, a specialist from LSU came in and evaluated Emily, re-ran tests and came in and told me she agreed that my sweet Emily was brain dead. The pediatric specialist who was assigned to Emily said they had to run the tests one more time to have her be declared legally brain dead and then they would pull her from life support.

I stayed with my baby girl all day and night. I also had Emily baptized. On November 20, the nurses came in and took her for the last test they had to do. She came back and they finally let me hold her. I was able to rock and love her for four hours. I sang to her and told her how much I loved her, read a couple of books to her and the social workers did a foot cast and footprints plus took pictures. At about 2:30 her blood pressure started dropping even with the medications they were giving her to keep it stable, so they paged the doctor. He came in and said she was settling in and going on her own so he had them turn everything off. She lived for thirty minutes without life support and passed away at 3:15 P.M.

The next day, Child Protective Services contacted me to talk. While I was talking to them they told me she had been shaken and asked me what I did on the morning of November 17. I told them that I went to work and left Emily with her father. That was all they disclosed to me.

Four months later her autopsy report finally came in. Emily's father was arrested and charged with manslaughter. He was given a plea bargain for "shock probation" (he got sentenced to ten years in state, but got out after three months), where if he screws up while out then he has to finish whatever time left in state with no possibility of parole or probation.

My daughter suffered. She had severe hemorrhaging of the brain, torn optical nerves, six shattered ribs, a neck injury and a fracture in her spine, among other things. My beautiful baby girl passed away due to SBS. Her death was ruled a homicide.

—*Danielle Fowler*

THE BRAIN

To understand SBS as a condition, one must understand the effect shaking has on a young, growing brain. The physical brain in an infant and very young child has the components of an adult, but the quality of it is different. First of all, the young brain is not firm like an adult brain. It is very soft and is growing in size and developing millions of new nerves daily. Each developmental process an infant acquires is the result of having a working, healthy brain. The act of shaking not only interrupts the growth process, but can irreparably damage it. The infant brain has higher water content (approximately 95 percent water vs. 85 percent in an adult).[1] The infant skull is also thinner and more pliable than an adult's. Finally, the infant brain has minimal myelin, which is the substance that protects the nerves. Myelin forms a protective sheath around nerves, much like the coating of an electric wire. Any disruption to these growing nerves can compromise the entire functioning of the nervous system.

To understand the intracranial (within the skull) injuries that severe shaking produces, we need to examine the layers of the brain. There is first the scalp, which provides warmth by producing hair (which in itself is a level of protection). The next layer is the skull, which is the armor that protects the vital parts underneath. The reason why the infant skull is malleable is that it has to be in order for the infant to squeeze through the birth canal. Six separate sections of bone are present: a frontal bone, two parietal bones, two temporal bones and the occipital bone in back. These bones are sutured together by nature and the spaces in between are called the fontanelles (otherwise known as "soft spots"). The skull does not fully fuse and harden until around two years of age. One problem of the pliable infant skull is that it lacks protection from impact. A hard hit can more easily transmit harmful forces deeper within the brain than an adult skull.

The next layer of the brain is the dural membrane—a tough, durable membrane that covers the entire brain. It is formally called the *dura mater* and is attached to the skull. It moves separately from the brain and can tear underlying veins and nerves. Any bleeding underneath is called subdural (below the dura). Any bleeding above it is called epidural (outside the dura). These terms are important in the upcoming discussions on falls and head injuries.

Deeper within the brain's layers is the arachnoid membrane, which is a thin, web-like layer that loosely attaches to the layer below it. There is a space underneath the arachnoid, which is called the subarachnoid space. This space allows cerebrospinal fluid to flow within the spinal column and the brain. Brain injury can cause bleeding within this space and is called a subarachnoid hemorrhage.

The final layer, the *pia mater*, adheres to the convexities (ridges) of the brain and is impermeable to fluid. It protects and cushions the brain.

The brain itself is made of gray and white matter, each serving its own function for movement and autonomic processes. The color difference arises mainly from the whiteness of myelin in white matter and the grayness of capillaries and neurons in gray matter. These matters are separate entities and shear off each other during violent shaking. Gray and white matter can also be torn more easily in infants and young children due to the softness of the brain. On a normal CT/MRI scan, the infant brain is clearly defined and symmetrical, with a clear differentiation of gray matter and white matter. Brain swelling from trauma (edema) diminishes or obliterates this difference and on a diagnostic scan appears as a patchy covering over the brain (hypodensity). Cohen and associates coined the term "reversal sign" to describe a state in which severe edema and tissue destruction makes the white matter of the brainstem, thalamus and cerebellum appear more dense than the surrounding gray matter portions of the brain.[2] This irreversible brain damage has also been termed "the black brain."[3]

Throughout the layers of the brain, blood vessels weave and are loosely attached. During a shaking event, these immature blood vessels can stretch and tear, causing bleeding within the membranes of the brain—most typically subdural bleeding. Multiple broken blood vessels seep fresh (or acute) blood into localized areas or spread over a wide area of the brain. Over a period of hours or days a clot will form, which is congealed subdural blood. The clot is called a hematoma. This clot expands and presses on the brain and physical symptoms will appear in an infant or child such as vomiting, lethargy, poor sucking ability, chirping cries, etc.

DIFFUSE AXONAL INJURY

The billions of nerve fibers that are within the brain can also be dramatically affected. These nerves are rapidly growing in infants and young children and violent shaking can stretch and tear these fibers, similar to how this motion affects blood vessels. Specific neurons, called axonal nerves, communicate with each other, sending messages that "teach" developmental information within the brain. Research has found that rotational forces and sudden deceleration movements (like in a motor vehicle accident or a shaking episode) cause axonal nerves throughout a large section of the brain (typically where the grey and white matter of the brain intersect) to be disrupted and break. This is known as diffuse axonal injury (DAI). Unfortunately, there is no cure when DAI occurs. Once an axon is broken, it remains broken. Most often, it is diagnosed microscopically—especially during an autopsy. DAI is the reason many infants fail to develop normally. The nerves that are in place to learn an activity are broken and stay that way. Mental handicaps and cerebral palsy are two examples of the aftereffects of shaking. These conditions in a baby are permanent lifetime consequences. They are also signs of brain damage, with a wasteland of previously healthy axons that can never be repaired. DAI is a very rare *cause* of death; instead, other consequences of brain trauma are the cause—oxygen deprivation, edema, etc.

When an infant is shaken to the point of causing physical harm, he or she will lose consciousness immediately. The brain is overwhelmed by the traumatic event and, like any head injury, shuts down quickly. Since infants and young children are unable to communicate their symptoms, parents and other caregivers may mistake excessive sleeping or irritability for normal behavior. Even when an infant is taken to a doctor, symptoms may be mistaken as the flu or another type of illness. Head injuries may not be suspected, so the infant is allowed to go home, where further complications may occur (or even further abuse).[4]

SUBDURAL BLEEDING

A subdural hematoma is a blood clot formed from an accidental, natural or abusive cause. Subdurals are the foundation for a diagnosis of Shaken Baby Syndrome and are typically bilateral (both sides). Subdurals are formed from rotational forces that occur when a child is shaken. In terms of physics, research has shown that the types of subdural hemorrhages that are seen in SBS involve a rotation of the brain that pulls and snaps the fragile bridging veins that cross the young child's brain. This is the action that causes the blood to spread and pool on the brain's surface. A rotational subdural is more likely to occur during severe shaking than a contact subdural, which will be described next.

CT and MRI scans can identify blood and injury with accuracy. Blood shows as a white highlight on scans, which is also called acute blood (also known as hyperdense). There may be older blood present which sometimes is called hypodense—appearing more grayish. Once doctors identify the location and size of subdural bleeding or bleeding in other locations of the brain, then surgery is typically performed to clear the blood. If the size of the subdural is small, surgery may not be necessary, since the subdural blood will naturally be resorbed by the brain.

Another way that a subdural hemorrhage can occur is from a blow to the head or a direct impact. In this instance, it is known as a "contact subdural." The mechanism for this to occur is often a fall onto a hard surface. Physics is brought into play here as well. The type of motion for a contact subdural is called a translational fall—from point A to point B in a straight line. When an infant or young child falls from an elevated surface and his or her head impacts a hard surface, a fracture may or may not occur. Beneath that fracture, a contact subdural may develop. The bleeding, especially in accidental falls, is typically epidural and necessitates immediate removal of the blood. Subdural bleeding in translational falls can be mass-occupying, meaning the hematoma expands and presses downward on the brain. Such bleeding needs surgical evacuation.

When an infant falls from an elevated surface down to a carpeted or hard floor, the chance of significant damage to the head is small. The greater the height (i.e. from a parent's arms), the greater the potential for head injury.

If an infant was playing in a walker and happened to roll downstairs while he or she was still inside, then that would be a rotational event, where possible subdural bleeding occurs. There is the physical manifestation of acceleration/deceleration in rotational falls (similar to motor vehicle accidents) and bleeding in any rotational fall can be bilateral.

An interhemispheric subdural hemorrhage is very specific to shaken baby cases, as the blood actually cleaves between the hemispheres. Because of the whipping motion during shaking, blood goes right up the middle—between the left and right hemisphere of the brain. Interhemispheric bleeding is seen in the posterior (or back) section of the brain. In 1978, Dr. Robert A. Zimmerman first correlated interhemispheric subdurals with violent shaking.[5] It is also not a good finding prognosis-wise, since subsequent CT scans of Zimmerman's patients found that 100 percent had cerebral atrophy (brain shrinking).

CHAPTER 4

Body Injuries

EYE INJURIES

According to Dr. Alex Levin, "The overwhelming body of literature supports a conclusion that severe hemorrhagic retinopathy in otherwise previously well children without obvious history to the contrary (e.g. fatal head crush) suggests that the child has been submitted to abusive repetitive acceleration-deceleration trauma with or without head impact."[1]

Retinal hemorrhages (RH) are the centerpiece of eye injuries that typically occur in SBS. Such hemorrhages cannot be seen with the naked eye. An ophthalmoscope is needed to view them, because the retina is situated at the very back of the eye, behind the globe. A normal retina includes an array of blood vessels and multilayered membranes. Retinal hemorrhages that result from violent shaking events can develop in front of the membranes (preretinal or subhyaloid), between the membranes (intraretinal) or below the membranes (subretinal).

The characteristics of retinal hemorrhages can be superficial and will manifest as splinter-type or flame-type hemorrhages or larger ones that are called dot or blot-type hemorrhages. Light retinal hemorrhages can disappear from anywhere within a few days to a few weeks. The larger hemorrhages can last several weeks. Retinal hemorrhage cannot be dated with any accuracy. When SBS retinal hemorrhages are present they are typically too numerous to count and extend from the back to the sides of the retina. This is the appearance of retinal patterns of SBS.

On direct observation by an ophthalmologist or via a retinal camera, SBS retinal hemorrhages have been called centrifugal—as though blood has been splattered across the entire retina.

The majority of retinal hemorrhages in shaken children are bilateral (both sides effected). One eye may have more hemorrhages than the other; having an equal number of hemorrhages in both eyes is not needed to satisfy a diagnosis of SBS.

The posterior pole of the retina is stationed at the very back, in the area where the optic nerve leads to the brain. Retinal hemorrhages in SBS commonly extend throughout the entire retina, beginning at the posterior pole and going out to the periphery (the edge of the retina). Accidental falls may produce a few retinal hemorrhages. These do not spread out, are few in number and are very light in size and shape. They are also confined to the posterior pole.

Studies have shown that the mechanism for producing hemorrhages in the retina comes from a tractional pull on the eye globe during a shaking event. The globe of the eye pulls back and forth on the retina, thus producing extensive bleeding within the retina, as well as possibly other damage.

It is believed that approximately 80 to 85 percent of infants and children who are shaken have diffuse retinal hemorrhages. In lethal cases the retinal hemorrhages are typically more extensive. Some children who are severely shaken may not have retinal hemorrhages or the hemorrhages are few and are limited to the posterior pole.

Retinal hemorrhages can appear in other types of trauma (such as birth injuries and motor vehicle accidents) or disease (blood disorders, leukemia, meningitis, etc.). But the types of retinal hemorrhages that are seen in other situations are very different from the ones seen in SBS. They are fewer in number and confined to the posterior pole of the retina. This is important to note, especially when perpetrators of shaking incidents try to explain away infant injuries as "accidental," such as a fall from a small height. The more violent the impact on the child, the more numerous the diffuse retinal hemorrhages.

When retinal hemorrhages are diagnosed, the discovery should be a part of a larger investigation of an abusive act. Such a diagnosis should not be the basis for an immediate judgment call of abuse. Other conditions need to be considered, laboratory testing performed and medical history checked within the child's family.

Another ocular injury that is highly specific for SBS is optic nerve sheath hemorrhage. The optic nerve extends from the brain to the eye globe. It transmits visual messages from the retina to the brain, where it is converted into meaningful information. The optic nerve is the cornerstone of human sight. To protect it, the nerve is surrounded by a membranous sheath. When bleeding underneath the sheath is diagnosed in infants and children who are being assessed for abuse, the finding is highly suggestive of a shaking case.

Repetitive acceleration/deceleration injury can directly affect the optic nerve and may ultimately cause optic nerve atrophy, which leads to permanent blindness. One reason why optic nerve sheath hemorrhage is so unique in SBS findings is the lack of correlation to short falls. There are no documented cases in the medical literature of optic nerve sheath hemorrhage that connect it to short-distance falls. So when a baby is diagnosed with this particular ocular finding, or if it is noted on an autopsy, it then becomes problematic for a perpetrator's defense if he or she is using the excuse that the baby "fell."

There are three other optic injuries that correlate directly with severe shaking: retinoschisis, retinal folds and vitreous hemorrhages. These are consequences that are seen in so few other conditions in childhood that they are a clear association with abuse.

RETINOSCHISIS AND RETINAL FOLDS

What are retinoschisis and retinal folds? During shaking events, it has been previously noted that tractional pulling on the eye globe is thought to be the mechanism for causing retinal hemorrhages. That same pulling or tugging causes a splitting of the retina. This separation (or schisis) is a result of the retinal traction that severe shaking brings about. A retinal fold is caused by the same means, but instead of splitting, the retina folds onto itself. Though severe, injuries such as these can be surgically corrected but some infants and children can be permanently scarred with vision loss.

There have been very few cases of accidental traumatic injury that have caused retinoschisis or retinal folds, the majority occurring from crush injuries.[2] In medical literature, there have been only *three* outlier cases of retinoschisis and retinal folds appearing in infants and children from accidental causes—one toddler reportedly had a TV fall on him[3], one infant had a twelve-year-old child fall on her[4] and a two-year-old was fatally injured by a three-story fall to pavement.[5] All of the children died. An outlier case is one where a scenario is presented that is outside the realm of prior medical knowledge. These are highly unusual and should be investigated thoroughly. There has been some question about the veracity of the accidental cases I mentioned.

VITREOUS HEMORRHAGES

The vitreous body (eyeball) is filled with vitreous fluid—there should be no blood in the vitreous. When vitreous hemorrhage is noted, there are also commonly retinal hemorrhages. These adjacent hemorrhages can bleed into the vitreous, or the vitreous can be torn as well from the shaking mechanism. Non-accidental trauma, such as shaking, is a key reason for vitreous hemorrhages.

The final eye problem that can occur in SBS is blindness from occipital cortical damage. When a child has damage to the occipital part of the brain, it may cause lasting visual problems, since this is the area that controls how vision is processed (in the occipital lobe at the very back of the brain). The child's pupil may have reaction to light and may be fully functioning, but the brain cannot translate the information because of occipital damage; blindness is the result.

MEDICAL DIFFERENTIAL DIAGNOSES IN SBS OCULAR INJURIES

Alex Levin, MD, one of the top child abuse ophthalmologists in the world, has listed the following medical conditions that produce retinal hemorrhages in children. This is not an exhaustive list, but the main ones that are found:

- Hypertension
- Bleeding problems/leukemia

- Meningitis/sepsis/endocarditis
- Vasculitis
- Cerebral aneurysm
- Retinal diseases (eg, infection, hemangioma)
- Carbon monoxide poisoning
- Anemia
- Hypoxia/hypotension
- Papilledema/increased intracranial pressure
- Glutaric aciduria
- Osteogenesis imperfecta
- Examinations in premature infants with retinopathy of prematurity
- Extracorporeal membrane oxygenation
- Hypo- or hypernatremia[6]

ACCIDENTAL TRAUMA
DIFFERENTIAL DIAGNOSES

How can accident-related RH be seen as different from shaking RH? In 2009, Togioka and team did a PubMed search with the keywords "shaken baby syndrome," "child abuse" and "retinal hemorrhages." There were sixty-six articles that met inclusion criteria. They found 53 to 80 percent incidence of RH with abusive head trauma. With proven severe *accidental* trauma, there was a 0 to 10 percent finding of RH. They reviewed mechanisms such as convulsions, chest percussion from CPR, forceful vomiting and persistent coughing. In the absence of any other condition known to cause retinal hemorrhaging, they found .7 percent, 2 percent, 0 percent and 0 percent respectively. So when these mechanisms are offered as an excuse for the diagnosis of retinal hemorrhage (as defense experts often attempt to suggest), it has been shown to be an extremely rare occurrence. Even then, these types of hemorrhages are not the kind seen in abuse—instead, they are light, confined to the posterior pole and few in number.[7]

Let's now look specifically at various claims that have been utilized in the courtroom in recent years:

BIRTH TRAUMA

Birth trauma retinal hemorrhages exist. In fact, they are found in 30 to 40 percent of all births, but they are resorbed within two to four weeks. They are also light, small and confined to the posterior pole of the eye. When a three-month-old has diffuse retinal hemorrhages and the defense asserts that these were caused by birth, there are studies that show this is not plausible.

One particularly relevant study was recently published in France. Laghmari and his group prospectively reviewed over 2,000 newborns for the presence of retinal hemorrhages. In their study, they used indirect ophthalmoscopy within twenty-four hours after birth in all newborns at various hospitals. Overall, 31.8 percent of newborns had some form of retinal hemorrhages. These hemorrhages were confined to the posterior pole of the eye and were few in number and size. Vacuum-assisted births had the largest percentage of retinal hemorrhages (38 percent) and cesarean births had the fewest (20 percent). Infants with retinal hemorrhages were reexamined weekly until the hemorrhages resolved. Annual ophthalmologic follow-up was also scheduled in these children. Their most critical finding was that two-thirds of hemorrhages had disappeared by one week after birth. Retinal hemorrhages had resolved in *all* newborns within four weeks.[8]

INJURIES FROM FALLS

When Dr. Betty Spivack testified in a dual appellate hearing in Kentucky to determine if SBS was a verifiable diagnosis, she discussed retinal hemorrhages. She made the statement, "Retinal hemorrhages have a much stronger correlation with abusive head trauma than unintentional head trauma, even when the unintentional injury is severe."[9] So, if there is a fall from a great height, there may be retinal hemorrhages seen that are similar in number and magnitude to ones seen in shaking injuries. In a study from 2008, Kivlin and associates reviewed motor vehicle crashes.[10] They studied ten children, younger than three years, who died in motor vehicle crashes. Eight had retinal hemorrhages which extended to the periphery. Three of the children had retinal folds, which are more commonly associated with a diagnosis of Shaken Baby Syndrome. Six had internal membrane bleeding, but none of them had any splitting (retinoschisis). Some even had optic nerve sheath hemorrhages. But what this study found was that one can't blame major retinal hemorrhages on a short fall, a rebleed of an underlying condition or something trivial. There needs to be a severe injury—like violent shaking.

Also from 2008, Trenchs and his researchers conducted an important study that looked at retinal hemorrhages in head trauma resulting from short falls.[11] There were 154 children who were studied and 80 percent of the falls were from a height equal to or less than four feet. The most common fall was from a stroller, followed by rolling off a bed. Ten percent had evidence of intracranial injury. Three children had retinal hemorrhages, all unilateral (one eye). All the hemorrhages were associated with an epidural hematoma, where there was also a midline shift to the brain. This is a severe injury where the epidural pushes onto the brain and it shifts to one side. Since only three patients had retinal hemorrhages (1.9 percent of the total), this equates to a very low chance of developing very specific retinal hemorrhages due to a low fall.

Vinchon and his team found that the lack of retinal hemorrhages in accidental falls, compared to severe findings in inflicted trauma, is statistically significant.[12] This confirmed an earlier study of his.[13] They found that, when confessed incidents of child abuse were studied next to accidental falls in public places, the predictive value of the presence of retinal hemorrhages was 96 percent. When combined with the presence of subdural hematomas and lack of impact the predictive value was 100 percent.

Not Just a Fall

I had dropped my eighteen-month-old son off at his babysitter (my brother's wife, Amber) that morning and headed to work. My job was within walking distance from her house. I was at work at about 8 A.M. when I heard the page from the overheard speaker. I was in a friend's office when I picked up the call. The babysitter was panicked and said that my son was unresponsive and I needed to get over there fast. My friend could see the panic in my eyes. I told her to tell my boss that I had an emergency and ran out the door. I didn't even stop to get my purse or my car. I ran to her house. Her neighbor had called 911. I got there just as the medics did. I ran into the house and carried him out. He was limp and mumbling and I remembered how strange his eyes looked. It wasn't until later that I understood he was having a seizure. The medics immediately put oxygen on him and transported him to the nearby telephone company's parking lot where we were met by the life flight team. They immediately took my son to the back of the chopper and I didn't see him again until we reached the hospital.

Amber had two children of her own. The boy was about nine months old and the older girl was eleven. The younger child was at home when the "accident" occurred and the older one was at school. Amber told me that my son had climbed on top of the highchair, had fallen off and hit his head. I believed her. He liked to climb and getting on the lid of his highchair was nothing unusual.

The medics who were the first to arrive were very reassuring. The life flight medics were all business. I couldn't even recognize their faces after the flight until they stopped in to see how my son was doing in the hospital. They had a huge part in saving my son's life. When we got to the hospital he was whisked to see a pediatric internist. I remember she was very cold to me. My face was probably swollen from crying, but she seemed to have no empathy and at the time I didn't understand why. They told me and my partner that our child had to be rushed to brain surgery. He had a massive blood clot and his brain was swelling. We waited almost eight hours with family and friends. Amber waited too and she kept repeating to us that she was so sorry. We did nothing but reassure that everything would be fine and it was an accident. When surgery was over, they allowed only me, my husband and mother-in-law to visit him. His tiny head was completely wrapped in gauze like a turban. He was on a ventilator and had so many tubes coming out of his arms. It was like something out of a nightmare. I couldn't imagine the pain my child had endured to require such medical intervention. The nurse was angry. She pulled his diaper off and started asking me where the red marks came from. There were bruises on his waistline area that matched perfectly to the fingertips of a small hand. I started crying, saying, "I don't know. I don't understand. Those bruises weren't there this morning when I left him. I didn't do it. My son's dad would never hurt my son."

The nurse began to soften as she was beginning to put the pieces together that we had nothing to do with the shaking. They asked me to keep what I saw to myself and not to share it with the people in the waiting area. I was so shell-shocked I still didn't quite understand that Amber was a suspect. I left the room to collect myself and give our family and friends an update. That is when I saw two policemen step off the elevator. My partner's mother grabbed my arm and said they were there to find out the truth. Amber was arrested that evening. I watched them take her out in handcuffs. After that initial evening, the hospital staff changed their attitude toward my family. The care they provided to my son was exceptional. Only special people can be members of the ICU staff and we met some amazing ones. My son was in a medically-induced coma for at least ten days and he had an ICP bolt in the back of his skull to monitor the pressure. He was in the hospital from the 28th of November until the 26th of December, when he was transported to a rehabilitation facility in Bethany, Oklahoma, called the Children's Center. He was in rehab for three weeks when they decided he would recover best in a home environment. At his time of release from rehab:

- He was beginning to crawl again.
- He could barely use his right side, due to a stroke from the blood clot.
- His eyes were not tracking properly due to retinal hemorrhages.
- He was on seizure medications, although the only seizures occurred during the hospital stay.
- He was eating thickened liquids.
- The speech therapists taught us how to teach him to sign as he was not speaking except for a few basic words: Mama, Dada, etc.

One memorable person from the hospital stay was a nurse named David. My partner's mother called him "Negative Nancy" because he always gave us the worst possible outcome so that we didn't get our hopes up. One afternoon he sat down in my son's room with my husband and I and said, "Do you understand that 80 percent of marriages do not survive a tragedy like this? A special needs child can be a huge burden on a relationship." I was feeling pretty crazy at that point so I laughed and said that we shouldn't have any issues there, because we were not married. Neither David nor my son's father found it to be very funny. We weren't married at the time but after our son was released from rehab we got married on February 8, 2008. One night, probably two days into the ICU stay, *my son's pressure stats were very high. The resident on staff rushed him back to have a CT scan. When the doctor returned, he said it would be a miracle if he made it through the night. All I can remember is leaving the room, crying hysterically, and running to the chapel to pray. My husband has never been much into religion but he was right on my heels and I remember he just sat there silently with me as I cried and prayed for God to let us keep him.*

A huge ice storm hit the Tulsa area while he was in the hospital. Almost all of the surrounding areas were without power. My mother-in-law and two older children were staying in a motel down the road because the power was out at my house. My son was still on a ventilator and he was being cared for by a new nurse. She was very young, probably in her early twenties. The power started flickering. I asked her what would happen if the power went out and if there was a glitch in the backup generators. I was worried he wouldn't be able to breathe. She was on top of it and she ran and got one of those handheld CPR bags and stayed by his side until the power stopped flickering.

Amber confessed to the police officers that she became angry with my son for throwing a toy and hitting her child. That is what triggered the shaking. She confessed that she shook him upside down, which explained the bruises, and then threw water on his face to wake him up after he started seizing. This part makes my stomach turn. She had such disregard for my son that she called her sister over before she called me, and her sister called 911. My baby could have died because she was too worried about being caught. The District Attorney was pushing for fifty years in prison, because the doctors didn't expect my son to make it. For the first week, the doctor said there was a fifty-fifty chance and if he did live he wouldn't be the same child. His brain function might be severely limited. He might never walk, talk, etc. But he defied the odds. Though I feel this is totally wrong, the DA changed the plea deal to twenty years in prison. When Amber is released she will remain on probation for an additional twenty years. The DA wanted Amber to be in prison until she could no longer bear children. We attended every court hearing. At first she looked somber and scared. Then she turned defiant. For the last hearing a friend of mine made T-shirts with my son's picture on the back and our titles, like Mom, Grandma and others. The judge acknowledged us during her sentencing and asked us if we agreed to the terms of the plea deal. It made us feel somewhat in control when things were so out of control.

Immediate family has become very bonded. My husband, his mom, his sister and our three kids are very close. We have become extremely protective toward all three children. My twelve-year-old did not have her first away sleepover until a few months ago. My brother and I don't speak. He sat with his wife's family during the court proceedings. They vehemently defended her and said she didn't do it even though she confessed and was taking a plea deal. He abandoned my niece and nephew. A Department of Human Services social worker wanted to place them in our care as foster parents. We were good with it until they told us we would have to take them to visit their mom and I fell apart. I just couldn't do it. My boss was going to foster them. It would have been a great environment for them. But the Indian Nation stepped in and said Indian children had to be placed with an Indian family. They ended up with Amber's parents. I will say my husband and I have our worst arguments over our son's care: future therapies, teacher issues, social issues. It takes a strong couple to survive something as devastating as SBS. I'm lucky to have found a true soulmate and we lean on each other. My other children suffered immensely while my son was in rehab and after. I regret it so much that their needs were pushed to the back burner, but I was so focused on making my son normal. I was so naïve to what SBS really does to the brain. His aggressive nature and quick temperament make it hard for him to have a close relationship with his brother and sister. My oldest is fifteen and he can read between the lines and calm his brother down when he is on the verge of going out of control. He is older, so I think he has more patience than my daughter. At times my daughter gets frustrated with her brother's behavior. I try to reinforce that, no matter what, after we are gone they only have each other and they will always have to watch out for him.

My son is now seven. He has been diagnosed with ADHD and a speech disorder. He is weak on his right side and he wears an Ankle Foot Orthosis brace. He still has weekly therapies and we are always trying the latest medical interventions. He takes medicine to control the ADHD and it has significantly improved his behavior *at school. He was placed in Special Ed because his behavior was out of control. Then we had a twelve-week neuro test completed that confirmed the ADHD and speech disorder. I don't think he will ever be able to participate in a normal class, because there are too many children and it is sensory overload. Being in a support group helped me realize that it's okay if he is not exactly like his peers. My friends who were there when the abuse occurred, who sat by us while we cried at the hospital, are incredibly loving toward him. When we make new friends with kids they don't understand and just think he is a brat. They don't comprehend the outbursts or the overstimulation. So it has made me intolerant and I would rather not make new friends than have my child criticized. I feel life today is wonderful, because he is here and we love him and are incredibly grateful God let us keep him with us. My husband's mom is a godsend. She truly is an angel. She backs up our therapy decisions and takes him to his appointments while we work and he loves her so much. Someone asked me the other day if I thought my son could live a normal life and I said, "Yes, with lots of hard work." My brother was incredibly supportive. He is a marine and was stationed in Broken Arrow when the abuse occurred. He was married with two children but still found time to visit and help with whatever we needed. He lives in Japan now with his family, but he is the only one of my siblings with whom I still communicate since my son was abused. My other brothers and sister became very divided from the SBS trauma.*

My son's abuse had a horrible effect on our lives, but we have each other and learned how to pick up the pieces and make it work. Amber's children were affected so badly, not only by losing their mother but by their dad leaving. SBS is like a fire that just destroys everything in its path.

—*Melissa Walker*

OPTIC NERVE SHEATH HEMORRHAGE

As previously noted, optic nerve sheath hemorrhage is very specific to Shaken Baby Syndrome and is a common finding during an autopsy. There is bleeding below the sheath that covers the optic nerve. Bhardwaj and his team found that a diagnosis of optic nerve sheath hemorrhage in 72 percent of examined children was associated with abusive head trauma.[14] This important conclusion was also confirmed by Wygnanski-Jaffe and colleagues where they showed a significantly more common association of optic nerve sheath hemorrhage and SBS (P is less than .0001, which is less than one in ten thousand cases and very significant).[15]

Eye findings related to SBS have been researched in greater detail in recent years. Therefore it is particularly important that physicians and ophthalmologists educate themselves appropriately on the implications of intraocular injury, because of the possibility of child abuse. Through keeping themselves up to date on the latest medical research, performing recommended examinations by the American Academy of Pediatrics and ruling out all differential diagnoses, ophthalmologists will be able to make a significant contribution as part of the interdisciplinary team that is needed to work with families and young victims.

BODY FRACTURES

When a child is shaken, it may be an isolated incident or he or she could be caught up in a cycle of abuse. Fractures are seen approximately one third of the time, depending on the type of fracture. Two of the most common are skull and rib fractures.

Skull fractures come about from impact after shaking. When a perpetrator shakes an infant, he or she may slam the infant down on a hard floor, against a wall, etc. Besides the trauma to the brain that is caused by shaking and impact, a skull fracture may occur.

There are different types of skull fracture. The most basic type of fracture is a linear one, which is a simple straight line that crosses through the full thickness of the bone. Infants and young children may sustain a depressed, or "ping-pong," fracture due to the immaturity of the elastic skull.

The depressed skull fracture occurs when a small area of skull is displaced inwardly (much like a ping-pong ball that stays depressed when pressed upon). These types of fractures can occur when a child is hit with something or impacts against an object. Depressed fractures have also been seen when a child accidentally falls onto an object, such as a small toy. The shape of the fracture can even take on the shape of the object that has made the injury.

A *comminuted* fracture is one where a section of the child's skull breaks into small pieces. This is caused by a major blow to the head. In newborns, comminuted fractures have been produced from vacuum extractions at birth, but this is a very rare event.

Growing skull fractures are associated with underlying trauma in the brain. When a mass is formed and grows, it can press against a simple linear fracture and cause it to expand. This is a rare complication of head trauma and is generally seen only in infants and young children. Growing skull fractures are considered an emergency, since the brain can herniate (or extrude) through the fracture site.

In the case of shaking, there may be signs of both old and new skull fractures, where an infant or child has been caught in a cycle of abuse.[16]

Skull fractures in infants and young children occur in accidental situations, but any fracture must be thoroughly evaluated by medical and law enforcement professionals to rule out abuse. Several issues must be addressed, including: timeline of injury, nature of injury, height of fall (if this is reported), hardness of impact surface, plausibility of story, underlying brain trauma (significant for abuse), type of fracture, witnessed fall, etc.

Rib fractures present a different problem for the caregiver reporting the injury, because these fractures are highly associated with child abuse. Because infants and young children's ribs are supple, it requires a great deal of force to cause breaks in the rib bones. Typical abusive fractures of the ribs are lateral (on the sides) and posterior (in the back), because of the way that a perpetrator's fingers grasp the child. There have been few reports of accidental rib fractures in cases of CPR, and these have occurred in the anterior (front) portion of the infant rib. There have been no reported cases of CPR-induced posterior rib fractures.

Rib fractures occur (as previously noted) in approximately 30 percent of SBS cases. During a shaking event, the perpetrator often squeezes an infant or child hard, which can cause rib fractures. When a medical exam (chest x-ray) finds rib fractures and there is no reasonable story presented by the parents or caregivers, then child abuse should be the first line of thought among medical professionals. Laboratory tests can rule out other types of medical conditions from which a child may suffer (e.g., osteogenesis imperfecta, rickets and other bone deficiencies), but abusive acts are the number one cause of rib fractures in infants and young children.

Radiologists can also determine if new or old rib fractures are present based on x-ray images. Older, healing fractures appear to have globs surrounding them, which are actually calcium deposits that formed in the healing process.

The final type of fracture that shaken babies can develop is the metaphyseal lesion. Infants and children have growth plates (epiphyseal plates) at the end of their long bones (elbows, wrists, ankles, etc.). These plates are actually growing tissues and help determine the length and shape of the mature bone when the child reaches adolescence. Growth plates are fragile and can be "fractured" by abusive acts. When a child is violently shaken, his or her arms may flail in the air, which can lead to injury of the growth plates. These types of fractures may not be seen immediately after a shaking event, so a series of x-rays may help diagnose the injuries as calcium begins to form. Metaphyseal lesions (occurring in the metaphysis [wide part] of the long bone) are also known as "bucket-handle" or "corner" fractures depending on the angle of the x-ray image. Growth plate injury can also occur from pulling or twisting arms and legs. Injuries to growth plates, depending on severity, can cause premature growth arrest and deformity.

DIFFERENTIAL DIAGNOSES IN FRACTURES

There are many diagnoses of problems, diseases and injuries in infants and young children that are known to cause fractures, including diseases such as osteogenesis imperfecta, copper insufficiency, rickets, osteomyelitis and others. These conditions can be diagnosed through lab testing and medical work-ups. When fractures are present in infants and young children (especially pre-mobile infants), the frontrunner diagnosis to be considered is child abuse. If the fracture is accidental, then the history of the injury should be appropriate for the present fracture. Was the injury witnessed? Or was it suddenly discovered? As in any potential child abuse investigation, it is vital that story of the accident be well described.

A lump on the back of a five-month-old's head, which turns out to be a skull fracture and was "just found" makes no sense. The infant's head needed to have impacted something, or something impacted it.

CONSEQUENCES OF SHAKEN BABY SYNDROME

It is a sad and alarming fact that between 60 and 70 percent of infants identified as having been shaken are faced with dire consequences, including death. The rest may seem to recover well from being shaken but still have residual effects. Truly, the lives of not just the victims, but their entire families change as a result of a brief act of violence. Millions of dollars are spent each year in the rehabilitation of shaken infants and toddlers. The expenses include costs for equipment and services, costs for daily care and, even more importantly, emotional costs.

In the next chapter, some of the main consequences that a shaken infant may face will be discussed.

CHAPTER 5

Serious Consequences

ATTENTION PROBLEMS

Because the brain has some resiliency in response to traumatic injury, there are children who experience minimal after-effects following an incident of shaking. One such effect might be an Attention Deficit Disorder (ADD) with or without hyperactivity. With an attention disorder, children may appear to ignore what a parent or caregiver is saying to them. They may also be easily distracted and need careful monitoring and clear instructions on adult expectations.

Certain stimulant medications can help a child experiencing attention problems to focus by counterbalancing the overproduced stimulating chemicals of the brain. Parents and caregivers should consult their physicians to discuss behavioral or medical options to assist with their child's needs. Before a diagnosis of ADD is formally made, the child should also receive psychological testing and evaluation. School personnel should be made aware if a child is diagnosed with ADD, so that special programs or consideration can be arranged.

BALANCE PROBLEMS

Balance is controlled by three areas of the body's nervous system—the basal ganglia, the cerebellum and the inner ear (fluid in the eustachian tubes of the ears maintains a consistent level for balance to effectively occur). Damage to any of these areas may result in poor balance. When a balance problem primarily stems from the inner ear, masking agents— such as a device that produces "white noise"—can assist in maintaining balance and coordination.

Physical and occupational therapy can help correct deficits in a child's balance. These deficits may cause a child to have difficulty standing or walking in an uncontrolled way. Coordination therapies and strengthening therapies can allow for smoother mobility.

BLINDNESS

Many types of visual deficits may develop as a result of SBS. Retinal hemorrhaging may resolve without any lasting ill effects, but may also leave permanent scarring with partial or complete blindness.

Cortical blindness relates to injuries in the cortex of the brain. Cortical trauma results from any type of brain injury, including contusion, edema or hemorrhage. The eye and optic nerves are functional, yet the brain's cortex is unable to effectively process visual information. There are several types of visual deficits that may result from cortical injury, such as gaze disorder (strabismus), visual field defects or total blindness.

Cortical injury usually results in severe loss of vision. Any injury to the occipital region of the brain may threaten vision, because this is the area that controls that function. Visual deficits may also occur in conjunction with other disabilities, such as cerebral palsy (CP), wherein a child is more likely to experience optic atrophy, lazy eye (amblyopia) or eye jerks (nystagmus).

Children affected by visual disability or blindness caused by SBS will benefit from regular visits to an ophthalmologist who is experienced in the area of ocular injuries resulting from child abuse.

CEREBRAL PALSY (CP)

This condition identifies a group of disorders that affect a child's motor skills, such as the ability to perform and control normal movements. Poor balance, weakness, stiffness and lack of coordination are all aspects of CP.

A child may be affected on different sides or various parts of his or her body. Hemiplegia is CP that affects an arm and leg on one side of the body, diplegia affects both legs and quadriplegia affects all four limbs. These are all considered "pyramidal" (spastic) CP as the pyramidal tract of the brain is often affected. Muscle control may be spastic (rigid movement), hypotonic (floppy movement) or ataxic (poor balance and coordination).

Extrapyramidal CP occurs when there is damage to the basal ganglia section of the brain. Muscle control will be athetoid (no control) where the limbs move in an abrupt and involuntary fashion. The majority of children diagnosed with extrapyramidal CP have a concurrent diagnosis of being mentally handicapped.

CP in infants and toddlers is diagnosed after certain developmental milestones fail to be met and there is abnormal muscle tone and abnormal movement. There is no exact measurement that can predict the eventual severity of the effects of CP, though by age two a child can be diagnosed as hemiplegic, diplegic or quadriplegic.

Parents and other caregivers are encouraged to allow the infant or toddler to socialize with other children, especially other children with disabilities, because this will emotionally support the child's instinctual need for independence from within a largely dependent body.

DEAFNESS

Children who are shaken may suffer damage to the eighth cranial nerve, which controls hearing. Damage may also affect the bones of the inner ear and the cochlea, which converts sounds from mechanical impulses to chemical and electrical impulses sent to the brain.

Children's hearing may be tested with an audiology follow-up. Deficits in hearing range from a mild impairment to profound deafness. Children may be left with some residual hearing that may be amplified with the assistance of a hearing aid.

Regular visits to an audiologist and speech therapist will help these children who are deafened from shaking to make the most of this particular disability.

DEATH

Death in SBS most commonly occurs as a result of cerebral edema and/ or hemorrhaging with resulting uncontrolled increase of intracranial pressure. Children under the age of six months have a greater risk of dying as a result of being shaken and overall, infants and young children have a 20 to 25 percent chance of dying after a shaking incident.

There are also children who suffer a "late death." These are children who have suffered massive brain injury and die years later, such as a child with only brain stem function which ceases. Or a child who succumbs to increased intracranial pressure and a shunt that can no longer support her neurological changes. Or the child who dies from pneumonia after living with devastating neurological damage for twelve years from being shaken at five months. The outcome for shaken infants is something that can never be predicted. There are children who are expected to live, expected to die, make recoveries that are called "miracles" and others whose young bodies cannot take the trauma of living with their injuries. Providing a hopeful, loving environment is the best any caregiver can give, no matter the days, months or years.

EMOTIONAL PROBLEMS

A subtle complication of SBS is a child who experiences subsequent emotional problems. This is subtle because of the fact that it is one category where a shaking incident may never be discovered or diagnosed. There are children who are shaken, become unconscious, may experience lethargy or vomiting and then recover. Years later, subtle complications will be present without parents or caregivers knowing the basis for such complications. Emotional problems might range from explosive anger to self-injurious behavior to depression. Later in life, a child who has been shaken may develop an attachment disorder. Psychiatric evaluation and treatment may be needed as a shaken child grows.

The harmful effects of abuse can be lessened. Loving family members offer structure and guidance to a child whose basic trust issues were dramatically altered. Parents and caregivers should watch for changes in their children. Therapists and other mental health professionals can help with understanding emotional problems and guide with treatment options.

A Behavioral Issue

My son was three months old and suffered subdural hematomas, seizures, retinal hemorrhages and buckle fractures in both legs. He was misdiagnosed with spinal meningitis for two days before he was transferred to a hospital in Springfield, Illinois. There, he underwent a full body scan and MRI, which showed bleeding in his brain and behind his eyes. I wasn't given this information at the first hospital. I told the nurses that he wasn't looking at me and I was told that it was because of the medication.

I found out at the Springfield hospital that he was blind, because of the bleeding behind his eyes. The next day the Department of Children and Family Services (DCFS) arrived with the Springfield police, accusing me of hurting my baby. Alone and scared and being threatened with having my baby taken away was the worst feeling ever, because I knew I didn't hurt my child. He spent two weeks in the hospital.

I figured out a male friend of mine was responsible for the abuse of my baby. I had to take a lie detector test to prove I had nothing to do with the abuse. The DCFS worker did a home visit and after getting my results I was cleared. She went to the state police to get something done. She fought to have the person responsible brought to justice and we were finally close to an arrest. But that was only the beginning.

I moved nearer to my family, where there were people I knew I could trust. My son had a neurologist, an ophthalmologist and physical and speech therapy, so we were busy. At five months, he had to have surgery to relieve pressure on his brain due to "slow bleeders" from being shaken two months earlier. Then he spent another two weeks in the ICU with more therapy and weekly CT scans in Chicago (two hours away).

My son made great strides, but there were developmental delays which led to special education classes beginning in preschool.

He also had sensory and behavioral issues, which resulted in him getting kicked out of not one school in first grade, but three. School through high school was rough for him, but he now has a community job at one school. He asked for a job, brought his résumé and they found a place for him. He now works ten hours a week and it has been a perfect job match. My son wants to drive but can't, because he has a visual impairment and a seizure disorder.

My son has big dreams of getting a college degree but won't be able to take collage classes, because he functions academically at a third grade level. He wants to get married, because he told me, "I don't want to die alone." I hope someday he can find that special someone. As I look back on what happened to my child, I realize all the hopes and dreams you had for your baby can be taken away in seconds at the hands of another person.

My son asked why he couldn't see very well when he was around ten. I told him he was a survivor of SBS. He got angry and blamed me for going to work that day. It was one of many days that I cried. The guilt and anger have not gone away in twenty-two years. Everyone says you need to forgive, but that hasn't happened yet and I don't think it ever will.

One day he and my grandson were watching a television program. My grandson asked him why he had to sit so close to the TV. My son told him it was because a man shook him and then said, "When I get older we are going to find him, because he needs to pay." That was another day I cried. I wish the court system felt the same way.

The person who hurt my baby did get six years in prison, but only after I gave my victim impact statement. They wanted to give him six months with time served. Someone from the state's attorney office alerted the media to the plea bargain. I talked to the media about not being happy with the plea. Finally, the judge threw out the plea and he got six years. My son's abuser got out of jail over fifteen years ago. My son got a life sentence—somehow that doesn't seem right.

My son receives Supplemental Security Income and has home-based services where personal support workers assist him with being part of the community. He also goes to community college to take

reading classes, because he still hopes he will get his reading level high
enough to get that degree. I never discourage him from dreaming
and always encourage him to advocate for himself. Life was forever
changed on September 9, 1991, and it affected our whole family, but
most of all it changed my son's future. This is a journey I can only
wish no one else ever has to take.

—*Brenda Justi*

GASTROINTESTINAL PROBLEMS

Children who are shaken are frequently left with oral motor dysfunction and hence are unable to chew or swallow. Damage from shaking causes poor oral coordination and functioning as controlled by the brain. A child may aspirate (or breathe in) food or liquid instead of swallowing, or may experience gastroesophageal reflux where food is regularly brought back up the gastroesophageal tract (from the stomach into the esophagus). This can cause severe irritation in the tract from the caustic effects of stomach acid and may lead to excessive weight loss in the child.

When a child has such problems with eating and processing foods, a gastrostomy tube (G-tube) may need to be placed directly into the stomach. One type of G-tube is the percutaneous gastrostomy (or PEG) tube. A needle is inserted into the stomach and the PEG is passed over the needle, all done under anesthesia.

Finally, children who have been shaken may have problems with processing food in their intestines and bowels. They may experience constipation. Changes in their diet, medications and laxatives (prescribed under a physician's care) may help alleviate such problems. Registered dieticians are also invaluable resources.

Betrayal by a Loved One

I was dating my daughter's father for two years. We were high
school sweethearts. I moved into his family's house for just one
month. Chris proposed to me just nine days before my worst day

ever. My daughter had just turned three months old and I left her with her father for my first day in Nursing Assisting Class. He was alone with her for ten minutes, so that his mother could run to the store. By the time I got home, she was already on her way to the hospital. She was not breathing for five minutes before Chris started CPR.

Chris waited until the cops showed up in the ICU the day after her injury to confess to abusing her. Since I had a runaway record back when I was sixteen, Child Protective Services [CPS] came in and questioned my mom to find out what might have happened. Both Chris and I were nineteen at the time. Two plainclothes cops came in and questioned me for three hours and then took Chris and questioned him. When he finally confessed, I was in tears and he was escorted from the hospital. Then I was asked by CPS to obtain a non-contact order, keeping him away from me and my baby. He was formally arrested on February 24, 2000, and they released my daughter from the hospital. When it finally came time for court, he pled not guilty to first-degree assault on a child, which carried a sentence of ten plus years. He pled guilty to second-degree assault on child and got sentenced to forty-six months. He was released after just twenty-six months for good behavior. The only thing that is required of him is to stay away from us.

As you can imagine, there was a major effect on the family. I can only work part-time, due to all the appointments that my girl has, the constant hospitalizations and her declining health.

My daughter turned fourteen this past October. She just had her twentieth surgery. She has had three brain surgeries, several G-J tubes inserted, two Baclofen pump changes, surgery on her teeth, tendon releases and many, many more. She is 100 percent total care, which means she can't do anything for herself. She has a feeding tube and an intrathecal pump, which gives her medicine twenty-four hours a day. She wears diapers, gets nothing by mouth and has a mental age of three to six months of age. She will never walk, talk, go on a first date, get married or have children of her own.

Life today is a day-by-day struggle. Her health is slowly getting worse. We were granted a wish from the Make-A-Wish Foundation and she went to Walt Disney World this past May for her wish. We are unsure how long she will be with us, but we enjoy every minute with her. My daughter has the support of me, her younger sister, her younger brother, my boyfriend of almost five years, grandparents, aunts, uncles, several other family members and very close friends, including the local music scene in Washington State who totally fell in love with her.

—*Shannon Stiles*

HYDROCEPHALUS

One complication of traumatic brain injury is an excessive build-up of fluid in and around the ventricles of the cranial space. Cerebrospinal fluid (CSF) is constantly being produced and absorbed in the brain. If there is a problem with resorption, CSF backs up and causes brain, and subsequently head, enlargement.

Hydrocephalus is controlled through the use of a shunt, a small tube inserted into one of the ventricles of the brain. The opposite end of the shunt is placed in either the abdominal cavity or the jugular vein for drainage and resorption. Shunts may malfunction over time, becoming clogged, and then require replacement or repair. Shunts may also become infected. Eighty percent of infections, if they develop, will occur within six months of the shunt placement surgery. Persistent headaches, nausea and vomiting will be signs of problematic shunt functioning.

Another treatment for the build-up of CSF suggests a rerouting within the ventricular system by endoscopic third ventriculostomy. Such a procedure is much more invasive but the long-term success rate is high, especially in children over two years of age. Usually, infants will initially receive a shunt placement and then be offered endoscopic treatment later.

HYPERSENSITIVITY

Infants and children who have been shaken can be hypersensitive in various ways. Hypersensitivity to touch means that an infant cannot distinguish between types and degrees of touch and can withdraw in a self-regulatory fashion. Patient, loving hands will eventually help the infant accept a caregiver's touch. Hypersensitivity to sound can keep an entire family tiptoeing. Infants with this condition frequently wail with discomfort when distressed by noise. Hypersensitivity to temperature relates to a dysfunction in the body's self-regulatory and circulatory process. Frequently hands and feet will become cold or hot. Caregivers will need to be extra conscious of this when dressing a hypersensitive child.

LEARNING DISABILITY

Children in this category may appear to act and think normally until they are faced with regular mental processing challenges in the classroom. This is another subtle complication from a shaking incident that is rarely discovered. Children with learning disabilities cannot process complex information adequately or smoothly. Writing, reading, mathematical computations and other types of learning can become significant hurdles.

Great care and patience is required when working with a child with a learning disability. Such a child will probably require an individualized educational plan (IEP) whereby many disciplines will come together to develop the right tools to effectively educate the child. There are several types of learning disability: visual (problems distinguishing shapes or colors), verbal (problems with word or sentence formation), reading (misreading or problems with pronunciation), attention (poorly follows instructions) and computational (problems with math). Learning disabilities can be diagnosed by psychological testing.

MENTAL HANDICAP

After a child is shaken and if there has been significant brain trauma, he or she may not have the ability to learn like other children. Children with mental handicaps have below-average intelligence, meaning their intelligence quotient (IQ) falls below 70—the average IQ being 100. IQ may actually drop as the child becomes older.

Mentally handicapped children may later learn to care for themselves, live on their own, go shopping and hold jobs. But in a small percentage of cases, the brain damage is too severe and they never become able to care for themselves. Children can be mentally handicapped in conjunction with other SBS injuries, such as blindness, deafness or CP. Evaluation and planning by a team of professionals is vital for the successful functioning of a mentally handicapped child and other family members. Such a team should consist of a pediatrician, speech therapist, clinical psychologist, special education teacher, social worker, etc. In this situation, a properly constructed IEP will maximize intellectual and social potential. Parents and caregivers should focus on gross motor skills, such as running, swimming and playing ball, as fine motor skills have the potential to be unsuccessful and frustrating for the child.

MICROCEPHALY

This condition is defined by a head circumference that is two standard deviations below the average for gender and age. Shaking can cause an infant's brain to slow down its rate of growth. The protective skull will slow down in tandem. Microcephaly in itself renders a poor prognosis. Most of these children will be severely disabled or have other physical complications.

PERSISTENT VEGETATIVE STATE

With the exception of death, this is by far the worst consequence of SBS. Though rare, this condition is emotionally the most difficult for an infant's family. When an infant's brain suffers severe damage, it may go through dynamic changes, such as excessive fluid build-up, ventricle atrophy, chronic hemorrhage, etc. In response to such trauma, the brain may shut down, leaving only the brainstem to function. Thus the child has no awareness of the outside world. Activities such as eating and drinking, moving spontaneously in bed, reacting to sights and sounds and sometimes even breathing are all very limited or impossible. The child is in a persistent vegetative state, where the body can only be kept alive artificially with breathing tubes, feeding tubes, etc. The child's body will continue to grow, but there is little hope for rehabilitation and death can be expected within months to a few years.

RESPIRATION DIFFICULTIES

Another devastating consequence of SBS is that a child's brain may be damaged in an area that controls the function of the throat. For example, if the gag reflex is lost, the child cannot clear his or her lungs. A child may also aspirate, or breathe in, saliva or food and could ultimately develop pneumonia. A tracheostomy is an operation done to provide an alternative route for breathing. It involves surgically cutting a hole and placing a tube in the child's trachea. This opening bypasses the mouth and throat and allows for a separate airway. Tracheostomy tubes can be temporary or permanent. Those that are permanent are more for children who have severe problems with aspiration.

Families will need to learn the details of caring for a tracheostomy tube, which includes regular suctioning, cleaning and dressing. For chronically debilitated children, there may ultimately be a need for ventilator support. A ventilator is an apparatus that breathes for the child. This is a life-sustaining measure, yet makes the child more susceptible to lung infections.

SEIZURES

Also known as convulsions, seizures can be a feature with any brain injury diagnosis. Seizures occur from a sudden flurry of neuron activity which blocks normal brain functioning. A common entity with cerebral palsy and epilepsy, they are one of the main consequences of SBS.

Electroencephalograms (EEGs) measure brain activity during a seizure and when seizures are absent. Most children with epilepsy and CP have abnormal EEG patterns.

There are several types of seizures that a child may experience. *Generalized* seizures (formerly known as *grand mal*) are the most demonstrative of seizures and involve the entire cerebral cortex of the brain. There will be tonic-clonic seizuring. The tonic element of the generalized seizure will produce body stiffening and loss of consciousness. The clonic elements of the generalized seizure alternate between relaxation and tensing of the body's muscles. Often, incontinence and deep sleep follow generalized seizures.

Partial or *focal* seizures (formerly known as *petite mal*) are limited to a small area of the cortex and produce involuntary, sudden movements in one area of the body. They occur in a way that is non-intrusive to the child.

There are several types of partial seizures. *Simple* partial seizures occur when the individual experiences an unusual sensation, including sudden, jerky movements of one body part, distortions in hearing or seeing, stomach discomfort or a sudden sense of fear. Consciousness is not impaired. *Complex* partial seizures are characterized by impaired consciousness. During such seizures a child will appear dazed and purposeless behaviors called "automatisms" may be observed, such as random movements, staring or lip-smacking. *Generalized absence* seizures are characterized by lapses in consciousness for several seconds. During this time a child will appear to be staring into space with eyes rolled upwards. They may evolve into other seizure types, such as complex partial or tonic-clonic.

Brain injury in SBS may also be followed by infantile spasms. These spasms, unlike normal startle reactions, occur when an infant's head suddenly drops forward while its trunk and legs "jack-knife" upward. They occur frequently throughout the day and disappear around age twenty-four months. Infantile spasms can lead to a more disabling condition called Lennox-Gastaut syndrome, which is characterized by frequent seizuring. Finally, *status epilepticus* is characterized by a steady set of seizures where consciousness is not regained between convulsions. Any seizure that lasts more than five minutes should be viewed as a medical emergency. Shaken infants often present in hospital emergency rooms with an initial diagnosis of status epilepticus.

Seizures in infants who have been recently shaken are associated with blood in the subdural and subarachnoid spaces of the brain and intracranial pressure. As the intracranial injuries resolve, there should be a resolution of the seizures as well, though some infants may experience twitching or jerking in the face, hand or leg. Lastly, a fever in a brain-injured child can bring about a seizure (febrile seizure).

Seizures can be very troubling for parents and caregivers, but knowing what to do during a seizure can change a situation of panic into one of structured calm. Being prepared for seizures is the main thing that parents and caregivers can do for their child. The following pattern of activities is a positive system to use when seizures occur: calm, turn, allow, time, support and document.

First, the adults should remain calm in order to give maximum support to the child. Next, the adult should carefully turn the child onto his or her side in order to avoid a choking hazard. Then they must allow the child to go through their seizure without restraint. Light touches and calming words can help both the caregiver and child (if conscious) remain calm.

It is important to time seizures, both when they happen and how long they last. A child's neurologist will need such information. When the seizure is finished, the child will need loving support. Emotional security is an important element in seizure management.

Finally, the caregiver should document the type of seizure and whether there were any complications. Caregivers who have questions about the seriousness of a seizure should contact their pediatrician immediately.

Most seizures can be controlled with anti-seizure medications. Ketogenic diets have been known to help control seizure activities. When a person fasts there is an accumulation of ketone bodies (ketosis) which in addition to increasing the body's acidity level (acidosis) can control seizures. It is often used when antiseizure medication does not effectively control seizures or when medication is not a treatment preferred by a parent or caregiver.

Ketogenic diets dramatically reduce carbohydrate and protein intake and maximize fat intake. Careful monitoring needs to occur using a registered dietician. To get to the state of ketosis, a child must go on a fast. The ketosis balance within the body must be maintained and caregivers need to be thoroughly educated. Often times, such diets begin if a child is hospitalized with a medical condition related to an injury as a result of a shaking incident. The child can be carefully monitored in a controlled setting. Some parents and caregivers of shaken children are true advocates for this diet and state that it cuts down not only the number of seizures their child experiences but the amount of medication that is taken as well. It is best to read about this subject carefully and discuss it with a medical provider before any intervention is begun.

Adrenocorticotropic hormone (ACTH) injections are an invasive treatment for seizures but seem to be effective when other treatments fail.

SPEECH PROBLEMS

Shaken infants who have sustained traumatic brain injury before beginning to talk may be left with the potential for later development of speech deficits. Often the problem will manifest itself when the children reach school or when their speech is tested when they are older. Speech disturbances appear in many forms. Aphasia occurs when children are unable to process information and cannot express themselves effectively. Problems with articulation may be due to difficulty with facial and mouth control. A child caught up in a pattern of abuse may have had an injury to the frenulum of his or her mouth (the thin membrane attached from the underside of the tongue to the floor of the mouth). Such a child may be "tongue-tied" as a result, whereby articulation can be challenging. Children with CP or who are mentally handicapped may suffer from stuttering (dysfluency). Often, the more excited a child becomes, the more he or she will stutter. Children should never be reprimanded for stuttering, but may need to be reminded to slow down the speed of their speech.

TOTAL PARALYSIS

Some children who survive a shaking episode will not have the benefit of limb mobility and may be confined to a wheelchair for the remainder of their lives. Such children may have sustained a spinal cord injury or an injury to the brain, which coordinates movement. They will be dependent on their caregivers for everything and will not progress through developmental milestones. There may be more tantrums in children with total paralysis as they are unable to move freely and toddlerhood is an important time to be more independent.

Physical and occupational therapies may allow for maximal use of limbs in paralyzed children, but often, neuromuscular messages are not transmitted or are slow to transmit. Such a dramatic injury may or may not affect the child's vocal cords and capabilities for chewing and swallowing. Feeding tubes may be required in children with SBS who are unable to eat effectively. If there are no developmental delays or mental handicaps, children can ultimately learn to use speech boards if there is a speech deficit. Ventilators are often required, because the basic instinct of respiration can be altered in shaking injuries.

Paralysis affects the entire family financially, emotionally and socially. Care at a regional rehabilitation center can allow families to slowly adapt to the changes brought on by paralysis and to learn vital information associated with caregiving.

CHAPTER 6

Consultation and Follow-Up

Miracle Child

When my daughter was born, she was a healthy baby girl. But at the age of sixteen months, our lives changed forever and our nightmare began. On September 2, 2006, I left my little girl with my then-boyfriend to go down the street to the market to get milk. I was gone less than twenty minutes. When I returned home, there were emergency vehicles everywhere and my daughter was in the back of an ambulance. I asked my boyfriend what happened, and he said she just stopped breathing. I wasn't sure why she stopped breathing; she was a healthy girl. I rode in the ambulance but I wasn't allowed in the back with her. The paramedics stood around her, blocking me from seeing her. At this point I freaked out and couldn't wrap my mind around what was happening. Because my boyfriend wasn't her dad he couldn't ride in the ambulance with us.

We arrived at the hospital, where my daughter was placed in the trauma room. My boyfriend came to the hospital with his mother. He sat right beside me and held my hand. My family and I were placed in the waiting room in the ICU. Later that night, the doctor came in and took my parents and me to another room. There were security guards and a nurse on both sides of the door. The doctor sat me down and told me my baby's head was injured and she just got out of surgery. She was injured by Shaken Baby Syndrome and was in bad shape. I dropped to my knees and became hysterical. The security guards would not let me out of that room, because I couldn't calm down.

When I grew quiet, I was told what happened and that I would be allowed to see my daughter. They told me to be prepared since she was in a coma and on life support. I walked into her room. There were tubes in her nose and throat and machines everywhere. The child I once had who was full of joy and energy was now lifeless—she couldn't speak or even move. She just laid there. My heart had never been so sad in my whole life. I never felt so much pain, hurt and anger as when I laid eyes on my daughter in that condition. Later that night, after everyone knew what happened, my boyfriend left the hospital and left my daughter on her deathbed.

She had swelling of her entire brain, a skull fracture, cortical blindness, severe developmental delay, traumatic injury to her head and brain, bruises around her neck, subdural hematoma (which means blood collections pressing on the surface of the brain) and retinal hemorrhage (which means bleeding behind the eyes because of torn blood vessels). She was shaken hard enough to break the veins that bridge from the skull into the brain, which put her in a coma and on life support. She was supposed to die from her injuries.

The doctors told me most babies that come in with these kinds of injuries don't make it past the first twenty-four to forty-eight hours, and I should think about letting nature take its course. I could not pull the life support plug. I couldn't make that kind of decision—it was way too hard. I told the doctors, "My kid is going to bury me but I'm not going to bury my kid." Then they let me hold her while she was in a coma and on life support. They said they only allowed that to happen if they knew the child wouldn't make it. I held her and it was the hardest thing ever, to hold her that way. Her life was slipping through my fingers and there wasn't anything I could do but pray to God for a miracle. After being in a coma and on life support for nearly two weeks, my baby beat the odds, woke from her coma and started taking breaths on her own. Then she was weaned off life support. When they took the tube out of her throat, I heard her first cry and it made me cry too.

At that moment, I knew my little girl was going to live through this. However, after waking up from her coma, she wasn't the same child at all. She couldn't do anything anymore. She couldn't even swallow her own saliva. A tube had to go in her mouth every five to ten minutes to suck the saliva out. The hospital ran several tests on her and her brain was still too swollen and it was determined that more than half her brain was damaged, which is a lot. The doctors told me she would always be mentally handicapped and wouldn't ever be able to do anything—talk, walk or function in any way. She would be in a vegetative state her whole life. I said, "Not my kid," which they didn't believe.

She spent four weeks in one hospital and then was transported to another hospital for extended rehab for another four weeks. She had around-the-clock therapy to make her stronger.

My daughter came home at the very end of October 2006. We still had a long road ahead of us. Even though I was thrilled and thankful to have her home, she was not the same little girl I remembered. She had been forever changed. She had a feeding tube and a kangaroo pump, due to her not knowing how to eat. She was also put on seizure medication, because of the brain damage. She has a seizure disorder (called Lennox-Gastaut). Her seizures became uncontrollable and a test showed she had eighty-eight seizures in one eight-hour period.

The first two years were the hardest. We were in and out of three different children's hospitals, as well as several therapy sessions. She was even in an early intervention program to help her get stronger.

Today, my daughter is a miracle. She now walks, runs, talks, plays and functions well. She is not mentally handicapped. She does everything all the doctors said she would never be able to do. She beat the odds and did the impossible. No more feeding tubes and she has been seizure-free for two years now. Her vision has gotten a lot better, but it is still unknown how much she can see. But she can see more than everybody thought she would be able to. She goes to school and loves it. She also roller skates on her own. She attends "Step to Your Dreams," which is a therapy clinic, and she really enjoys it. There, she receives Hippotherapy, which is horseback riding. She can count and say her ABCs. Though more than half of her brain was damaged, everybody is amazed at what my daughter has been able to achieve in a short period of time. But she still faces challenges every day. I'm not sure what the future will hold for my daughter, but God let her live for a reason and for that I'm very thankful.

—Randi Shepherd

After a child has been shaken, there is a multitude of medical and social personnel involved in his or her care. An effective team of individuals will work collaboratively to assure the best possible outcome for a shaken child and his or her family. Some members of the multidisciplinary group will be consulted for only a short time, while others will follow the child for months or years. It is vital that families of shaken children are comfortable enough to ask pertinent questions or share their feelings with any member of the multidisciplinary team. This provides not only a caring atmosphere, but a professional one as well.

Now let's look at various team members and their roles:

AUDIOLOGY

For a child with suspected hearing loss, the audiologist will administer a hearing test and, based on the results, will make formalized recommendations for treatment. A brainstem auditory evoked response (BAER) is a type of hearing test that is done during an electroencephalogram (EEG). An audible click is produced and a neural response from the brain should be seen in the form of sound waves.

Hearing tests can indicate mild, moderate and severe hearing loss. If there is some residual hearing available, hearing aids can improve the child's potential to hear sounds and voices. Cochlear implantation has also been found to be useful in both children and adults with hearing loss.

CHAPLAINCY

Hospital ministry provides great comfort for families in need of emotional and spiritual care. Chaplains are available for all types of needs: to pray, to listen, to handhold, to guide and to administer communion.

Most hospitals will have a quiet meditation room or chapel where families may gather for prayer or worship services. Chaplains are an important part of the hospital interdisciplinary team to assist families and others through emotionally difficult times. Prayer groups and guidance can also support hospital personnel and clinicians affected in their own way by SBS.

GASTROENTEROLOGY

Because brain injury may cause subsequent problems for a child's gastrointestinal process, a gastroenterologist may be consulted. This type of specialist will help determine if feeding tubes or surgery are necessary (especially if there was abdominal trauma related to the shaking incident). Chronic gastrointestinal problems are followed up on an outpatient basis with a gastroenterologist.

NEUROLOGY

Because the brain is such a complex organ, injury to any of its parts may cause significant problems. Seizuring is one example and is a result of faulty neurotransmission. Neurologists are specialists who can help manage seizures and other neurological deficits experienced by hospitalized and outpatient children.

To help ensure a favorable brain response, neurologists will track a child's EEG, prescribe medication, aid in the interpretation of CT and MRI scans and so on. Outpatient management will depend on the severity of neurological difficulties the child is experiencing. Visits may occur on a regular basis or may only be a few times each year.

NEUROSURGERY

A neurosurgeon can determine the best method for stopping intracranial bleeding. Shunts, burr holes (a small hole drilled to drain hematomas) and craniotomies (surgeries where a bone flap is temporarily removed to access the brain) are ways to evacuate collections of blood within the cranium. Neurosurgeons will not only perform the surgery, but also will follow up with the child after hospitalization to assure successful management of intracranial trauma.

NURSING

Though not a specialty that is formally consulted, nurses take care of a shaken child and help his/her family from the child's first appearance in a hospital emergency room. Nurses provide the backbone of the medical care a child receives and often assist with the emotional needs of the family.

Often the first medical contact with the child and family at a hospital, nurses are in a unique information-gathering position. Their documentation of the initial injury history can make the difference in how cases proceed.

In an outpatient or hospital setting, nurses are in an important position for early identification of families at risk for SBS, recognition of victims of SBS and management of patients suspected of SBS.

Nurses can also make a difference in how a family remembers the experience of the child's hospitalization. They can create special touches for injured children by placing soft toys in their hospital beds, by comforting with a touch and by soothing with calming words. These are the types of empathic medicine unique to the profession of nursing.

NUTRITION

When a child is unable to eat, because of brain trauma and other abusive injuries, a nutritionist will work with a gastroenterologist to supply the child with the appropriate types of nutrition. For example, *parenteral* nutrition is a type of feeding that utilizes an IV in a child's upper chest or a PEG tube in the child's stomach.

Sometimes children are unable to chew food, even if they knew how prior to the shaking incident. In this case, alternative means will be found to provide nutrition, such as a liquid or soft food diet. Nutritionists allow for the child to maintain the calories necessary to grow and rehabilitate.

OPHTHALMOLOGY

Since most shaken children have intraocular trauma, they will be seen by ophthalmologists. There are so many different types of ocular injury that may occur to a shaken child that it is usually wise for the child to be seen by a pediatric ophthalmologist. These specialists often have expertise in child abuse-related injuries and will be able to provide state-of-the-art care. Surgery may even be needed to correct damaged vision, i.e. detached retinas. Otherwise, frequent outpatient appointments will assist in managing injuries to the eye caused by shaking.

ORTHOPEDICS

Unless there have been concurrent fractures in a child who has been shaken, orthopedists may not be used until later in the child's development. As a child grows, there may be complications in the child's limb movement. For example, a child with cerebral palsy may experience hip subluxation, whereby the hip becomes dislocated. Surgery can hopefully correct this in order to avoid osteoarthritis later.

Orthopedists can guide parents and caregivers in the appropriate support of legs, feet, arms and hands, i.e. brace support. Strengthening exercises can also be suggested.

PEDIATRICS

Residents and/or ER physicians will provide initial care and the child's pediatrician will then be notified of the incident and will formally admit the child to the hospital in person or, if the admission is in the middle of the night, over the phone. The pediatrician then performs the day-to-day management of the child, writes orders for other specialists to become involved and arranges for special procedures.

In an intensive care unit, the child may have a medical director who also writes orders and is key in managing the child's care. Children who survive shaking tragedies will follow up with their pediatricians when they are discharged from the hospital.

PSYCHIATRY/PSYCHOLOGY

Hospital emergency rooms often have a mental health component to their care teams. Psychiatrist or psychologist involvement in this initial process is important because these specialists will support families of shaken children. They may also have a chance to interview or converse with the perpetrator of the shaking crime. Thorough documentation can then play a significant role in efforts to prosecute such cases.

Ongoing therapy for family members is beneficial and psychiatrists or psychologists can offer such therapy.

PULMONARY/RESPIRATORY THERAPY

Proper brain functioning is one of the keys to proper lung functioning. Children who are shaken may need to be intubated if they are unable to breathe on their own. Pulmonologists will be involved to offer guidance with the management of heart and lung functioning. If the child will be ventilator-dependent, these specialists will provide follow-up care as well.

Another important caregiver in the hospital setting is the respiratory therapist. Duties include checking blood gases, setting appropriate oxygen flow and interpreting vital oxygen counts. Respiratory therapists can also help arrange home oxygen for children going home.

SOCIAL WORK

Social work can provide a great deal of care and comfort for families affected by illness, injury and death. Social workers have a multifaceted role in the management of a shaken child. A social worker will be a member of the team that initially evaluates the injured child and interviews the family members. Child Protective Services will become involved, and social work may or may not be the discipline to coordinate their involvement.

Social workers also provide brief counseling and support for families affected by SBS, arrange homecare services and transportation, follow up with community agencies, arrange short-term extended care facility placement (if necessary) and assist with financial services.

Social workers have a much different role today than in years past. They work along with other disciplines to maximize family integration and advocate for the child. These dual roles may sometimes be contradictory. Social workers are often seen as working against a family in an abuse case, by taking away the children involved, and sometimes also their siblings, while the investigation proceeds. What is paramount is the safety of the child.

PART 2

SBS In Depth

CHAPTER 7

Victimology

Using a criminal profiling term, we now will conduct an in-depth examination of which infants and children are most at risk to be shaken. *Victimology* has to do with the relationship of a victim to the perpetrator of a crime. For adults, it is an examination of every facet of their lifestyles, background, health and physical characteristics. Using this information, criminal profilers hope that through an in-depth examination of the victims, they might understand the perpetrators of crimes better and ultimately lead to their apprehension. For profilers, victimology is important in the overall investigative process since it discloses who the victims are, as well as their personal histories, social habits and personalities. More importantly, it reveals why individuals are chosen as victims.

For some people, the term "victimology" is a blaming one. But this is far from true. One can't place fault on an infant or child for crying or exhibiting normal developmental behaviors. This term is used to explain the traits children have that spur caregivers to shake them violently.

Victimology also provides ideas as to why certain infants are chosen as victims. In adult crimes, especially involving serial killers, the perpetrator may hold back from choosing a victim until he meets one who satisfies his needs, which allows him to fulfill a fantasy or desire. Yet in child abuse there is no fantasy, unless it's a fantasy of torture. Child shaking victims are usually chosen subconsciously. Although there is a conscious decision to violently shake a child, the act of choosing the victim is important as it gives an insight into how the offender thinks, which subsequently affects how he or she acts. For example, a mother's male friend wins her affection, in part, by engaging with her children and in due course becomes her partner. But, if the male friend actually has disdain for children, then the children may be targets of his anger and control when left alone with him. There is also the situation in the home of the "runt," that one child who is simply not liked by one or both parents. In a daycare setting, assessing the motives of an employee who shakes a child is more difficult. However, by looking at the victim, there may be telling characteristics that the child brings through no fault of his or her own, such as being new to the daycare, being sick or lonely, crying easily, etc.

Investigators can assess how subjects are acting at the time of crime scene walk-throughs or during formal police interviews. With this evaluation, they may be more likely to pinpoint a perpetrator based on the victim's behavior and the person's relationship with the victim. If there is not enough evidence to make an arrest yet, investigators may be better able to predict the future behavior of the subject, possibly leading to a successful prosecution.

Certain concepts that are related to victimology (method of approach, method of attack and risk assessment) can be used in physical abuse crimes against children. Asking questions regarding the child's personality (i.e. easy to soothe, cries a lot, has temper tantrums), investigators may be able to determine how he or she was approached by the caregiver. Questions such as, "What did you do when he started crying?" and "Before she stopped breathing, what were you doing with her?" will be asked. What, using the words of the caregiver, was the victim doing prior to the 911 call? So, not only what the *caregiver* was doing, but what the infant or child was doing is examined. In terms of method of attack, perpetrators of child abuse crimes use different methods to inflict pain. For example, a parent who wouldn't think of hitting a child might shake a child. Or the caregiver who chooses a scalding bath as punishment for a toilet-training toddler might also shake a child. Perpetrators choose certain methods that they believe will control and punish. Finally, there is risk assessment. Who are those most at risk to shake? This is not directly possible (specifically in regards to shaking as a mechanism of abuse), but indirectly by considering certain characteristics of perpetrators of child abuse. This will be looked at in the next chapter and in the prevention chapter, but risk assessment can be done on multiple levels. Hospitals can provide education to parents about the dangers of shaking and hospital social workers can be involved for emotional support and guidance if there are concerns that either parent is not bonding well with the baby. Parents often use risk assessment in evaluating daycare providers, but they need to know what questions to ask. This is not always fail-safe, as there have been SBS cases after daycare owners reported they were licensed (and were not) or reported there were no problems with children in the past several years (but there were complaints by parents), etc. Finally, parents are often blinded to risk assessment on each other. A father might not pick up on the stresses that raising children can cause for the mother. Or the mother may believe the boyfriend who offers, "I'll be fine and I'll call you if I need you," but fails to commit to that promise.

It is important to use the study of victimology to not only understand perpetrators, but to assess victims of SBS to predict abuse as well. To begin with, we need to look at the basic physical makeup of infants, as previously discussed: weak neck musculature, larger head-to-body ratio than adults and an immature, soft brain. With all these characteristics, you have a recipe for a disastrous outcome when shaking occurs.

Also previously noted, a shaken infant has a 25 percent death rate and a 60 percent rate of lifelong complications. These are important statistics, because it gives all professionals involved in the care of the child an insight into what lies ahead. The prognosis is poor and, because of this, doctors can do all they can to extend a child's life or make it better, while police and prosecutors can start working on criminal charges. This relates to victimology, because children who are hospitalized after being shaken have the universal link to a violent person. Someone shook the child, caused enormous damage to the child and the details need to be tied together to hold the person responsible.

Another aspect of SBS victimology is the fact that babies cry to communicate. This becomes problematic for certain caregivers who have problems with control issues. If the caregiver is unable to calm or manage a crying baby, then it will be much easier to physically manage that crying (i.e. shaking), than to figure out ways to stop it. A crying child is the number one reason why perpetrators shake. Research has shown that infant crying peaks at around four months of age, beginning a regular pattern at two months.[1] The younger the child, the more susceptible he or she is.

Full of Life

My daughter was twenty-one-and-a-half months old at the time of her abuse. She was so smart. She was walking, talking and just so full of life! I had just started going back to college after a four-year break and was twenty-four. I had only been in school for about two weeks. On September 13th, 2006, I had my first English quiz. My close friend, Steve, didn't have class that morning, so he said he didn't mind watching my daughter. I left early for school that day to study in the parking lot before class. I was bound and determined to get straight A's.

On my way home from class later that day, I called home to check on my daughter and talk to Steve. I had a twenty-five-minute drive home, so I figured I could chat with him a little bit to make the drive home seem faster. I had worked a lot the weekend before and I was off that evening, so I was very excited to get to spend the whole day with my baby girl. When I called, Steve answered. I asked how my daughter was, and he said, "I don't know; I think something may be wrong." Then he told me she wasn't breathing right. I didn't quite know what he meant, because he seemed very calm. But I knew something was wrong. I called 911, since I was so far away from home.

I arrived at the hospital the same time as the paramedics. I asked what was wrong with my baby. No one really had any answers. I did hear one man say, "We don't know." It seemed like an eternity, but I think it was about forty-five minutes when a doctor came out of the room to tell me they suspected there might be head trauma, because her pupils weren't dilating. I wasn't quite sure what that meant or if it meant the injury was severe, but I knew her condition wasn't good.

The scans came back. The doctor asked me to come into another room. I didn't want to go, because I think I knew in my heart it was going to be bad. He asked me to have a seat. I felt like I was in one of those movies where they say, "You might want to sit down for this." At first I didn't want to sit, but I told myself, if it was bad news, I'd better be sitting, because I might faint. Then I heard the words, "Someone shook your daughter violently. If she survives, and that's 'if' she survives, she will be severely disabled."

Her whole life literally flashed before my eyes. I prayed that she would get through it, that it wasn't as bad as they said it was. They life-flighted her to a major hospital in Toledo, Ohio, about an hour away from where I live. She died at 10:31 P.M. on September 14, 2006.

My hospital experience was very professional, caring, non-judgmental and positive. Everything that was done was in the best interest of my daughter, myself and the legal side of things. The doctor on duty recognized quickly that my daughter's symptoms appeared to have been caused by being shaken violently. I believe the life-flight to a larger hospital was a way to keep her alive long enough to see specialists and allow for family to have time to gather and be by her side. It was readily apparent that her injuries were too severe to do any emergency surgeries or anything along those lines. They never provided me with false hope but also weren't quick to write her off either.

While at the local hospital, I was questioned by authorities. After questioning, I rode with family to the new hospital. It was the longest one-hour drive of my life. Meanwhile, investigators were questioning Steve at my apartment. It is my understanding that they convinced him to come to the station to write a statement. It was then that they were able to hold him on the basis that he violated his parole. Apparently he had a curfew and admitted to investigators that he had stayed the night at my apartment. Over the next two days they interrogated him. On the second day he admitted to shaking my daughter.

He was charged with murder. The Friday before the trial was to begin, he took a plea deal. He pled "no contest," that is, he did not admit guilt but did consent to the judge finding him guilty. The stipulations of his plea deal were that if he had good behavior while incarcerated, the state could not make any recommendations at his parole hearing. If he had bad behavior, the state could then make *a recommendation. The judge found him guilty and sentenced him to fifteen years to life. He is eligible for parole in 2021. Our family is allowed to petition the parole board and make any recommendations we feel appropriate. The man who shook my daughter, whom I trusted and who told me over and over he loved me, who treated me like a queen, is in prison. And my daughter is dead.*

Our world has been turned upside down. Not only has this affected our family, but also our friends and anyone who has come across our story. We have trust issues. We are paranoid. We miss my daughter. I've since had two more children who will never know their big sister. I will never be the same again. I miss my happy, carefree ways. I have anxiety. I blame every little problem in my life on what he did to her and to me. I have lots of support, yet I often feel all alone.

I've found solace in having candlelight memorials on the anniversary of her death and throwing parties on her birthday with cupcakes and balloons. Every year we send a cupcake up to her in heaven, tied to a balloon. I've used online support groups and in-person support groups. I've never had counseling. I turned to awareness to help myself grieve. But mainly, I've learned to block out the thoughts of my daughter, of him. It often makes me sad, because sometimes it's now hard to actually remember her. Thankfully I have photos and videos. It's just not the same, though.

I'm finally back in college. I'm attempting to live as normal a life as possible but it's often difficult. I should graduate in May 2015, with my degree in diagnostic medical sonography. My other children are now two and five. My daughter would be nine years old if she were still alive. We recently had our "seven years in heaven" balloon release and candlelight memorial.

I miss her so much. She was my whole world. Never leave your child with someone you don't truly know and trust. It's now my purpose in life to try to put an end to child abuse and my cause is making parents aware of the dangers of shaking a child and that it can happen to anyone. There really is no way to describe the pain and horror of losing a child. I can only say, it's sort of like how you would imagine it, except it's real, it's not just a bad thought. You wake up every single day, getting hit with the reality of it all, that your child isn't

*coming back. You also have to tell yourself every day that you will
be with them someday. Shaking shatters lives! Never shake a baby!*

—Melissa Fell

While MeKenna was female, approximately 60 percent of shaken
children are male. The real reason is unknown, but a commonly held
belief among child abuse professionals is that, in a perpetrator's mind,
male babies aren't supposed to cry (even though they are babies). Male
babies are supposed to be tough and often are brought up that way. Their
victimology is driven by their sex—the fact that they are males.

If, after being born, there is a delay in an infant coming home from
the hospital (either due to low birth weight, illness or a birth defect complication), then the chance of the infant being shaken increases. The reason for this is believed to be that in the view of the parent(s), this infant
is "different." A happy, healthy baby was expected, but instead there was
a complication. This in and of itself can set the baby apart from one or
both parents. The emotional distance created by a problem birth can lead
to an abusive or shaking event.

Nearly three decades ago, Brenner and colleagues reported on
their review of 545 abused infants seen over a period of five years.[2]
Of these cases, 447 abused children were African-American and 87
were Caucasian. They found twenty shaken infants, eight of whom were
Caucasian and twelve were African-American. So, Caucasian infants
represented a disproportionately high percentage (9 percent [eight of
87] versus 2.7 percent [twelve of 447]). All social classes and races have
shaken infants. It is a syndrome that does not discriminate. Yet, in recent years, there has been a shift in the trend of race of the victim,
from Caucasian to African-American. In 2000, Sinal found that race
was not a significant factor in predicting SBS cases.[3] In 2011, Esnerio-
Jones found, in their study group, that African-American and Hispanic
children were the top racial groups in terms of SBS victims, followed
by Caucasians.[4]

The final aspect of victimology in the realm of SBS is who the infant is around on a day-to-day basis. Since infants are unable to choose
their parents and caregivers, this makes them totally vulnerable (or

totally secure in a loving home). The social habit of an infant is outwardly regulated. He or she has no control over day-to-day interactions with others, choice of food, etc. Even a toddler has very limited control—an example of this is refusing to do something and throwing a temper tantrum. Some babies cry more than others, some toddlers act out more than others. This "negative" aspect of personality will be seen by certain caregivers as a problem. With these caregivers, there are limited positive reactions to such negative outbursts. Caregivers who are in a controlling mindset don't believe that it is okay to leave a child alone in a room. They could ask for an "adult time-out" and call someone for help or do something to recharge their batteries, but they don't. They act instead, which is when victimology leads to a harmful (or deadly) outcome.

CHAPTER 8

Perpetrators

Consider the following people: a twenty-two-year-old male, a sixty-seven-year-old grandmother and a nine-year-old female babysitter. Could these individuals have the potential to shake a baby? What about a two-and-a-half-year-old male, a thirty-five-year-old soldier or a twenty-five-year-old female professional? Perpetrators of SBS can be teens or adults. Grandmothers, uncles, babysitters, siblings and daycare workers all have fallen into the category of perpetrator. New parents can be dangerously naïve about others who care for their infant son or daughter and believe that no one would ever bring harm to their baby. The idea that any caregiver can be a perpetrator of SBS needs to be reinforced, especially to new parents.

CASE STUDY: KILLER CHILD

A four-month-old female was put to bed for a nap. Later, the baby cried and her two-and-a-half year-old male cousin ran out of the baby's room. The baby's aunt found the baby crying and then the baby suddenly went stiff, became limp and stopped breathing. There were several metal toys scattered around the baby's room. Police were called and CPR was attempted, but the baby was dead on arrival at the hospital. The aunt reported to police that the little cousin said, "Hit the baby, Mommy...baby bad girl." The autopsy showed the infant had bilateral cheek ecchymosis (bruising). She also had multiple scapular hemorrhages, bilateral acute subdural hematoma and subarachnoid hemorrhage. The autopsy findings had no comment about the ophthalmology findings. When questioned about her son's feelings toward his infant cousin, the mother said, "Well, I know that he was jealous of the baby, that's all."

This case was part of an article about young child abuse perpetrators, entitled "The Battering Child."[1] I spoke with the author, Dr. Lester Adelson, a well-known and respected pathologist in Cleveland, Ohio. I asked him about his findings and if he believed that a two-year-old could injure an infant like this (I highly doubted it). He said he felt that it would be improbable for a very young child to kill an infant in this manner. My opinion was that the aunt shook and beat the infant to death and the young cousin was acting out and saying some of the things that his mother was saying to the infant. The article had an autopsy case number, but after speaking with the area coroner's office, I found that the case numbers were not documented the same way. Obituary checks in newspaper archives failed to turn up any leads. I presume that the adult got away with murder and blamed it on her young son—and the police accepted it as truth. It occurred in the 1960s, when cases like this were handled differently.

What about today's committers of SBS? Though there is a whole variety of people who have shaken babies, there are common characteristics of people more likely to shake and injure young children. These perpetrators are mostly young and male.

Approximately 60 to 70 percent of SBS offenders are male. There are several reasons for this. Studies have shown that men often respond negatively to the stimulus of infant cries simply through physiological reactions. Heart rate increases, subtle sweating begins, respiration quickens and so on. There have been some recent studies that have suggested that there's an equal balance of male and female perpetrators of SBS, but over the years, it commonly has been more often males.

On a social level, men do not have as much caregiving exposure as women; hence they will have fewer options from which to choose in caring for and soothing infants. Men might become more frustrated with the chores of caregiving and not want to perform certain duties, such as diaper changing.

Men are more likely to choose control and containment as a way of dealing with stressful situations, such as fussy or crying infants. They may not be emotionally flexible. Shaking can be employed as a way to control a seemingly unmanageable situation.

Control by Shaking

My son was born on April 20, 2001. He was born six weeks early, because I had a blood clot. We almost died, so I needed to get an emergency C-section. He was in the hospital for a month. He was born with three holes in his heart. One closed on its own, one needed medications to close it and the other closed when he was five. He needed to be on a breathing machine for two days and then needed an oxygen tent for a while. He also needed a feeding tube and was in an incubator.

My son came home on Mother's Day and he was the best Mother's Day gift ever. He had developmental delays after that. I decided to go back to work and my parents watched my child. On April 1, 2002, the day after Easter, my mother left to go visit family in Florida and other family members and I had to go to work. So I asked the guy I'd been seeing for about three months to babysit that day. He always seemed great with my son and I never thought in a million years he could ever hurt my baby. I thought I could trust him.

That was the only day I ever left my baby with anyone. It is also the day he got violently shaken five times. My son got yelled at for ripping his babysitter's car magazine. At the time of the abuse, my baby was only eleven-and-a-half months old (twenty days before his first birthday). The babysitter gave him a bottle and laid him down for a nap. At least the babysitter had some common sense to check on him and realized he was not waking up, so he called for the neighbor upstairs. They called 911 and they said that he was limp and unresponsive. I then got a phone call at work that something was wrong. They rushed him to the local hospital, did a CT scan and then said my son was in critical condition and needed emergency surgery. They transferred him to the Children's Hospital.

He was suffering from bleeding in the brain and left eye. When the doctor finished the surgery, he said my son was suffering from classic Shaken Baby Syndrome. At that point, it was all a waiting game. Nobody knew how he was going to respond to the surgery. When he woke up, he wasn't able to move the left side of his body, which signaled to the doctor that he was paralyzed on that side. They also noticed the pupil of his left eye did not react to light, indicating there was brain damage.

My little boy slowly started responding to food and stayed in the ICU for three days. He was moved to a regular room and stayed there a week. Doctors felt he needed intensive therapy in a rehabilitation hospita, so we were transported to the rehab hospital, where we stayed for three months. I was able to live there with him the whole time.

When he came home he continued to get intensive services. He is still in therapy and will always need some sort of treatment for the rest of his life.

My former boyfriend did admit to shaking my son five times. He also admitted he was sixteen years old and had lied to me, telling me he was twenty-one. So, they charged him as a minor and he was sentenced to one year in jail. He got out in nine months on good behavior. His records are sealed, because he was charged as a minor.

My son will always suffer from traumatic brain injury, abusive head trauma and cerebral palsy (on the left side of his body), he is legally blind without his glasses, he is intellectually disabled (aka mentally handicapped) and has a mood disorder, Attention Deficit Hyperactivity Disorder and seizures. He is able to walk but does have a lot of trouble keeping up and gets tired very quickly. He can only use his right hand, since the left side of his body is very weak. He has a lot of mood swings at times. This usually comes along with a traumatic brain injury.

Because of his traumatic injuries, we have been through hell and back and we still continue to have challenges every day. I believe that God got me through this and still does every day. God has something special in place for my son. He survived twice in the first year of his life. He is truly a miracle. I'm so proud to be his mother. I love my kids more than life itself. He is a survivor and my hero!

—TraciLyn Novello-Hodapp

Starling and Holden's 2000 study found that men, as the most common perpetrators of abusive head trauma, did not differ when comparing two geographic U.S. populations. Of a group of twenty-seven children who were shaken, impacted or a combination of both, fathers were perpetrators 45 percent of the time and mother's boyfriends 25 percent. Female babysitters were found to be the third highest offenders.[2]

PERPETRATOR'S BACKGROUND

What else in a perpetrator's background makes him or her shake? Typically, there are multiple life stressors present. During poor economic times, we often see an increase in child abuse rates. The numbers of Shaken Baby Syndrome increased during the 2008 U.S. recession. Dr. Rachel Berger looked at a pattern associated with the recession. She said there has been a rise in SBS cases and called it "striking." She wrote, "It was a perfect storm in a bad way, where we have economic stressors that are causing the removal of social service resources for preventing and addressing child abuse." She said she was not surprised by the association of her study and the recent increase in the number of cases of abusive head injury.[3]

Perpetrators also tend to have issues with their tempers. They will strike first and apologize later. Perpetrators are often first-time parents, so they tend to have limited choices in caregiving. Perpetrators may have a history of abuse themselves. Often, if you have been abused in the past that is what you know. And so abuse is used as a means of discipline. Finally, shakers are more prone to use alcohol while they are caretaking. In and of itself, this could impair judgment and increase anger due to lowered tolerance levels.

Next let's focus on some common patterns that are seen with perpetrators of shaken baby crimes.

SHAKING WHEN NO ONE IS PRESENT

The first American Academy of Pediatrics consensus statement on Shaken Baby Syndrome was published in 1993. In this statement they wrote, "While caregivers may be unaware of the specific injuries they may cause by shaking, the act of shaking/slamming is so violent that competent individuals observing the shaking would recognize it as dangerous."[4] Perpetrators know that they are inflicting harm on infants by violently shaking them, which is why such an act is not usually performed in the presence of others.

Most caregivers will hand an infant to another person in the house or at a place of employment when they become frustrated. When there is another person present to hand a crying infant, the infant will not be shaken. Yet some individuals are so egotistical that expressions of violence are normative and they will shake regardless of who is present.

UNATTACHED

A potential shaker can also be emotionally unattached. Some examples include a mother's boyfriend not related by blood to the baby, a father who has not bonded well with his child or a babysitter who doesn't have the emotional attachment family members do. Perpetrators may be jealous that a baby is not their own or that a baby cries in their arms and not in others people's. Schnitzer and Ewigman found that children who reside in households with unrelated adults are at exceptionally high risk for death by inflicted injury (not all SBS injuries). In their study, most perpetrators were male and most lived in the child's household at the time of injury.[5]

Most individuals who shake infants don't have reasons for what they've done. They haven't prepared an adequate story, nor do they typically call for help immediately once an infant begins to physically decline. They have to think quickly on their feet and come up with scenarios that they feel will be sufficient as an explanation.

UNREALISTIC EXPECTATIONS

Many parents and caregivers expect their children to perform above their level of development, such as a two-month-old standing, a six-month-old crawling or an eleven-month-old being toilet trained. When performance by an infant does not match what a caregiver expects, this can be a "trigger event" for shaking.

Within training programs in childbirth education, postnatal parenting classes and support groups, there needs to be instruction on the developmental aspects of infants and children. Well-child visits to pediatricians should always include a review of what a child has been doing and what parents and caregivers should soon be expecting.

YOUNG PARENT PERPETRATORS

People who shake infants are typically in their twenties.[6] Such individuals do not have significant experience caring for an infant. Young parents often do not have the maturity or mental resources to cope with their crying child and will be quicker to react, rather than pause to consider appropriate caregiving alternatives. There is sometimes an egocentric attitude of the caregiver—it's all about him or her, not the baby.

So young caregivers often assume the "Three I's" (inexperienced, intolerant and insensitive). An example of inexperience is the young male who does not have exposure to caring for young children like his female counterpart does. He also does not have a mental checklist of ways to soothe a crying baby that he can access if he is in the role of caring for an infant. Instead, he may have one or two soothing strategies. Even female caregivers may not be prepared for the role of "constant parent," which is often quite stressful.

Many caregivers, male or female, are less tolerant of crying children. Since crying is the number one trigger for shaking, this can be very irritating to the caregiver. He or she doesn't understand the language of babies. A perpetrator of SBS will often believe that an infant is "out to get" him or her when there is crying. He or she does not readily consider the physical or emotional needs of the infant and the many factors that will cause an infant to cry or be irritable. Instead, the infant's needs are ignored, which can give rise to further crying.

Finally, abusive caregivers are insensitive to the needs of children. They may have tried simple soothing techniques and were unsuccessful. It then becomes a burden and they become insensitive. The perpetrator makes the crying his or her personal issue. Their video game is being interrupted, their TV watching is being disturbed or something else is being ruined. They don't care. They are reactive to the incessant crying. They go through their strategies to soothe a baby very quickly and then explode.

Overpeck and associates found a strong correlation between childbearing at an early age and infant homicide. They felt that prevention programs related to child abuse should be targeted more actively to the adolescent population.[7] This recommendation is on track with other prevention initiatives that call for early training of young, less-experienced caregivers.

PRESENTING SITUATIONS AND STORIES

Next let's look at some untrue stories that perpetrators of Shaken Baby Syndrome make up and use, from the initial 911 calls to their trials. Many of these will be revisited in the Investigation and Prosecution chapter, in terms of how defense attorneys use these excuses in the courtroom.

Apnea

Apnea is the temporary cessation of breathing—the child is struggling to breathe. It is a typical sign of distress in shaking injuries. This is a common excuse that is given by caregivers who claim they were reviving infants from episodes of apnea, so they gently shook them out of the apneic crisis. The caregivers may even seek praise for acts of heroism for saving an infant's life who was struggling to breathe. In truth, infants can easily become apneic *after* an episode of shaking. This often complicates a medical diagnosis, as providers might not consider abusive trauma in an initial work-up. In past decades, parents and other caregivers were actually instructed to gently shake infants or children who were not breathing in order to revive them. This has since been removed from cardiopulmonary resuscitation (CPR) classes.

Apnea is rare in infants, especially if they were born healthy and are going to their pediatricians for regular "well-baby" check-ups. The excuse is often, "I found my baby not breathing and I shook her to revive her." Certainly, loving parents may panic if they find their child not breathing, though it is hard to believe that such a parent would severely shake the child to revive him or her. Light pats or rubs on an infant's back and gentle strokes on the face are techniques to be used if apnea occurs. In more urgent cases, parents should call 911. If infant mouth-to-mouth resuscitation/CPR is known, it should be performed after calling for emergency assistance.

Apnea as a *result* of SBS has been studied and reported in medical literature as a finding indicating very severe brain injury. This condition is among a constellation of clinical indicators of trauma. In 2009, Macguire and his researchers found that when comparing accidental versus non-accidental injury, an infant or young child who arrives at the hospital not breathing is *seventeen times* more likely to have been abused.[8]

"I Found the Baby That Way."

Perpetrators of shaking crimes have made statements such as, "I don't know what happened to the baby; I found him that way," even though the baby had intracranial bleeding and retinal hemorrhaging. It is an easy excuse to make, since it is one where the caregiver blames imaginary forces for the baby's decline. Prior to the 1960s, hundreds, if not thousands, of infant injuries or deaths were attributed to "congenital malformation" or "aneurism." For the family doctor or pathologist doing an autopsy, there wasn't the connection of brain bleeding with abuse. Today, science knows better, but caregivers often still use this excuse to place blame on the child.

"The Baby Was Choking."

If a baby is choking and the caregiver is trying to dislodge food that is caught, why would the shaking be violent? Even in panic situations, most people know to turn a baby face-down to clear an airway. If a baby was shaken face-down, the position would lessen the acceleration/deceleration forces on the baby. This is when a sharp investigator will have the caregiver recreate the event on video to show what happened.

Cardiopulmonary Resuscitation (CPR)

Another "heroic measure" that has been disproved as a viable explanation for injuries seen in SBS is the use of CPR. This is a typical defense strategy. The fact that an infant has retinal hemorrhaging does not mean it was received during an episode of CPR. Hemorrhages are underlying and appear beyond any efforts of resuscitation. At time of trial, many defense attorneys or experts will claim that an infant was not shaken, but his or her parent/caregiver should be recognized for their attempts to save the struggling baby by giving CPR. There are no known medical journal articles or research that can substantiate shaken baby-related eye injuries from CPR. Even prolonged CPR may only cause minimal, pinpoint retinal hemorrhages. It is a very rare occurrence. In chapter 11 we will explore the research studies on CPR and SBS that have been written to counter this courtroom excuse.

Delay in Seeking Medical Treatment

This is a very common occurrence in SBS abuse cases. Often, delay in getting medical attention for a severely injured young child is due to ignorance. As a child is characteristically rendered unconscious after being shaken, the perpetrator might believe that he or she is sleeping. It isn't until actual signs and symptoms of head injury appear (vomiting, seizures, going limp, etc.), that the perpetrator panics and seeks help or calls someone else. Another possibility is that the perpetrator realizes that he or she has inflicted injury, sees the signs and symptoms and simply ignores them. Such delays typically cause a worsening of the underlying damage. A frequent scenario in SBS cases is that 911 isn't the first to be called. Instead, calls are made to the parent who is not at home. This further complicates the situation and makes for additional delays in getting medical attention for the injured child.

Describe a Situation Not Matching the Infant's Injuries

Stories or explanations that accompany a shaken infant to the emergency room are frequently erroneous. A common excuse used is that an infant fell from a couch or bed. Articles from the past three decades have proven the lack of serious injury in falls from one to four feet. Even falls down flights of stairs or from a few stories rarely produce life-threatening consequences. Police investigators need to compare a story of injury given at a hospital with the actual scene where the injury took place to determine the rigidity of the landing surface or if there was a crushing injury with the fall and so forth. Medical providers should approach inconsistent stories professionally, stating something like, "Your daughter's injuries are very serious. We do not usually see this in falls [out of arms, off a bed]. In order to treat her in the best possible way, could you tell us if anything else might have happened?"

Falls

When a caregiver reports that a child has fallen from a bed or a couch and becomes injured to the point of needing to be hospitalized, I realize that this is the most common excuse that abusers use. It is used because to the caregiver it simply makes sense. Perpetrators of SBS are unaware that infants and young children have malleable bones and extra subcutaneous fat that actually protects them in falls from heights. They believe that any kind of fall (even the short ones) could be damaging to a young child, so this is why the short-fall excuse is so common—it is one of ignorance.

If a caregiver reports that a child has fallen from his or her arms, then the adult has placed him or herself within the "accident." Again, this makes sense to a caregiver and needs to be recreated with a doll. There have been legitimate cases of infants being crushed by an adult falling on them, but the injuries will look different from SBS-type injuries. Also, injuries to the adult in the fall would be noted. In the recreation of the "fall," an investigator will look at the surface the caregiver and the baby landed on and the objects around them that were disrupted or broken, etc.

Finally, infants (and especially toddlers) are susceptible to falls down stairs. Depending on the mechanism, there should be bruises on the child's body from impact on the individual steps of the stairway, especially if the steps are uncarpeted. This type of fall is rotational. There will be rotation of the head and possibly the brain. So if the child happens to have a subdural hemorrhage from the fall, it is a feasible finding. Retinal hemorrhages, if present, should be limited to the posterior of the retina and few in number. This type of fall should also be recreated during a police investigation.

Play

Playfully jiggling a baby back and forth or tossing in the air will not produce SBS either. This activity of tossing a baby up in the air is often something laypeople question in terms of being harmful. Some perpetrators have suggested that rough play was the cause of a baby's injuries, having no idea that this is not one of the causes of SBS.

Rarely Confess to Shaking

Most individuals who shake use excuses (an infant fell from a bed) or minimize the actions they took with the baby. Most shaking offenders will seek the path of least resistance as it is a part of human nature and stems from a childhood fear of "getting caught." Perpetrators of shaking crimes will seek the path of least legal resistance as well, whereby they will lie to avoid prosecution and punishment. Often there is a "saving face" element to lying or minimizing one's actions, as individuals want to be seen in a good light by significant people in their lives.

Always Changing the Story

My daughter was born on August 30, 2007. She was a happy, healthy, average baby, weighing 6 pounds 5 ounces and measuring 19 ¼ inches long. She scored all nines on her Apgar test, devised to rate the health of a newborn (nine is a near-perfect score). She was a little fussy due to colic, she had tummy aches and I was constantly changing her formula per her pediatrician's orders. At only six weeks old, I began to notice she was more lethargic and having a hard time taking her formula. She was throwing up and began looking pale. Her eyes also appeared glossy and sunken. I continued taking her to her pediatrician, who thought it was formula related. So we continued making changes.

On the night of November 2, 2007, her father woke me and said "The baby isn't breathing; we need to go to the hospital." Immediately I told him to call 911. He thought we could get there faster than the ambulance. I picked up my beautiful daughter, who at that time was pale, slightly blue, limp and lifeless, and we sped off to the emergency room. Upon our arrival, they immediately took her and began trying to get an IV in her. They had her on oxygen and were asking what happened. Unfortunately, I was asleep and could only tell what my then-husband had told me. He was telling the doctors he was also asleep and heard a bag rustle and fall on her face, thus causing her to stop breathing. Little did I know at this point that his story would change many, many more times. The doctors decided my daughter had a brain tumor and sent her to Savannah for surgery. Once we arrived there, the doctors told me they wanted to place an external shunt in her brain. They felt she had spinal fluid building up and putting pressure on her brain; therefore the shunt would drain tea-colored fluid and my baby girl should be okay. After they placed the shunt, I went in to see her. The shunt was draining, but it was not tea colored, it was blood red.

At this point, I was told someone had shaken my little girl. She had several subdural hematomas; she had retinal hemorrhaging and blood was putting pressure behind her eyes and on her brain. She was unable to even take her bottle, because she had lost her suck reflex. She was unable to perform even the natural behaviors of an infant: crying, sucking, etc. She was completely silent with her eyes closed, not making any noises or moving at all. This meant someone close to her hurt her. My beautiful, happy little girl was now a victim of child abuse. Who could have done this to her? Why? What would make someone hurt such an innocent little girl?

She endured several surgeries while in the hospital to relieve the pressure from the blood, and to also place a G-tube in her belly which would be her only source of nutrition. It took about two weeks before I even heard her cry again. That was the happiest moment for me during all of this, just to hear her cry. Unfortunately, she spent many more months doing just that. The one thing that probably caused her abuser to inflict injuries in the first place was the only thing she was able to do.

A full criminal investigation was launched on everyone who had ever been in contact with my baby. The doctors began to act differently toward me. They would not speak to me directly about anything regarding my daughter's care. Police officers and investigators questioned me endlessly about my girl and myself—where I was, what did I do, also about her father and his behavior and habits. The questions concerned what happened to her and who did it. I was looking for the same answers myself. The Department of Family and Children Services stepped in as well. They questioned us and investigated where we were living. During all of this I was being accused of hurting my daughter, the worst thing a mother could go through.

During the investigation she endured many more surgeries while in the hospital. A subdural peritoneal shunt was placed in her brain to alleviate the pressure and continuously drain the blood from her brain. She had surgery on her eyes to remove blood that had built up behind them. She has also undergone many, many more surgeries since coming home from the hospital and throughout the last six years. She had strabismus surgery on both of her eyes as a corrective measure from the blood damaging her retinas, causing her eyes to no longer work together. She has had hip surgery twice, because she developed hip dysplasia due to her injuries. She had surgery to keep her from constantly projectile vomiting.

My daughter has lifelong health issues due to being shaken. She developed cerebral palsy, epilepsy, spastic quadriplegia, visceral hyperalgesia, nearsightedness, cortical vision impairment, right-side body weakness, myoclonus, torticollis and she cannot regulate her own body temperature, because that part of her brain is damaged.

On November 24, 2007, we were no longer allowed to be alone with her at the hospital. I was told someone else had to take over guardianship of my daughter until the investigation was complete or she would go to foster care. My aunt and uncle graciously accepted taking care of her while the investigation was going on. For this I will always be thankful to them; she would not have survived in foster care due to her injuries. She was released from the hospital with hospice services; they did not expect her to live at all. She was sent home to die. I was told she would be a vegetable for the rest of her life. "She will never walk, talk, smile, coo or do any of the things that normal babies do. This is it for her."

Finally, after I was subjected to lie detector tests, more badgering and questioning, on February 14, 2008, her father was arrested and charged with cruelty to children and aggravated battery. He was later indicted by a grand jury in May of 2008. We were told by doctors that due to the amount and coloration of the blood drained from my daughter's brain she had been shaken about five times. I had only left her alone in her father's care five times since she had been born.

He changed his story many times during the investigation, from the original plastic bag on her face, to a diaper bag falling on her head, to even saying he dropped her. We had a second opinion doctor come in whose exact statement was, "She would have had to fall from a thirteen-story building to sustain the injuries she has." Her father failed the lie detector test the investigator performed and even became abusive toward me after she went in the hospital.

Through working very closely with the district attorney, we decided a plea bargain would be the best way to ensure he was found guilty. The DA suggested that it was too difficult to prosecute and guarantee a guilty verdict when there were no eye witnesses to the shaking. Once her father was finally arrested, I was then able to begin the fight to get my baby back with me, where she belonged. I had to work very closely with DFCS to achieve this. I went through family counseling, also many agonizing family team meetings with DFCS. In these meetings I would be asked, "With you being such a young mother, I am shocked that you even want her back at all. Why do you want her, and why do you want to go through all of this to get her?" I was eighteen years old at the time of the abuse. The answer was simple and so very clear to me: "She is my daughter, and I love her and want her regardless of what condition she is in. I will do whatever it takes to bring my baby home."

Finally, her father was sentenced to five years in prison and five years probation for nearly killing his daughter. I do not feel this was justice for her at all. She will never be able to live a normal life because of what he did to her. She will suffer forever due to his actions, but after just a few years in prison he could return to his life. That is so unfair. Of course I wanted a higher punishment for him, but was unable to achieve it for her.

He served his time and was released in 2013 and has since resumed life as if his daughter does not exist. Justice? I think not.

Finally, after a year of working very closely with DFCS and being taught by home health nurses at my aunt's house, I was able to bring my girl home. She has endured countless surgeries due to her father's abuse and she has been through numerous therapies, with still more to come. All this has helped her along the way. She is now six years old, and by the grace of God and hard work, determination, a loving family that never gives up on her and her own strong will, she is a survivor, a fighter and has not given up one step of the way. She was given a five-year life expectancy and surpassed it. She has developed by leaps and bounds compared to her original prognosis. She still has her G-tube, but is able to eat some things by mouth as well. She drinks very small amounts from her sippy cup.

She began kindergarten this year and absolutely loves school and her teacher. She is a very happy little girl. She has not started walking yet, but boy, does she try. She has crawled a few times and gets upset when she can't get where she wants to go by herself, and that is when she tries the hardest. She has some vocal skills, she knows how to say "momma," "uh huh" and "no." She has recently started identifying colors and tracking with her eyes. She absolutely loves sweet potatoes. She has a fantastic personality and an attitude to go along with it. She loves watching cartoons and even giggles and laughs at them. She has endured way too much for a child her age, or any child at all, but continues to fight and never give up through it all. She has always bounced back from whatever barrier has been put in front her, whether it is surgery or sickness. My daughter is the strongest person I know and has without a doubt made me the person I am today. Each morning that she wakes up is a reminder that God is good and she is an inspiration to everyone around her.

She is on a daily medication regimen to control her seizures and spasticity but, even with all the medications, she still struggles. She was recently placed on a ketogenic diet to help control her seizures, which it does, but she cannot eat the foods she loves and that is one of the times she is happiest, eating her sweet potatoes. Each winter, she ends up in the hospital for days at a time. It always seems this is when her temperature drops, her seizures get increasingly worse and she struggles the most during the winter months. She has spent the last two Christmases and many other days throughout the year in the hospital due to her injuries.

During this last stay I was informed that the remainder of my daughter's healthy brain (she only had about a dime size amount remaining after the abuse; the rest had atrophied or was fluid) is beginning to slowly atrophy. This is why we are seeing the health issues we are now. Even with this new development, she is fighting through these changes as well. She is home from the hospital, just went back to school and she is still her happy, fun self and continues to progress on a daily basis. Only God knows what is in store for her in the future, but she will fight every step of the way.

Everything my daughter has been through was completely unnecessary. This was all caused by the hands of someone who was supposed to love, protect and care for her—her father. This should have never happened to her or any child. Everyone needs to know the reality of Shaken Baby Syndrome: this is real and it does shatter lives daily. It is okay to walk away if you are frustrated, to call someone to come help you, whatever you need to do to not shake the baby. This can be prevented, but to do so everyone must know that shaking does hurt babies regardless. It does not matter if it is only once or five times. There are always alternatives to this. Crying

never hurt a baby, but shaking does. Always remember Shaken Baby
Syndrome is 100 percent preventable, but it is not curable.

—Candace Hinkle

Rough Handling

Light shaking and blows to an infant's back to dislodge an object (as identified previously with choking) will not produce SBS. Innocuous activities such as these were thought to be damaging and played a significant role in the diagnosis of SBS when it was initially described by John Caffey and for many years afterward. But studies and witnessed events have proven otherwise. For SBS injuries to appear, there needs to be substantial violence while shaking an infant. A caregiver who is being considered for a shaking crime will often minimize the force that he or she used on a child in order to both "confess" and lie at the same time. The caregiver might even describe him or herself as being "rough with the baby."

A tactic that police investigators can use during questioning is to mention something like, "Maybe you shook the baby lightly." The investigator knows something that the perpetrator probably doesn't—that it takes a significant amount of force to cause the symptoms and injuries seen in SBS. Since the perpetrator doesn't know this fact, the investigator gets him or her to admit to the shaking by suggesting, "Well, it seems that you were struggling emotionally when the baby was crying—maybe you just shook him a little?"

PERPETRATOR DILEMMAS

What are the traps that perpetrators fall into? There are strategies that police investigators can use to their advantage in pursuing SBS cases. Here are the common steps that lead to shaking:

1. *Alone with the child*
   This issue is important, because if an individual was getting frustrated with a crying baby he or she would typically give the baby to another adult who is present.

2. *Crying/behavior issue present*

Triggers to shake a toddler include a toileting problem or a temper tantrum or getting into household things. With babies, the issue is crying. Because of these issues, the infant or child is shaken.

3. *Hope that the child will respond*

The perpetrator has shaken the baby or toddler to an extent that renders the child unconscious. The caregiver now hopes that the baby will respond, thinking "What have I done?" The child has been seriously injured and the adult just hopes that he or she will get better right away. Because of this delay in seeking treatment, the perpetrator doesn't want to get caught, so he or she will pace around trying to come up with a story (or excuse). The caregiver does not call 911; instead he or she calls the mother or father and asks, "What should I do? The baby is not doing too well." So the caregiver comes up with a lie. This delay in seeking treatment for the child is often hours, not minutes.

4. *Create a story*

During the delay in seeking treatment, a "creative" story is born. The excuse is typically very far-fetched to professionals, but caregivers try to connect the idea of a fragile infant to an ordinary occurrence—such as a short fall.

5. *Rarely confess to the shaking event*

It is a rare moment that a perpetrator, responsible for injuring a child, will confess and say, "Yes, I shook the baby and shook him very hard."

RESEARCH STUDIES ON SBS PERPETRATORS

In 1990, Dr. Randall Alexander wrote about serial abuse in shaken children. Often, shaking a child is not an isolated incident. In many abusive households, a child is shaken again and again. Repetitive shaking may build up in intensity over time, with the final assault having a lethal result.[9] This was confirmed in a 2010 study of French perpetrators of SBS.[10]

In 1986, Bergman wrote about the increased percentage of male perpetrators by a proportion of approximately two to one.[11] This trend has not changed since initially noted, though a study will be examined later in this book that assessed one county in the U.S. and found different results.

In 1995, Gessner showed that shaken baby rates are 3.5 times higher with perpetrators who are in the military.[12] There was also a new shift in this finding, as Gumbs and colleagues described the overall rates of abusive head trauma in military families as very close to civilian populations when using the same definition.[13]

In 1999, Brenner stated that Caucasian children have a higher rate of Shaken Baby Syndrome.[14] In 2011, Parks and others from the Centers for Disease Control and Prevention reported a new trend shift toward African-American perpetrators.[15]

Starling and colleagues had three studies (1995[16], 2000[17], 2004[18]) discussing the relation of perpetrator to victim, comparing populations and the time interval of onset of symptoms. They found that fathers accounted for 37 percent of the abusers, followed by boyfriends (20.5 percent), female babysitters (17.3 percent) and mothers (12.6 percent). The 2000 study compared a Southern population of victims with those of a Western population, and found that men, particularly fathers (45 percent) and mothers' boyfriends (25 percent), are the most common perpetrators. Finally, in a fascinating study, Starling and colleagues looked at thirty-year retrospectives of SBS perpetrators and found that 68 percent of the perpetrators admitted to shaking their victims. In 91 percent of the victims, symptoms appeared immediately after the abuse. They also reviewed impact injuries and found that most perpetrators admitted to shaking without impact. This was confirmed as they found a relative lack of skull and scalp injuries on victims, which suggested that shaking alone can produce devastating symptoms and consequences.

In a surprising study in 2005, Theodore et al found that parental shaking of very young children as a means of discipline occurred among 2.6 percent of children less than two years of age.[19] They performed computer-assisted, blind telephone surveys of mothers in North and South Carolina. The statistical findings were startling—"For every one child who sustains a serious injury as a result of shaking, an estimated 150 children may be shaken and go undetected." This was, and continues to be, a very important paper that shows that shaking is being used by parents as a mechanism for punishment. There are several things that the reader can note about this study. The subjects of the surveys were mothers, so it is unknown the number of fathers, mothers' boyfriends, etc., who are also shaking, as men are twice as likely to shake infants and young children. Alhough the estimated undetected number of 150 children are being shaken, the rotational effects on the child's brain are not strong enough to hospitalize the child. That isn't meant to say that the child isn't being physically harmed, but the authors are comparing actual hospital admissions of shaken children with those mothers who have reported a shaking (or multiple shakings). In serial shaking episodes, often the intensity of the shaking increases, so the potential for harm increases as well. Finally, the authors reported a significant decrease in the number of reported shakings after a prevention campaign was initiated, but their area hospital rate of SBS diagnoses stayed the same, which may mean that the mothers were less likely to disclose incidents of shaking.

In 2010, a French study (Adamsbaum et al) questioned prisoners who were convicted of SBS crimes (66 percent males). They talked about how a third of them confessed to serial shaking (or their term, "habitual shaking"), where they would shake their infants again and again at home and that was their way of controlling behavior.[20] Ultimately each baby developed symptoms and needed to be hospitalized. When the forensic investigators asked the prisoners about aspects of the shaking, "[it] was described as extremely violent (100 percent) and was repeated (55 percent) from 2 to 30 times (mean: 10), because it stopped the infant's crying (62.5 percent). Impact was uncommon (24 percent)." The men also reported that their victims would be rendered unconscious immediately or symptoms would appear within several hours after being put to bed. The perpetrators reported that the shakings occurred over a period of weeks to months.

In another recent study in 2011, Debra Esernio-Jennsen and associates looked at multiple issues among perpetrators of SBS, including perpetrator gender, victim outcomes and perpetrator legal outcomes.[21] The sample size was small—thirty-four identified perpetrators—and they found that there were an equal number of men and women shaking babies. This appears to be a new trend. The median age for female perpetrators was thirty-four years and the male perpetrator median age was twenty-seven years. More male perpetrators confessed to shaking and were more frequently convicted than female perpetrators. Esernio-Jennsen found that two-thirds of the victims were male (which coincides with other victimology studies). Finally, most likely due to the strength differences of perpetrators, victims of male perpetrators had more serious injuries, more serious neurosurgical intervention and suffered worse clinical outcomes.

In 2013, Gumbs and fellow researchers looked at military families and found that the trend of SBS that had formerly been much higher in that particular subset (see Gessner) was now shifting toward the pattern seen in general society. In *Pediatrics*, Gumbs reported that the ability to access a large database of "abusive head trauma" cases gave the ability to link investigative results. Gumbs and associates used the same case definition codes as civilian populations and, in doing so, found that the military population was consistent with the civilian population. They noted that the infants most at risk were the same as at-risk civilian family infants, i.e., infants with parents in lower military pay grades, infants with military mothers and infants born prematurely or with special needs. They recommended that such at-risk families be a part of military family support programs.[22]

So, the studies we have discussed (though not all-inclusive of the most recent perpetrator studies) appear to show a change in some trends. Several studies have highlighted an increase in female perpetrators of SBS, a rise in African-American perpetrators and a leveling off of the traditional imbalance of perpetrators in the military. Evaluating research papers on perpetrators allows us to consider how we can best prevent and warn about the dangers of shaking infants and young children. These trends also help in the investigation process, by targeting those who may have a propensity to shake.

PERPETRATOR CASE EXAMPLES

Next, let's look at some of the unique cases involving shaking that have made national headlines over the years.

The Youngest Convicted SBS Perpetrator

In 2010, a ten-year-old girl, who was the daughter of the owner of an unlicensed daycare center, shook a baby at the daycare. While she was with another girl (age seven), she planned to play catch using the baby. The seven-year-old girl wanted nothing to do with it. The ten-year-old then shook the baby violently several times and the baby later died at the hospital. After a year of working on the case, the prosecutor charged the girl with second-degree murder (when she was ten). The girl's mother was also charged for being an accomplice, because she had tried to cover up the crime. This was a very rare case, as the previous youngest individual to be prosecuted was a twelve-year-old girl who also shook a baby to death.[23]

The Brumfield Case

One-year-old Olivia Madison Garcia allegedly hit her head in a fall as she tried to climb out of a playpen. She was staying overnight at a friend of her mother's. The woman who was babysitting her was Amanda Brumfield. When Olivia supposedly fell, she received a three-and-a-half inch skull fracture and intracranial bleeding. After a two-hour delay, she was finally taken to the hospital, where she later died. Doctors determined the little girl had died after being shaken and impacting on a hard floor. Amanda Brumfield was arrested; she was originally charged with first-degree murder and aggravated child abuse charges, but was acquitted of those. The prosecution claimed that not only did Brumfield shake and drop Olivia, but she didn't call for help until two hours after the injury. She was later found guilty of aggravated manslaughter and sentenced to twenty years in prison.

This case would not have made national headlines if not for the fact that Amanda Brumfield was the estranged daughter of actor Billy Bob Thornton. She was the nation's first celebrity-connected SBS perpetrator. Brumfield's mother, Melissa Parish, was married to Thornton in the late 1970s. Brumfield and her father never had a close relationship. At the time of Olivia's death, Brumfield herself was married and had two daughters. Olivia's mother was Brumfield's close friend.[24]

The Smith Case

In 1997, Shirley Ree Smith was convicted by a California jury of the murder of her seven-week-old grandson, Etzel Glass.[25] On the night of Etzel's death, Smith was staying with her daughter Tomeka, the infant's mother, along with her two other young grandchildren (an eighteen-month-old brother and a four-year-old sister) and two of Tomeka's sister's children. Around midnight, Tomeka fed, changed and washed baby Etzel before placing him to sleep on the living room sofa. Baby Etzel shared this sofa with his siblings. Smith was also in the living room, sleeping on the floor. When Tomeka put Etzel to sleep at 11:30 P.M., he appeared healthy.

In her two interviews, Smith recounted different versions of the events that followed. First, Smith told a hospital social worker, Linda Reusser, that she awoke after 3 A.M. when Etzel's brother had a nightmare. After comforting the child, Smith went over to check on Etzel. Etzel didn't respond to her touch; she picked Etzel up and his head "flopped back." She then gave Etzel "a little shake, a jostle to awaken him," to which Etzel did not respond. Reusser described the shaking to the jury as "a quick jostle," a "smooth motion." At this point, Smith stopped speaking. When Reusser prompted Smith to continue, she said "something like 'Oh, my God. Did I do it? Did I do it? Oh my God.'" Smith's daughter Tomeka turned to Smith and said, "If it wasn't for you, this wouldn't have happened." Smith didn't say anything.

Smith told a slightly different story to the police who interviewed her as part of the criminal investigation. Smith stated that her grandson woke from his nightmare sometime before 3 A.M.; Smith rose and checked Etzel, who was fine. Then, past 3 A.M., Etzel's sister rolled off the couch and fell onto Smith.

Upon waking, Smith noticed that Etzel's diaper needed changing. After going to the bathroom to take her medicine, Smith picked up Etzel and saw he had "spit up" around his mouth and his head was "flopped back." Smith said something to Etzel and he didn't respond; he was not breathing or moving. At first, Smith told the police she "shook" Etzel, but then corrected herself and said she "twisted" him back and forth to get a response. When asked about her statement to Reusser, Smith denied saying that she had "shaken" Etzel.

Smith then carried Etzel, who was not responsive, into Tomeka's room. Smith and Tomeka called 911. Over the phone, they were instructed to give Etzel CPR, which they did. When firefighters and paramedics arrived, Smith was "apprehensive" and stated that she thought Etzel had fallen off the couch. Etzel was clothed and warm, but he was not breathing and had no heartbeat. The paramedics began CPR. Three of the rescue squad noticed blood in one of Etzel's nostrils and one consequently thought Etzel had suffered an injury. When an ambulance arrived, two more technicians administered CPR on the way to the hospital. Etzel appeared "chalky." They arrived at the hospital at 3:50 A.M.

Soon after his arrival, he was declared dead. The attending physician suspected that Etzel had died of Sudden Infant Death Syndrome (SIDS). The only injury the paramedics noticed was fresh blood in one of Etzel's nostrils.

An autopsy revealed signs of recent trauma to Etzel's brain. When the autopsy surgeon lifted Etzel's brain out of the skull, she saw fresh blood on top of the brain (subdural blood). The subdural blood measured one or two tablespoons. The surgeon also saw a fresh blood clot between the hemispheres of Etzel's brain and recent hemorrhaging around the optic nerves. Further, she found a small quantity of fresh subarachnoid blood. Finally, the surgeon and her supervisor noticed a small bruise at the left lower-back part of Etzel's head and a recent abrasion at the same site.

Dr. Carpenter, the autopsy supervisor, stated that Etzel had died by being violently shaken. According to Carpenter, he reported that death from violent shaking could have occurred in one of three ways: (1) massive swelling of the brain, (2) massive bleeding sufficient to crush the brain stem or (3) a sudden shaking "so violent that it destroys the vital centers in the brain and is a quick death." Here, Carpenter opined that death occurred through the last process, as Etzel's head had undergone whiplash from chin to chest. The death occurred too quickly for visible trauma to develop on the brain stem itself.

Dr. Carpenter explained the basis of his opinion as the recent trauma to Etzel's brain and the absence of other causes. The subdural blood, the subarachnoid blood and the blood around the optic nerves showed "violent trauma to the head sufficient to cause the death of the infant." The bruise and abrasion had, in Carpenter's opinion, "very probably" occurred during shaking, as the head collided with a hard, rough surface.

The alternate causes of death that Carpenter considered didn't make sense to him. First, Carpenter ruled out SIDS because "[a case] is never called SIDS if there is any suspicion of trauma to the infant." Second, Carpenter ruled out that a fall from the sofa onto a carpeted floor could have caused Etzel's injuries or death. Third, Carpenter considered the evidence of an old injury to Etzel's brain, such as birth trauma, as the cause of death. While he could not exclude the old injury as contributing to Etzel's death, the old injury was "not sufficient to cause death in that the infant had apparently sufficiently recovered from this injury and was appearing to look normal to others."

The prosecution at Smith's trial called two other board-certified doctors, who testified that violent shaking was the cause of death. Notably, the prosecution's witness on rebuttal, Dr. Chadwick, had published articles on how to distinguish between falls and abusive injuries in children. Based in part on his own research, Chadwick concluded that a fall from the sofa was "extremely unlikely" to cause death. Chadwick also explained that the old trauma was not the cause of death, because old injuries do not cause sudden death without a specific pathology that was absent in this case. In short, Chadwick saw "no other natural or unnatural cause except the injury that would explain [Etzel's] death," and, therefore, believed that Etzel died from SBS.

The defense's two expert witnesses, by contrast, stated that the necessary physical evidence of Shaken Baby Syndrome was lacking. Dr. William Goldie believed the cause of death was SIDS. Dr. Richard Siegler believed that the death was traumatic, but that it was impossible to isolate the cause of death between the recent and the old trauma. Significantly, both Goldie and Siegler would only diagnose Etzel's death as SBS on a finding of visible injury to the shorn region of the brain stem. Even if death were instantaneous, Goldie said that hemorrhages in the neck or brain stem would be present.

The jury resolved this conflict among the experts' opinions against Smith by convicting her. The California Court of Appeal, after reviewing the medical evidence, affirmed the conviction because "[I]t was for the jury to resolve the conflicts" in that evidence. The California Supreme Court denied review. On federal habeas review, the Magistrate Judge recommended denying Smith's petition for the same reason as the California Court of Appeal. Notwithstanding the tragedy of Smith's case, it was the jury's province to choose between the conflicting expert opinions. The district court accepted the recommendation and denied Smith's habeas petition.

Another California court, however, granted habeas relief on the ground of insufficient evidence of causation. They wrote:

> *Claims of insufficient evidence are judged according to a familiar*
> *standard: we ask whether, 'after viewing the evidence in the light*
> *most favorable to the prosecution, any rational trier of fact could*
> *have found the essential elements of the crime beyond a reasonable*
> *doubt.' To grant habeas relief, the opinion set aside the qualified*
> *opinions of the prosecution's experts by misconstruing the basis for*
> *their opinions. '[T]heir testimony was that death was caused by*
> *the shearing or tearing of the brain stem and'—according to the*
> *opinion—'they reached this conclusion because there was no evi-*
> *dence in the brain itself of the cause of death.'*[26]

In October 2011, the U.S. Supreme Court reversed the California Court's decision and stated that the lower court was wrong, since Smith's jury had convicted her based on the evidence at hand. They also said that Smith should serve her remaining prison term.

Shirley Ree Smith did return to prison and remained there three months before her sentence was commuted by California governor Jerry Brown. Smith walked free in April 2013.

CASES OF DELAYED PROSECUTION

There have been many SBS cases where arrests have been delayed or evidence was not adequate to take a case to trial. The following are two examples of cases that were originally stalled, but ultimately went forward.

The Hang Bin Li Case

In Flushing, New York, around midnight on October 22, 2007, Hang Bin Li, the father of ten-week-old Annie Li, violently shook her and then slammed her head into a nightstand. Six years later, he was found guilty of manslaughter on February 1, 2013.[27] What were the complications in bringing this father to justice?

On that fateful night, Li called 911 and said Annie was sweating, not moving her arms or legs and making gurgling sounds. Li was an immigrant from China and two days later was being interviewed by police through the use of an interpreter. Li claimed that he had "accidently bumped her head on a nightstand" and once he noticed that Annie was in distress, he called 911.

Four days later, Annie was declared brain dead and taken off life support. She suffered a fractured skull, leg fractures and significant brain injury. Her father was arrested and ultimately ended up on Riker's Island, where he awaited trial for five years. A plea deal of reckless endangerment was offered to Li, but it was refused. Instead, he went to trial in 2013.

Li's defense attorneys claimed Annie had a variant of osteogenesis imperfecta, which would have explained her fractures due to the possible fragility of her bones. But the jury did not accept this as an excuse and convicted Li as being responsible for causing the death of his ten-week-old daughter.

Li was ultimately sentenced in Queens Supreme Court to five to fifteen years in prison. District Attorney Richard Brown's statement read, "The sentence imposed today is a measure of justice for the defendant's ten-week-old daughter who was senselessly killed by the person who was supposed to protect and nurture her: her very own father. Instead, she suffered a violent attack and death at his hands. It cannot be stated too often that infants are fragile and must be handled with care. Never shake a child."

The Poore Case

On April 16, 1981, a three-month-old baby was pronounced dead at West Virginia University Hospital in Morgantown, West Virginia. Twenty-six years later, his father went to trial for his murder.[28]

Richard Alan Poore was accused of shaking his son, Richard Jr., to death because the baby was crying. But this determination was made when an arrest warrant for Poore was issued in July 2006. The reason why the case was delayed so long was because the baby's autopsy report was misplaced before it was completed and given to law enforcement investigators. It was only after the report was discovered that officials re-examined the case. Poore heard about the warrant and turned himself in to police in August 2006.

While awaiting trial, Poore remained in prison for nearly three years. In 2008, Poore was convicted on a charge of first-degree murder for having shaken his son. At trial, direct evidence was submitted—a telephone conversation that Poore had with another person which was overheard by the victim's older sister. The crux of the phone call was that Poore told the other person that he "did not mean to hurt the baby but only wanted him to quit crying."

But Poore's conviction was overturned in November 2010 by the West Virginia Supreme Court of Appeals. There were several reasons why this happened. First of all, the autopsy slides from 1981, which should have been available for further study, had been destroyed by the state's Office of the Chief Medical Examiner. The new chief medical examiner did not sign the final 1981 autopsy report. And the doctor who did sign the report never testified.

The original autopsy reported that the manner of death could not be determined. This was understandable, as the nuances of SBS were unknown at the time.

Another trial was scheduled for 2012, but Poore and his attorneys decided to plead guilty to a charge of felony manslaughter in the death of his son. He was then sentenced under the law in effect in 1981 (which was one to five years in prison). Because he had already been in prison for 1,060 days, he was released under "time served."

Although Poore was ultimately held responsible for the death of his son, I believe this is a case that highlights the necessity of keeping track of paperwork that could bring justice for a child.

CHAPTER 9

Controversies

There are many myths and controversies surrounding SBS that are argued in hospitals, police stations and courtrooms. However, injuries from child abuse have been well documented over many decades and have now become an exact science. SBS is one form of child abuse that is more difficult to understand and diagnose due to the complexities of the brain's response to traumatic injury.

With improved understanding of the characteristics of SBS and when recognition of the true facts of SBS are more fully incorporated into our society, juries will not have such a difficult time deciding the guilt or innocence of the accused. Research and prevention work needs to be more amply supported in order to affect such change.

Simulation studies on shaking cannot be performed on infants, living or deceased. Instead, the medical community bases its conclusions about what happens to an infant who has been shaken on autopsy results, perpetrator or witness accounts, mechanical studies, accidental injuries to children and other factors.

CONTROVERSIES BEGIN

In 2008, Dr. Norman Guthkelch, the neurosurgeon honored for having been the first physician to describe the effects of shaking infants, wrote an affidavit on behalf of a *defendant* in a shaken baby case. The prosecution dismissed the charges against the father. When Dr. Guthkelch was in his nineties, he spoke with Deborah Turkheimer, an advocate for those in prison wrongfully accused of shaking their children. Guthkelch was asked to begin to review "unjust" cases of shaking. Guthkelch continued to review the medical literature on SBS and in an interview for a paper for the Medill Justice Project, he said, "I realized that what I had described was being made into a completely different disease. We've assumed the cause of shaken baby syndrome on the basis of a few cases."[1]

I spoke with Dr. Guthkelch and not only congratulated him for saving countless lives since addressing the problem in 1971, but urged him to reconsider his stance. He said that there were those who had been wrongly accused and in prison. I agreed with him that, over time, there may have been a few isolated cases of this, but for the most part SBS is accurately diagnosed and prosecuted. Guthkelch held firm and said, "Well, one is too many."[2]

The defense side's smokescreen that is often seen in today's SBS criminal trials picked up significant speed with the 1997 trial of Louise Woodward, the Boston-area au pair who was convicted of shaking eight-month-old Matty Eappen to death. At that trial, the defense enlisted a high-profile team to support the nineteen-year-old caregiver. The defense attempted to paint a picture showing that the young English au pair couldn't have done the act for which she was accused. The team used tactics such as attempting to show the victim's mother as uncaring and callous and identifying a wrist fracture on the boy as being two weeks old. This was the true start of the shaken baby conflict between prosecution and defense—one that persists to this day. The smoke that has been created by defense experts has darkened. Each year there seem to be new finite conclusions written that can be pointed to in the courtroom as fact. No wonder acquittals happen. No wonder prosecutors throw up their hands and settle.

The issues surrounding SBS are now the focus of a growing discussion even within the medical community. Doctors and pathologists who, ten or more years ago, might normally have diagnosed a shaken baby, now aren't sure. Or they are hesitant to make that professional assessment. They ask questions, "Is the trauma I see abusive trauma or accidental?" "Should I be looking for an underlying disease that I'm not readily seeing?" and "Is this a medical condition that mimics SBS?"

Why aren't shaken baby cases clear-cut anymore? There are many complications within these controversies. Has the original diagnosis changed? Yes and no. On the "yes" side of the spectrum, the diagnosis has become better known. Years of research and countless peer-reviewed articles have been published to validate and strengthen the model of SBS. What a leap science has made from Caffey's hypothesis of SBS being caused by "playing," "jostling" or "rough-housing." We know better today about those innocuous activities, thanks to research. So the diagnosis has changed. On the "no" side, the methods for causing these injuries (subdural hematomas and retinal hemorrhages) have remained the same. It is and has always been violent shaking of an infant or young child—pure and simple. Dr. Guthkelch got it right in 1971. I firmly believe he had no reason to change his mind thirty-seven years later, since the same type of abuse is still happening today. In fact, through today's prevention efforts, his original diagnosis has probably saved countless lives. For that he should be proud.

Are there innocent people who have been imprisoned for shaking crimes they didn't commit? Yes; these cases may be rare but misdiagnoses are possible. The portrait of SBS is a montage of various disciplines coming together. Later in the book you will read about differential diagnoses, which are "rule out" diagnoses that physician consider prior to making a final, definitive one. Police investigators do the same in order to assess if a crime has been committed. Prosecutors even have differentials that need to be evaluated, such as the type of charge or whether to charge at all based on the facts of a case. A simple fracture in a child is much easier to assess than SBS injuries. True, the players go through the same steps looking at differentials, but when a child has been shaken the picture becomes much more complex. Many more specialized physicians are involved and they may even disagree among themselves. To get the final diagnosis of SBS right, the team, both individually and collectively, need to be thoughtful, since the ultimate end involves an accusation toward another person.

Next we will discuss several scenarios. These examples highlight the excuses that are often proposed in SBS-related cases. Depending on the source, such excuses are either strongly-held beliefs or attempts to confabulate and confuse the medical/legal process. I hope that readers will consider these usually false notions when rendering decisions.

BLEEDING DISORDER

While certain viable bleeding disorders cause excessive bruising and rare brain bleeds, these conditions almost never appear in shaken children. But a defense witness may differ. Bleeding disorders are also known as disorders of hemostasis, where a child has problems forming blood clots to stop bleeding and will bleed longer. Bleeding disorders are either genetic or acquired. Most genetic bleeding disorders are noted at birth. A clinician can identify acquired cases of bleeding by taking a history, performing a detailed physical examination and ordering necessary laboratory tests.[3]

There are multiple types of rare bleeding disorders including von Willebrand disease, hemophilia A and B, Factor II deficiency, Factor V deficiency, Factor VII deficiency, Factor X deficiency, Factor XI deficiency, Factor XIII deficiency, etc. The severity of bleeding depends on the type of disorder.

When a child is brought to a doctor's office or an emergency room with unexplained bruises, bleeding disorders should be ruled out. Such bruises should not have patterns to them, such as lines (cord) or palm impressions, which would be signs of abuse. Asking caregivers about the trauma that produced the bruises is another important step in ruling out/ruling in abuse. If a child has an intracranial bleed, abuse is high on the list of differential diagnoses, especially if the child is under one year of age and has additional injuries, such as fractures, retinal hemorrhages, burns, etc.

Some defense experts propose that child victims had no vitamin K injections at birth. While some states do not require vitamin K at birth, most hospitals provide this as a preventative measure. Laboratory tests to assess the presence of proteins produced by vitamin K can confirm a problematic condition.

Research has shown that bleeding disorders are very rare in abused children, especially ones who present with intracranial hemorrhage.[4] If a diagnosis of a bleeding disorder does appear, it doesn't automatically rule out the presence of abusive trauma. Some children with bleeding disorders may be at higher risk of abuse. Epidemiological studies have shown that not only are bleeding disorders very rare, but SBS-like findings (subdural and retinal bleeding) are exceedingly rare—with a probability of one in five million.

CARDIOPULMONARY RESUSCITATION (CPR)

Although there have been claims that chest compressions used during CPR cause diffuse retinal hemorrhaging in infants, there are many studies that have been done over the years to discount this claim. Defense attorneys will sometimes claim that clients of theirs should be viewed as heroes because they attempted to save the life of a mysteriously unresponsive young child by using CPR. These attorneys may also claim that the finding of diffuse retinal hemorrhaging is a result of CPR compressions. Keen prosecuting attorneys will prove otherwise. After being shaken, infants may become limp and unresponsive. Perpetrators of such crimes will panic and perform CPR on infants who already have retinal bleeding from being shaken.

Fackler and associates did a study in 1992 on piglets, utilizing chest compressions with these animals. There were no retinal hemorrhages found as a result of the compressions.[5] Levin reviewed six studies on infant CPR and retinal hemorrhaging and stated that, in the absence of disease or traumatic injury, there is no such condition as CPR-induced diffuse retinal hemorrhaging.[6]

Two studies in the 1990s described retinal hemorrhages in infants following prolonged CPR.[7] A rise in intrathoracic pressure during CPR produces a subsequent rise in retinal venous pressure, causing hemorrhage. This condition only happens in extremely rare cases, is commonly unilateral, stems from prolonged resuscitation efforts and produces minimal retinal hemorrhages in the back of the retina. Because the mechanism of shaking very often causes widespread bilateral hemorrhages, it shows that extreme violence is required.

DIPHTHERIA/PERTUSSIS/ TETANUS (DPT) VACCINATION

In years past and in very rare circumstances, some infants who received DPT vaccinations developed meningism (irritation of the lining membrane [meninges] of the brain). These infants with a marked reaction to the vaccination usually had a fever, became irritable and cried inconsolably for many hours. There were claims that infants died as a result of a reaction to the injection (some have even attributed the reaction to shaken baby-like injuries). A defense attorney may use pediatric vaccination records as an exhibit to show that on the day the child deteriorated, he or she received a "deadly vaccine." What medical and legal professionals often do not consider is that a crying, fussy baby reacting to the effects of a vaccination is the one most likely to be shaken or abused.

There is a federal law that provides compensation for the parents of infants who have died as a result of any type of vaccination. This may or may not be supported by autopsy findings. A few parents of shaken infants have claimed compensation from the Federal Vaccine Injury Program, stating that the DPT injection had caused "encephalopathy" with resultant convulsions and brain damage. However, there is no independent evidence that the vaccination has ever caused subdural bleeding, brain swelling and bruising or retinal hemorrhages.

The American Academy of Pediatrics formed a consensus committee in 1996 and verified that whole-cell pertussis vaccine has not been proven to be a cause of brain damage.[8] Activated pertussis in the vaccine is known to be contraindicated in children with seizure disorders but, for a healthy baby, DPT is a safe, effective prevention measure.

Since 1998, pediatricians and family doctors routinely give the DPaT vaccination, whereby the whole-cell pertussis virus is no longer included. Rather, it is the acellular form that is now part of the vaccine blend. This rules out the possibility of potential harm and puts to rest this SBS myth trying to be legitimized in the courtroom.

EXTERNAL BRUISING

Because a majority of infants who have been shaken do *not* have external bruises, there can be a delay in the process of diagnosing SBS. Infants will present to a hospital's emergency room with symptoms of lethargy, swollen fontanelle and fever and are worked up for a blood infection or some other cause. Externally, a shaken infant may appear healthy, since all the damage is internal.

The lack of bruising is another classic theory of "no abuse" that defense experts frequently use. The victim had no external bruising, hence he or she was not abused. Only about 40 to 50 percent of infants and children who have been shaken have external bruising.[9]

Often, the only bruises that *do* appear with SBS are fingertip marks on an infant's back and chest (or around the arms) where the perpetrator held the child during the shaking. Close examination of an infant's entire body by medical providers will assist in properly diagnosing a shaken infant.

Bruising in photos or scans can be made clearer if the contrast of the image is adjusted with imaging software. Often, fingertip marks that are invisible to the naked eye can be made very clear with specialized software.

Family members of a child being evaluated for abuse may make statements that the child "bruises easily" or that there is a history of family bleeding disorders. If patterned bruises are noted, such family statements are likely a mask that an abusive event has taken place.[10]

LUCID INTERVAL

A lucid (awake) interval is the medical term for a period of apparent normality that may intervene between traumatic brain injury and unconsciousness. This means that an infant or young child was injured from some known or unknown reason, recovered, was crawling and acting normally and then just collapsed and died. This argument is frequently put forth by defense attorneys and expert witnesses who state that a shaken child will appear normal after a traumatic injury and therefore anyone who had access to the infant during a twenty-four to forty-eight hour period could be the perpetrator.

This theory has been unfounded where the injury findings of lucid interval do not match those of SBS injuries. Infants who are shaken are shaken on a continuum. Science does not know the length of time that is required to cause even subtle intracranial alterations. Nor does science know the force required to produce such subtleties. What *is* known is that infants showing the signs and symptoms of SBS have been shaken extremely hard and for an extended period (ten to fifteen seconds or more). Science also knows the severity required to produce a concussion.

Regardless, a child who has been shaken severely enough to cause injury to the brain will not be lucid or without symptoms. There will be unconsciousness immediately or within minutes. It is after this period that cerebral edema may develop and intracranial bleeding will form into the clots called subdurals (which often occur simultaneously with each other). In these cases, there is intracranial pressure and a lack of oxygen and blood flow within the brain and the child likely can die.

Children who experience less severe shaking with mild to moderate injury to the brain will display emotional or physical changes that a regular caregiver should question, i.e. irritability, poor feeding, lethargy and/or vomiting. Typically in these cases, there will be immediate loss of consciousness and a slowness to wake.

"NICE PARENTS"

It is well-known that parents or caregivers who are most liked by their child's medical providers will be at least risk for child abuse in the eyes of the provider. In early medical literature about injuries in young children, doctors viewed parents as being the last cause for trauma seen. Terms such as "spontaneous" and "unknown origin" graced journal pages. Cases continue today in hospitals, clinics and courtrooms of parents who appear as upstanding, confident and loving, yet who are perpetrators of shaking and other child abuse crimes.

Physicians and other professionals may be hesitant to inquire about the possibility of abuse to avoid offending or wrongly accusing parents and caregivers. If all pediatricians and emergency room doctors would consistently consider a differential diagnosis of child abuse on all injuries in children, then a more thorough examination, assessment and interview could be accomplished, and a greater number of children protected.

"SHAKEN BABY SYNDROME DOES NOT HAPPEN."

Many medical professionals are skeptics when it comes to SBS. They believe it is not a syndrome because of the fact that a minority of the cases recover "fully." However, SBS is an appropriate diagnosis whenever an infant experiences intracranial and intraocular damage from being shaken, regardless of the outcome.

Some professionals believe that an adult cannot shake a baby hard enough to kill that child, even though this line of thinking goes against a large body of evidence accumulated over the past two decades. They refer back to the 1987 Duhaime study that questioned the existence of pure SBS and concluded that "severe head injuries commonly diagnosed as shaking injuries require impact to occur and shaking alone in an otherwise normal baby is unlikely to cause shaken-baby syndrome."[11]

The main author of the Duhaime study, pediatric neurosurgeon Christine Duhaime, and her colleagues used mechanical dolls with rubber necks to assess the forces of violent shaking. Some study participants shook the dolls, performing pure shaking without impact, others shook and struck on a pillow-like surface and others shook and struck against a metal rod. Those who struck the doll against a metal rod showed that the impact was ten times the amount of impact to the brain of shaking alone. So defense experts use this study to say that an individual can't cause injury or death from pure shaking—you need impact. They don't consider shaking to be abuse anyway; what is more important is if there was impact or not.

Years later, Dr. Duhaime disagreed and publicly said that pure shaking is still abuse. She added that her study simply found that there would be significantly more damage to the infant brain if there was impact on a hard surface after the shaking. The other issue with the Duhaime study is that it was performed with dolls that lacked many of the physical attributes of a live infant.[12]

One of the shortcomings of this study was the model that was used. The hinge joint of the model infant cannot duplicate the motion and rotation of a human infant head and neck and the damage which is caused within the cranium. The substance and myelination of an infant brain cannot be duplicated by models either. Two recent studies (Cory and Jones[13]; Wolfson et al[14]) asserted that the Duhaime study was faulty in the construction of the doll that was used. The researchers adjusted some parts and found that the shaking outcomes changed and the model's neck dramatically altered the rotational accelerations and velocities that were achieved. These were two very important studies, since they called attention to the problems of the original Duhaime study in attempting to compare the doll to a live infant.

There are well-documented cases of witnessed shaking without impact, perpetrator confessions (though such admissions are largely minimized) and video-recorded animal studies. If no impact injuries are found at autopsy, then pure shaking should be considered. Even if an infant was tossed onto a bed after shaking, the forces of this type of impact are not thought to render significant injury.

Many parents and professionals affected by SBS believe that the shaking versus shaking/impact controversy is one that is irrelevant. Shaking a baby is abusive, pure and simple, and is deserving of strict punishment. The fact that adults can seriously injure or kill a baby by shaking him or her is widely supported by medical professionals.

There are also individuals who believe that innocent people are imprisoned as perpetrators of shaking crimes due to findings of intracranial injuries and retinal hemorrhaging. Defense attorneys will often attempt to explain away such injuries as an infection or pressure in the brain resulting from such innocent causes as accidental smothering or congenital seizures. SBS is a syndrome of combination injuries and should never be diagnosed or prosecuted in light of a singular medical finding.

One mother recounted her opinion of how this defense can affect the outcome of a trial: "I had obtained a list of licensed daycare providers from the Department of Human Services. At 4:35 P.M. on April 12, 2005, I received a telephone call from my daughter's daycare provider advising that my little girl had stopped breathing. Upon my almost immediate arrival at the home, I found my daughter in the ambulance with the paramedics. They would not let me in to be with her 'due to the circumstances;' however, I was told to put my car flashers on and follow the ambulance."

"After we arrived at the hospital in Altus, Oklahoma, I saw a paramedic carry my daughter out of the ambulance in his arms. Her head was in the palm of one hand and her bottom rested on his forearm. He immediately ran inside. When I got inside the hospital, they wanted me to do paperwork but all I wanted was to see my daughter. They would not let me in her room until they stabilized her and I refused to leave, so they got me a chair to sit in the hallway.

"At one point I was taken to the side of the room by the doctor and told the good news that there were no bruises on my baby. He would not give me any further information other than they had to fly her to Tulsa. When he could have started relieving the fluid on her brain, he instead refused to treat her and sent her to Tulsa.

"She was life-flighted to a children's hospital, where she was immediately seen. Our family was taken into the room and advised that she had a 1 percent chance of survival, and that it was the worst case of Shaken Baby Syndrome he had seen in the state of Oklahoma. My baby had a bruise on her chin, a baseball-sized bruise on her pelvis, a bruise on the back of her head, and it was later stated she had been shaken so hard that it broke her body temperature gauge as her brain was shoved into her spine.

"On April 13, the licensed daycare provider, on her own, went to the police station and gave a two to three-hour video and audiotaped confession. Part of that confession included her showing her husband in the interrogation room what she did to my daughter. "I shook her until she went blue in the face, gasped and went quietly."

"On April 14, at 9:55 A.M., my daughter was pronounced brain dead. Cords were detached and I held her for the last time, as her little life perished before my eyes.

"The defense attorney in this case openly states on his website he does not believe Shaken Baby Syndrome exists. I know it was the only argument they could even attempt, but still it is shocking and traumatizing to hear and to live through the emotional turmoil of the trial.

"After her public defenders saw the caregiver's confession tape, they withdrew from serving as her attorneys. Then a new defense attorney stepped in and persuaded a jury to find the caregiver not guilty of first degree murder with no lesser punishment."

SHAKEN BABY SYNDROME RESULTING FROM PLAY/ROUGHHOUSING

When SBS was first coined and described, in detail, as a syndrome in 1972, Caffey proposed that swinging or bouncing a baby, along with a multitude of other play activities, might cause associated injuries. But what is known today after years of research is that SBS occurs from violent whiplash motions on infants by adolescent or adult hands. While certain play activities are harmful in terms of potentially injuring an infant through careless handling, these activities do not cause SBS. At trials of SBS perpetrators, defense attorneys often raise the question to defendants about rough play, which puts doubt into the minds of jurors. Most people believe that if you are rough with a baby, then the potential for injury is high—which the defense will use to their advantage.

BED/COUCH FALLS

Over the past several decades, falls in infancy and childhood have been detailed in medical literature. Falls from short distances, such as couches or beds, do not produce significant injury to infants—especially when a fall is onto a carpeted surface. An infant placed in the middle of bed or on a large couch can only roll off if he or she has the ability to turn over.

Over the years, falls as an excuse for infant injury have been widely used by perpetrators of abuse. Such innocuous injury histories given by caregivers were believed until the 1970s, when studies on infant falls finally began. It is now known that shaking is the only *physical* mechanism that produces the combination of subdural hematoma and retinal hemorrhaging, other than falls from several stories or high-speed, unrestrained motor vehicle accidents.

IGNORANCE

A statement to investigators such as, "I didn't know shaking would hurt the baby," is a claim of ignorance. But the force needed to cause SBS discredits this excuse. To cause and allow an infant's head, arms and legs to whip violently back and forth is to breach one's responsibility as a positive, loving parent or caregiver.

Perpetrators often resort to shaking as the first and only method to try and quiet an infant in their care. Shaking and other forms of physical discipline are ways that adults attempt to exert control on a very dependent young child.

Most shaking incidents last at least fifteen seconds, with as many as fifty shaking movements. This particular time element coupled with the ferocity of the act surely discounts a claim of ignorance that the act was harmful. Rather, this intentional deed knowingly inflicts harm.

"I DIDN'T MEAN TO HURT THE BABY."

Perpetrators of shaking also use this statement as a defense to justify their actions. Chadwick has said that "an unintentional injury is one in which you [hear all that] occurred and inflicted injury is one where you won't always get the full story."[15] Of all pediatric trauma admissions to hospitals, 3 to 7 percent are inflicted injuries.[16] With inflicted injury there is also a delay in seeking care. The child may experience several episodes of shaking before that one time which finally causes irreparable damage. That child was deliberately hurt, as is any child that is shaken. Physicians, as well as juries, will often innocently believe a child's injury to be unintentional because of the need to believe in the goodness of parents and caregivers. This is a dangerous assumption and does not assist in protecting the child.

SIBLING ABUSE

Parents and caregivers have been known to blame other children in the home for inflicting SBS injuries, such as the victim's older brother or sister. There have even been reports of two-year-old siblings being accused by parents as perpetrators of shaking crimes.

There are several reasons why the theory of the young perpetrator fails. For SBS to occur there needs to be significant and sustained force. This is something young children are incapable of producing, as they do not have the strength to shake a baby hard enough to cause SBS injuries. For a two or three-year-old to violently shake a fifteen or twenty-pound baby, it would require a great deal of strength. This could mean trying to shake 20 percent or more of the child's own weight. Secondly, young children do not use shaking as a mechanism for injuring other children. They will bite, kick and hit. Shaking is a method of discipline that teens or adults use. Several case studies in this book will highlight incidents where children have been blamed for shaking episodes.

HIGH RISK PERPETRATOR

Although there are other reasons that may motivate a person to shake an infant, crying is by far the number one reason. Persistent crying occurs at all levels of our society, and perpetrators of shaking crimes come from all class levels too. Historically, child abuse and neglect has been more common in families with significant social problems, i.e. low income and/or unemployed. Some perpetrators are loving parents, some are childcare workers, some are drug addicts and some are violent individuals.

A crying infant can affect anyone—though not everyone shakes a crying infant. Concentrating on a group of individuals who are more "at risk" misses the need for prevention efforts across a continuum. Typically, SBS prevention efforts tend to respond to highly-publicized shaking cases, such as those occurring in daycare facilities, where an au pair is employed or with stay-at-home dads. Instead, attention should be given to the syndrome itself, its causes and how to prevent it from happening at all.

WHAT SHAKEN BABY SYNDROME IS NOT

Scientists are unable to conduct evidence-based studies on live infants. So we need to rely on the outcomes of those who have been shaken, on witnessed accounts and on those few and far between "nanny cam" videos. There has yet to be a fatal shaking event captured on film. There have been non-fatal events captured that would shock a layperson watching them. In these cases the children had no lasting physical effects, nor were they hospitalized. One can only imagine the forces that are used in fatal cases. There is a growing wave of "professionals" across the U.S. who have labeled SBS as the "so-called Shaken Baby Syndrome."

There are three studies that defense experts typically rely on: first, the Ommaya monkey study—they try to compare it to SBS injuries. This is impossible, because the infant brain is different, the type of acceleration/deceleration movement is different, etc. But still, defense expert witnesses like to use this study. Second, they use the 1989 Duhaime study. Finally, defense attorneys use the 2005 Bandak study, which looked at neck injuries in shaken infants (this will be looked at next).[17] Let's focus now on the ways that defense attorneys have attempted to explain such abuse in court.

DEFENSE ATTORNEYS' COURTROOM EXPLANATIONS

Birth Trauma

An important recent study looked at intracranial bleeding in term infants and how long it took for this to resolve. The authors found that the majority of subdural bleeds were small (averaging three millimeters in size) and had resolved within one month. Larger bleeds had resolved by three months of age. These were all confirmed by MRI imaging. This is an important study, as defense experts have posited that SBS injuries may, in fact, be the result of birth trauma. If the victim is over three months old and had no complications from birth (meaning never being diagnosed with brain injury and not being followed by a neurosurgeon) then the injury can't be blamed on birth trauma.[18]

Brain Hypoxia

In 2001, Jennian Geddes published a very powerful Part I/Part II/Part III article that shook up the child abuse world with her claim that shaking can damage the nerve fibers of the neck area that control breathing.[19] If this occurred, Geddes hypothesized that the subsequent lack of oxygen caused the brain to swell dramatically. In turn, the swelling caused brain damage of the kind previously blamed on direct trauma caused by shaking. She felt that minor shaking might later produce lethal consequences. Geddes believed it might not be necessary to shake an infant very violently to produce stretch injury to the brain's fibers. This became what was known as the "unified hypothesis."[20] Several years later, this hypothesis was challenged in a court of appeals and was struck down. Geddes gave evidence herself in court and stated that she didn't think she had the hypothesis quite right. She said she wrote the papers but never intended them to be used in the courtroom. She said she was unhappy to think that SBS cases might be thrown out based on her hypothesis being accepted as fact.

Hypoxic-ischemia became a buzz word in medical literature and was used in an article that focused on retinal hemorrhages from shaking. Binenbaum and his colleagues studied the severity of retinal hemorrhages and their association with "hypoxic-ischemic" brain injury patterns.[21] They used magnetic resonance imaging in young children (under three years of age) with inflicted or accidental head trauma. Retinal hemorrhages were graded on a scale from one (zero hemorrhages) to five (severe hemorrhages). The researchers also noted the type and location of the hemorrhages. They found that 86 percent of the children with "hypoxic-ischemic" brain injury patterns had moderate to severe retinal hemorrhages. Of the children without "hypoxic-ischemic" brain injury patterns, only 12 percent had moderate to severe retinal hemorrhages. The important finding was that severe retinal hemorrhages were only observed in children with inflicted injury. They concluded that with inflicted head injury (e.g. shaking), a distinct type of trauma occurs, which causes more widespread brain injury and more severe retinal hemorrhages. This is an important flag for medical practitioners to note when "hypoxic-ischemic" brain injury and severe retinal hemorrhages are diagnosed—it is most likely an inflicted injury (no matter what the reported "accidental" history is). Binenbaum and associates also found that "hypoxic-ischemic" brain injury is not a necessary factor for severe retinal hemorrhages to occur from inflicted trauma.

Short Falls

Short falls do not produce diffuse retinal hemorrhages, deaths are exceedingly rare and death is due to contact injuries. A recent study, spearheaded by Dr. David Chadwick, looked at The California Epidemiology and Prevention for Injury Control Branch database to assess all childhood falls (playground falls, falls off a chair, etc.)[22] The search yielded six possible fall-related fatalities in young children in a population of 2.5 million children over a five-year period. Only six, which calculated to 0.48 deaths per million children per year. Other databases in literature review produced no data that would indicate a higher mortality rate from a short fall. The chance of any given child dying from a short fall is approximately one in two million. Another study by Barlow in 1983 reviewed a ten-year span of falls from a tall height in children.[23] Of sixty-one children admitted for falls from one or more stories, 77 percent survived. Of the children who fell three stories or less, *100 percent* survived, and only 50 percent died when the fall occurred between the fifth and sixth floors. How is this possible? Infants and young children have more subcutaneous fat and their bones are more supple, so there is less mortality from a long fall versus when an adult falls from one or two stories. When a young child fell three stories or less, the Barlow study showed that everyone survived. If a defense attorney pins cause of death on a bed fall or couch fall, one needs to question the validity of this claim.

In 2001, Warrington and colleagues presented their findings of 3,000 different falls in infants and children. They reported that twenty-one injuries had findings of a concussion or fracture (less than 1 percent) and there were no intracranial bleeding injuries or deaths.[24]

Haney and associates surveyed parents of children younger than five years in an anonymous questionnaire. Out of a total of 307 eligible surveys, there were 209 falls reported for 122 children. Haney found that only 24 percent of those children sustained any injury as a result of a fall. The majority (85 percent) of injuries were a bruise or a bump. The most severe injuries occurred in two children who sustained concussions; only four children had permanent injury (a scar). They found that injuries were six times more likely when a child fell onto a hard surface compared to a soft surface. They determined that short falls rarely cause injury and that the excuse of a short fall in a seriously injured child should raise the question of child abuse.[25]

Finally, Thompson's comprehensive study in 2011 of the biomechanics of short-distance falls in homes concluded that children aged zero to four years did not sustain severe or life-threatening injuries. He looked at seventy-nine children and determined that, in falls from normal household furniture, there were only 2.5 percent who had serious injuries and these were dependent on greater heights, greater impact velocities and lower body mass index.[26]

One of the problematic issues with short fall deaths is that these are used often in court to assert the innocence of a defendant.[27] One particular case is often used as a "go-to" example of how short falls kill. Horace Gardner, a pediatric ophthalmologist, testified at a shaken baby trial and claimed that a witnessed fall backwards of an infant from a seated position resulted in subdural and retinal hemorrhages characteristic of SBS. Due to that, he felt that violent shaking was not necessary to produce the findings.[28] However, this was a fall reportedly witnessed by a five-year-old relative. It was not a valid fall account. Also, it is an outlier case, which makes it a low-level review. As an outlier case, it naturally becomes suspect and its validity should be questioned. Of the millions of minimal falls, topples over and trips each year, this is one that stands alone. It is a short fall that looks just like SBS and most likely is. It is just that it is presented in a way to attempt to refute the diagnosis of SBS.

Kirk Thibault is a biomechanics professor who testified in a shaken baby case several years ago that the severe intracranial bleeding and retinal hemorrhages that the victim in the case suffered could have resulted from a fall.[29] Later, though, when interviewed for the 2008 *Discover* magazine article "Does Shaken Baby Syndrome Really Exist?" he stated, "I don't know that shaking can't kill a child. I assume you can probably shake a child to death. I have no idea."[30]

Choking Episode

Patrick Barnes, MD, is a pediatric neuroradiologist who believes that choking in infants is often a cause for SBS-like symptoms. He feels that SBS is misdiagnosed and overdiagnosed. He reviewed a case of a four-month-old male with an ALTE (apparent life-threatening event) who was brought to the hospital by his father.[31] Supposedly, the infant gagged and choked on formula, which caused apnea (a cessation of breathing). The infant died and at autopsy was found to have subdural hemorrhage, interhemispheric subarachnoid hemorrhage, healed and fresh rib fractures, bilateral retinal hemorrhages with retinal detachment and marked cerebral edema. Barnes wrote, "the sequence of events in dysphasic apnea starts with aspiration of a feed or reflux causing paroxysmal coughing/choking. This produces a dramatic rise in intrathoracic pressure, which is transmitted directly to the intracranial contents during which intracranial vasculature becomes over-distended and damaged. If the buildup in venous pressure is sufficient, there may be disruption of the blood-brain barrier along with SDH, SAH, and RH."[32] So what Barnes claimed was that an infant's injuries that were the exact signs of typical SBS were actually due to choking. This conclusion also did not explain the presence of the *posterior* rib fractures.

Intracranial pressure

After a violent assault to the brain, swelling is common. A rise in intra-cranial pressure goes hand-in-hand with brain swelling. This pressure is occasionally transmitted down the optic nerve and affects the retina, causing pinpoint retinal hemorrhage at the posterior pole. This is called Terson's Syndrome (in *adult* patients). Does it occur in children? Do these hemorrhages look like typical SBS injuries? Are retinal hemorrhages from intracranial hemorrhages a frequent occurrence? Two studies report that Terson's Syndrome is limited to adults and fails to show in children. Morad et al. and Schloff et al. found no correlation with a rise in intracranial pressure directly influencing the presence of retinal hemorrhages in children.[33]

Literature Review

Defense attorneys and defense experts frequently use medical literature as evidence in the courtroom. They claim that if a paper has been published, then it must hold vital truth to support their assertions. One particular paper that is often cited in court is the 2003 SBS literature review by Mark Donohoe that was published in the *American Journal of Forensic Pathology and Medicine*.[34] This reviewed shaken baby articles from 1968 to 1998. It was an article that was embraced (and still is today) by some defense experts. It was also an article that was criticized by child abuse experts.

The Donohoe paper focused on a period of time when the term "Shaken Baby Syndrome" was not a keyword in the search engine PubMed. Donohoe criticized SBS due to its lack of evidence base. As mentioned earlier, researchers are unable to do controlled studies on live infants. But there have been hundreds of scientific reports in medical literature that I believe are valid when it comes to "proving" the existence of SBS, not to mention the clinical experience of thousands of doctors. Also, after the period of time that Donohoe studied, the level of complexity in journal articles grew exponentially. In her dissent in the Shirley Ree Smith case, Supreme Court Justice Ruth Bader Ginsburg cited the Donohoe article. I strongly feel that one needs to dissect articles and ask questions of them in order to accept or reject them.

New York Times writer Emily Bazelon caused another stir in 2011 with her article, "Shaken Baby Syndrome Faces New Questions in Court."[35] In this instance, the article was directed at the general public. It not only received a great deal of online comments, but it received additional press, as well as an *NPR* and *Frontline* documentary. Bazelon reviewed much of the typical information that is cited in court—the original Caffey articles, the 1987 Duhaime study, the Geddes articles, along with court case reports and interviews. It was a very complete article by Bazelon, featuring child abuse experts and defense experts; however, it featured many cases of those who felt wrongly accused and those who had alternate explanations for a condition that is well-established in the medical world.

Lucid Interval

Dr. John Plunkett made news in 2001 when he published a medical journal article supporting lucid intervals.[36] One of the highlights of his study was a video of a two-year-old who was riding on a toy horse. She fell off, hit her head on a concrete garage floor and later died. Initially she seemed okay, but her injury was a contact subdural, and not the bilateral subdurals that are seen in SBS. Plunkett also wrote that the girl had retinal hemorrhages, but these weren't described in detail (confined to posterior pole vs. extending to the periphery). This paper made big news in the child abuse field, where Plunkett was trying to state that if an infant dies from an accident, he or she may have a lucid interval and perpetrators may be wrongly accused. Plunkett usually testfies for the defense in child abuse cases and the United Kingdom has reopened hundreds of SBS cases. He has been one of the primary experts to testify on behalf of the defense. Recently, Plunkett testified in Ohio (*State vs. Carr*) that an adult can't shake an infant hard enough to cause a subdural, that neck injuries would be present and that a skull fracture could be obtained from a two-foot fall.[37] Nevertheless, the accused was found guilty.

Neck Injuries

In 2004, the Bandak study claimed that the levels of rotational velocity and acceleration on an infant's head called for in SBS literature would exert forces on the infant's neck far exceeding the limits possible without structural failure of the cervical spine (the base of the neck). Restated, if an infant or young child were violently shaken, there would be significant neck injuries, even fractures. Yet this finding isn't typically found in SBS injuries. Bandak, one of the authors, proposed that the head velocity from shaking would be the same as the free-fall head velocity of a three-foot fall. But the study was problematic, because the math was skewed. It went through publication and no one tested the G-force data until afterward, where it was found that the measured velocities were incorrect. Defense witness experts are still using this study as proof that there needs to be significant neck injury if a baby was shaken.

SUBDURAL REBLEEDING

At the 1997 trial of Louise Woodward, the nineteen-year-old au pair who was accused of killing eight-month-old Matthew "Matty" Eappen, Dr. Jan Leetsma (a forensic neuropathologist and defense expert) testified about the delayed effects of a head injury young Matty suffered three weeks before his death. He said that the baby re-bled into a previously created hematoma of the brain. In one of his recent publications, "Shaken Baby Syndrome: Do Confessions by Alleged Perpetrators Validate the Concept?", he said such confessions are forced across the board and he stands by his "rebleed" belief.[38] Another supporter of the rebleed stance is Ronald Uscinski, a pediatric neurosurgeon who often testifies for the defense.[39] Uscinski believes that children will suffer rebleeds months after a birth injury.

In the previous discussion on birth injury, we looked at how the resorption and disappearance of a birth subdural occurs after a month—not six or eight months. Uscinski also believes that retinal hemorrhages result from intracranial pressure. We already have addressed this—but Uscinski believes in his own rebleed theory, that a subdural from a birth injury causes intracranial pressure, which causes an infant to develop retinal hemorrhages. Yet it doesn't work this way in an infant or young child. The process doesn't go from point A to point B to point C. He wrote,"Just because subdural hematomas and retinal hemorrhages are present in virtually all the alleged shaken baby cases, does not validate that phenomenon even when the parent has confessed to the crime. I don't equate a confession in court with medical reality."[40] That is his belief and that's what he proposes.

What about subdural rebleeds, though? What actually happens to an infant who happens to have an old subdural that is resolving and it happens to rebleed? The majority of the time, nothing happens. Most rebleeding subdurals are only found when neurosurgeons perform radiographs on outpatient follow-up visits. There are typically no symptoms at all. Many defense experts try to argue this phenomenon from the opposite direction. A child develops a subdural hematoma from accidental or non-accidental cause. Depending on the size of the clot, it is either surgically evacuated or left to resorb in the brain. At follow-up outpatient visits, the child will typically have a CT scan to assess the size of the subdural. Sometimes, the subdural breaks and rebleeds acute blood. The child typically has no averse symptoms from this rebleed and surgery may be needed.

In the defense experts' viewpoint, the child is physically well with a subdural, but once it rebleeds from light jostling or a short fall then the child goes into extremis. This is adjusting reality for the purposes of making an excuse for abuse, and is simply not accurate.

THE "TRIAD" CONTROVERSY

Years ago, SBS would be confirmed if the presence of subdural hemorrhage, retinal hemorrhage and cerebral edema (or swelling) were identified by medical professionals. This triad of injuries has been challenged in court, especially if the child had one or two parts but not all three. Hence, the triad has been downplayed by abuse specialists and is no longer seen as pathognomonic (or definitive) of SBS. Even though the vast majority of shaken infants and children have all three, legal defense strategists have raised enough controversy in the courtroom to turn the tables on prosecution presentations to juries.

So is the triad the centerpiece of SBS? No other condition looks *exactly* like it—the classic bilateral subdural hematomas, the too-numerous-to-count retinal hemorrhages that extend to the periphery and the cerebral edema that develops from an assault to the brain. For years, the SBS diagnosis has held up in court and still does. The concept of why the triad works is that the majority of infants and children who are shaken have brain swelling due to intracranial pressure that occurs secondary to the shaking trauma on the brain, in addition to the blood clot that is present from intracranial bleeding. The majority of shaken children also have retinal hemorrhaging. Hence, the triad of injuries is in the *majority* of cases. Are there outlier cases? Of course there are and these need to be evaluated clinically, as well as investigated and prosecuted properly. For example, some cases have intracranial bleeding without retinal hemorrhaging. Many defense attorneys contend that skull fractures or subdural hematomas cause death in fatal cases. Instead, I believe it is the intracranial pressure in the brain shutting down that causes death.

VACCINATIONS

Viera Schreibner, PhD, is a retired principal research scientist with a doctorate in natural sciences. She believes brain and retinal hemorrhages may be due to the toxic effects of vaccines. She wrote, "Not only do vaccinations do nothing to improve the health of children and other recipients, they cause serious health problems and hardship for their families by victimizing the victims of vaccines."[41] She and many other defense experts believe that many of the symptoms attributed to SBS are actually caused by a vaccine-associated autoimmune reaction in certain children who are genetically susceptible. The majority of infants in the U.S. receive vaccinations without adverse effects and I believe that the subsequent research has shown Schreibner's claim to be false.

VITAMIN C DEFICIENCY

The idea that shaken baby injuries can result from a lack of vitamin C (Barlow's Disease) has been suggested by Dr. Michael Innis, an

Australian pathologist and hematologist.[42] He believes that vaccinations of infants may raise the blood histamine level, which lowers vitamin C, which could cause spontaneous bleeding. Innis is very anti-SBS and has stated, "I repeat, the diagnosis of Shaken Baby Syndrome or inflicted shaking/impact injury is a proven figment of the imagination of some in the medical profession and should be relegated to the scrap heap of history before it causes any more shame to the profession and disaster to innocent families."[43]

DIFFERENTIAL DIAGNOSES

In their thorough review of issues surrounding SBS, Narang and associates presented this scenario:

> *A three-month-old infant presents to the emergency room for... stopping breathing (apnea). The mother's boyfriend, who was caring for the child while the mother was at work, states that the infant was crying. When he gave the infant a bottle, the infant... choked and gagged and then...stopped breathing. He...shook the infant gently to revive the infant. When the infant began crying a short time later, he soothed the infant and waited for the mother to return home, which occurred some hours later. When the mother returned home later, the infant appeared pale and lethargic and so the mother and her boyfriend proceeded to a hospital for evaluation.*
>
> *"At the ER, the mother and her boyfriend denied any trauma for the infant in the prior three months of life. The mother denied any other problems in the child's medical history or any notable family medical history. On physical examination, the child was noted to have a small amount of swelling to the back of the head, but nothing else notable—no bruising, scars, or other lesions. A head CT scan performed in the ER revealed an acute (fresh) subdural hemorrhage (SDH) along the front of both brain hemispheres and in between them (interhemispheric) and developing cerebral edema (brain swelling). The child was admitted for further evaluation and management, and CPS was called. Further hospital evaluation, including whole body x-rays (a skeletal survey), revealed healing rib*

fractures on the right side of the rib cage. Ophthalmologic exam by
the pediatric ophthalmologist revealed severe retinal hemorrhages
(RHs) in both eyes. A child abuse pediatrician was consulted.[44]

Each discipline comes up with its own differential diagnoses. A shaken baby diagnosis is not based on an isolated symptom or injury finding. It is a total picture where multiple professionals become involved. If death occurs, the pathologist's report becomes the final puzzle piece. Looking at rib fractures, doctors will consider the different ways that these fractures could be present. Laboratory work would be performed, the family re-interviewed and assessed for a history of bone fragility, etc. Though rib fractures have a high inclination toward abuse, such a diagnosis needs to be examined thoroughly. So once all the pieces are adequately scrutinized, then the diagnosis of non-accidental injury will be made. This is especially true if no cause history is provided by the caregivers.

Given the fact that the infant in the case we just focused on had been healthy for the first three months of life, the mother and boyfriend had been the only caregivers and there was no family medical history, this made them appear suspicious to physicians, etc. This is when the police become involved—they don't need a differential diagnosis.

CHAPTER 10

Understanding Family Needs

What does a family go through after a shaking incident? How do parents pick up the pieces after their young child has been shaken? This traumatic incident is a life-changing one. One's trust as a parent or family member is deeply affected. Shaking crimes start with the question of "why did this happen?" and then go far beyond.

Let's first consider the effects on the perpetrator's family. They may question the validity of claims against the person accused of doing the shaking. A father might say, "I know my son couldn't have done this," or the wife believes in her heart that her husband is a great father and thinks, *how can he be the one accused of shaking our son*? Let's focus next on the psychological aspects of Shaken Baby Syndrome. These are common denial-related feelings that are normal during times of tragedy. Even when the accused is not a blood relation of the victim, his or her family is very affected. This has not been studied in research but I strongly believe it is a fact. The shaking event was a terrible act and now all family and friends connected to the perpetrator will be emotionally affected. They may stand by the accused and refuse to accept that the person is guilty. They may scour the Internet and try to find alternative theories to SBS in order to make their own beliefs become fact in their minds. They may discover research, commentaries and blogs that denounce the science of SBS and say, "See? You can't shake a baby hard enough to harm it."

This is true denial. It can become a viral process with even strangers taking up the cause. Alan Yurko, accused of shaking his son to death, gained quite a following of supporters. He started a campaign professing his innocence through letter-writing from prison. His case was ultimately overturned because of problems found in the medical examiner's report and in court transcripts.[1] Though he asserted a "vaccine defense," it was not the reason for his freedom (which was short-lived as he was arrested for an outstanding aggravated burglary charge).

What about the infant or young child's family? How does a shaking event affect them and how are they able to carry on "normal lives?" There is the potential for a destruction of the family unit. With an arrest, trial and sentencing (or acquittal) the family unit can never be the same. Families become ruined by breaches of trust. A caregiver was entrusted to provide good care for an infant or child and failed to do so. Not only failed, but caused injury or death. The guilt of allowing a perpetrator to care for a son or daughter is immense for many parents. In cases where a babysitter has shaken a child, the parents' relationship may be harmed due to how each parent copes with the loss. One parent might turn inward and stop communicating, while the other parent becomes an advocate for justice. This separation can lead to an ultimate breakdown of the couple's relationship. Or, such an experience will make the couple even stronger as they stand as a united front against the perpetrator who brought tragedy on their son or daughter.

If a shaking event ends with the death of a child, there are multiple grief issues that occur among families.

GENERAL LOSS—THE CHARACTER OF SBS

Not only is there the loss of the family unit, but there could also be the loss of freedom, loss of finances, etc. Shaken Baby Syndrome tugs at the very core of families and challenges them in ways they've never been challenged before. It is a road that no one asked to be on and one that pulls them away from their former selves. Instead of vacations, the family goes to an outpatient clinic for routine visits to the shaken child. To pay monthly bills and expenses from the experience, the family may take out loans or initiate fundraisers. In addition, there are issues of loss that no one thinks about after a baby is shaken.

There are multiple questions from family members: Why did this happen? How could this have been prevented? How can I live through this? Many of these questions may never be answered. These questions are being asked to make sense of a tragedy and are largely rhetorical, but they still need to be asked by the family. Such questions help with coping, but they also can draw families, especially parents, into an abyss of darkness if they don't have proper emotional support from others.

ISOLATION

Two families are affected: the victim's and the perpetrator's. Each may be isolated in the same way for different reasons. A perpetrator's family might ultimately be shunned by friends, other family and the community. Families may become estranged, feeling that there is a criminal in the family with whom no one wants to even be associated. The victim's family (especially survivor families) may experience isolation in terms of detachment from others. Some people have a problem with the stigma of abuse and don't want to be associated with it—even as friends of the parents. Court and trial appearances, follow-up medical exams, etc. become a part of the family's routine. Friends or even close family members may not be able to relate, so they drift away.

GRANDPARENTS

Grandparents are often very affected, because they've lost a grandchild to Shaken Baby Syndrome. If the child survives, then the grandparent might have new responsibilities for caregiving. If the child dies, then the grief of the loss takes an emotional toll. As a grandparent, you have not only lost a grandchild, but you've also lost a son or daughter if he or she is the perpetrator. The grief may lessen but the loss will always be present. The relationship with the son or daughter will never be the same as before.

SIBLINGS

Siblings have needs which often will be diverted as the entire family focuses on the victim and the perpetrator. But it's important to allow siblings to express their feelings and talk about what happened, so they can get confusing feelings out. Spending time with the brother or sister of a shaken child will also help direct positive attention to him or her. Whether the shaken child survives or dies, the sibling will experience loss very acutely, like others in the family. The sibling may have enjoyed caring for the baby or started to really bond with him or her. When tragedy strikes, that closeness is gone and it draws the sibling into a dark place for which he or she isn't prepared.

SBS has an emotional ripple effect on the entire family; for siblings this can be lasting. For many children, a shaking event is often a dramatic introduction into the darker side of life. Sometimes, siblings actually witness shaking events. This can lead to a lifetime of adjustment problems. Children may have physical reactions to the trauma. They may experience nightmares or night terrors, bed wetting and anger outbursts. This sort of behavior is regressive and is not unusual in the presence of an abnormal situation. The key for adults is to give the child support, normalization and even professional guidance if the physical manifestations continue.

It's easy for siblings to become lost during a case investigation and multiple trips to and from the hospital. Siblings have questions similar to those of adults: "Why did this happen?" "Is the baby going to be okay?" and "Could this happen to me?" are all common; in young children and teens they are amplified. Children have not had many of the negative life experiences that adults have. There are also after-effect issues. Families who are dealing with survivors of SBS are coping with weekly therapy, adjusting the home for wheelchair accessibility, etc., and have thus taken on a new lifestyle. Siblings are left to adapt. If the shaken child dies, there is grief surrounding the death.

What are some ways adults can help siblings cope after a shaking event? First, families need to make their home a place of refuge. For the siblings, home needs to feel normal and safe. By letting children talk about the violence that happened, they are allowed to share on their terms. Violence affects children on different levels and family members need to gauge what is intrusive and what is supportive.

Adults often become focused on a survivor's needs. They need to take time for the siblings on an individual basis as well. Spending time playing a game, going for a walk or having a special lunch together are examples of ways to make a sibling feel unique. Kids should not be pushed into talking about their feelings. There are stages of grief that each individual family member experiences uniquely. Sometimes children even blame themselves for what has happened to a younger sibling. If this occurs, parents and others should allow the child to talk and then reframe the act as the fault of the perpetrator and that the abuse could have happened at any point. While parents may wish to shelter siblings from the details of the shaking event, they should also be honest, using language that is age-appropriate for the child. For example, a mother might say, "Your daddy became very angry with Jacob when he was crying. He hurt Jacob and that is why he is in the hospital. The police are talking with Daddy and he may not be coming home for a while."

Life specialists are professionals in children's hospitals who work with children of all ages to meet them at their developmental level and guide them through a traumatic event. Play therapy and art therapy often supply a creative outlet that children can use to work through difficult emotions. Books on loss can be important ways that parents and others can help a child work through feelings.

Symbolism is a way for families to remember a child who has died. There are many ways that families can use symbolism to honor the life of a child. Siblings can be an important part of these events. Families can plant a tree, make a memory book, visit the child's gravesite (especially on the anniversary of the death) and more. Families can then process these special times afterward as needed.

Siblings in the Middle

My son was shaken in 1999 by his babysitter, Annette Perkins. He was four months old. From what I have been told, Annette picked him up from a nap around 1:45 P.M., got upset at him and began to shake him. Then she put him back into his crib, went to get a bottle of milk and when she came back he was having a seizure and having problems breathing. She then called 911. He stopped breathing three more times between her home and the hospital while in the ambulance and then again two more times in the ER.

I arrived at the hospital about two hours after he did. She never contacted me at work. She was finally told that she had to get in touch with someone and she decided to call my mom. We had known her and her family for over twenty years. When I arrived, my son was already on a ventilator and in a coma. They informed me that he was not breathing on his own, that he had several blood spots in his brain and that they didn't know if he would make it. He was going to be transferred to the nearest children's hospital. I was told to speak with the police who had been called. After speaking with them I was allowed to ride in the ambulance with him to the children's hospital.

When we arrived, my baby was admitted to the ICU. I was told that they would be doing a repeat MRI or CT scan in the morning and that the next seventy-two hours would be most critical. On the 22nd, they did a repeat scan and we learned that he still had brain activity and was in a medical coma. He had a few seizures while in the coma and they had to adjust the meds they were giving him.

On July 23, we were advised that a neuro specialist and an eye specialist would be coming in to look at him. The eye specialist informed me that my son had twenty-one blood spots between both his eyes and that all but one would heal. The one that would not heal would cause him to be blind in his left eye. At this point the police were called again and detectives were assigned his case; they informed me that they had enough to press charges against Annette for child abuse and attempted murder. They were going to arrest her that evening. I learned later on that she was taken into custody at around 10 P.M. and brought to the police station. She made a statement that said she had picked up my son and he was smiling and laughing at her and she got angry at one of her children and shook my son. She later recanted her statement and pleaded not guilty.

My son was in the ICU in a medical coma until July 27. On that day, they started to reduce the medicine that was keeping him in a coma. They started to remove the ventilator. On the morning of July 28, one week after the shaking, I was allowed to hold my son again. I was in tears, because it was one week almost to the minute from when I had held him last. We were told that while he was physically almost five months old, developmentally he was a newborn again. He spent another week in the ICU and then was transferred to the rehab floor where he began physical, speech and occupational therapy. We were given exercises to do with him for his muscles (because of the oxygen loss and the shaking, he had CP, traumatic brain injury, a delay in his development and a seizure disorder). He was given a swallow test that determined that he was able to swallow milk and some soft foods (we had just started jar foods), which was wonderful because this meant that they could remove his feeding tube. After four weeks in the hospital we were allowed to take my son home.

He continued therapy on an outpatient basis three times a week and also home therapy three times a week. In December of 2000, it was determined by his neurologist that he would need to have a shunt put in his head, because one of the clots was not healing. He was then admitted back into the same hospital for three weeks.

The medical professionals at the hospital were wonderful, letting me know what they were doing, telling me what I could do when he was in a coma (read to him, talk to him, play music for him and kiss him). They also kept my baby's abuser away from me (she had been calling every few hours and tried to visit him). They also corrected Child Protective Services, who had been given the wrong info (somehow they had been told that I had done this to my son).

The criminal part of this ordeal took a long time. The caregiver was charged at the end of July 1999, but the trial did not begin until the spring of 2001. The trial started on a Monday. Her attorney tried to get it delayed by not showing up until late in the morning. The trial went on that day, all day Tuesday and then into Wednesday. I was put on the stand and asked all kinds of questions, not only by the State's Attorney, but also by her attorney. She was claiming that my son had problems from the beginning, that I had caused this by bouncing him in a stroller and then finally that my brother (who was fifteen years old at the time) had hurt him the night before.

The jury got the case early Wednesday afternoon and had come to a decision by 3 P.M. that day. The verdict was guilty on the child abuse charge. Annette was taken into custody immediately and returned to jail. In August, I was allowed to make a statement and she was sentenced to ten years in prison. She had to serve at least eight and a half years. She was released from prison a few years ago.

My son being shaken had a huge effect on my family. I watched the light go out of my brother's and daughter's eyes; both of them had been so excited when he was born. My brother was excited, because there was another male in the family whom he could play ball with and do other boy things with when my son got older. My daughter took this very hard. You see, Annette was also her godmother. After her brother was shaken I was not home for over a month, so she was taken to a friend's house to stay so that I could deal with my son's injuries. Then, once we were all home again, she still didn't get much attention from me, because I needed to deal with my son's needs.

I trusted almost no one with my son. It took me a long time to even trust my own mom to take care of him. I found out years later that it was during this time that my daughter almost ran away. I was lucky that some friends of hers talked her out of it. I will say this much—my daughter loves her brother now more than anything in the world. She can calm him down with just her voice. He loves talking to her on the phone and they have a wonderful relationship. But it was very hard for many years and I know that she was jealous of him on many occasions. I had to finally get over my fear of trusting people and gave in to respite care when my daughter entered high school so that I could attend some of her school activities. I believe that doing this helped me and my daughter's relationship.

My son turned fifteen on March 2 and he is a very happy young man. He still has many issues, but he puts a smile on my face every day. He is in a wheelchair and can only walk using a Pacer walker. He is still in diapers and is on two seizure medicines. He has to have blood drawn every three months to check the levels of his medicines. He also wears AFOs [ankle-foot orthotics] on both legs.

I have been asked if I could go back would I change anything. I usually answer yes and no. Yes, I wish that this had never happened to my son. And no, I would not change him. He is a happy little person most of the time who still loves me and kisses me (how many moms can say that about their fifteen-year-old?). He loves music, game shows and spending time at school and with his family. He makes me laugh every day.

While every day can be a challenge, I have very wide shoulders. I have let go of the hate I felt at one point for Annette. I can't seem to forgive her, but I have let go of my anger and believe God will deal with her. I have only broken down once because of her, about four years ago. At that time, I had to take my son to the ER when I could not get his gums to stop bleeding, I didn't realize what the date was (it was the anniversary of the shaking event) until the nurse said it as I was signing papers. I completely broke down and could not stop crying. I was lucky that we had been to this ER before and I had gotten to know the minister there. They were able to get her and she came and talked to me. I know that my son may never live the life I had planned for him when he was born, but he is living his life and he enjoys it. He loves the wind and the sun, but doesn't like snow. He loves to learn new things and can talk your ear off. I am told that he is between a two and five-year-old, which as we all know can be a very fun age (and also a challenging age). He repeats a lot of the things that are said around him, so I have to watch what I say. He loves to watch sports and is a Michigan State University fan.

—*Ruth Clark*

Many hospice programs have community grief programs for families who have lost loved ones. There are also therapists and counselors in many cities and towns who specialize in grief work. Healing needs to happen and some family members have a harder time coping with loss than others. Finding community resources can allow the emotional healing to happen more effectively.

PART 3

SBS Best Practices

CHAPTER 11

Investigation and Prosecution

Kassica Harp

The weekend of April 14, 2000, was like every other visiting weekend we had. My husband picked up his children and brought them to our home. The boys came running in to say hello. Bringing up the rear was Kassica, a sweet twenty-one-month-old little blond-haired, blue-eyed girl. We enjoyed our wonderful weekend with the kids, never knowing this would be the last time we would ever see Kassica playing and full of life.

Sunday night we had to drop the children off with their mother. She was not there, but her fiancé Michael was. The kids were crying, saying, "Please, we don't want to stay." Kassica had to be taken from me, screaming, because she did not want us to go. We were beside ourselves leaving the kids with him.

Monday, April 17, is a day that forever changed our lives. The kids were taken to day care and school. Michael picked the kids up and brought them home. The boys went outside to play. From what we have been able to put together, he and the children's mother were trying to potty train Kassie (she was nowhere near ready). She had an accident and that enraged Michael. While changing her, he shook her violently and slammed her head into a wooden bedpost. He then laid her on the couch so he could take a shower. When he finished his shower, he found her having seizures and she was unresponsive and throwing up. He grabbed her and ran next door. The neighbors called 911. Kassie was rushed to the hospital and her mother was called. Shortly after that, we were called and we rushed to the hospital.

When we arrived, the halls were full of police officers, social workers and investigators. All we wanted to know was what in the world was going on. We found out that Kassie was in surgery having a burr drilled into her skull to relieve the pressure. Michael, the man who did this to her, sat in the waiting room watching the damage he did to this family unfold.

The first night is still a blur. The police interviewed my husband and me. The boys were placed in our custody immediately. We got them out of the hospital with other family members as quickly as possible, since they were only five and seven—they also had her eight-year-old step-sister. There were lots of MRI, CT and other scans. By the morning it was clear to the doctors what had occurred. Kassie had been shaken. This had been done on purpose and they were sure they knew who did it. Michael, her soon to be step-dad, a man who should love her, was arrested Tuesday, April 18, 2000.

That Tuesday, Kassie had more scans and was a little more awake than the night before. She was crying part of the day and moving around a bit, so we were hopeful. The doctors explained that we were in for a long haul. They felt things could turn bad quickly and that we should not get overly positive. They were honest and kind.

Tuesday was a long day and we just had to wait. Wednesday she coded once. It was so scary and heart-breaking. Describing it is impossible. We stood there helpless. It was so long just watching her struggle. She seemed to be getting weaker. Wednesday night we went to check on the other children, because we knew they needed us too. Since Kassie's mother would be with her, we thought it would be a good time to go to the other children.

We arrived early Thursday morning to find out that Kassie was having seizures again. While her tremors were small, I knew immediately it was not a good sign. I went and got the nurses and they started Kassie's medications again. She seized until noon that day. It was not a good day. They watched her closely. She coded two times that day, but they were able to get her back. They ended up doing an EEG and the results were not good at all. It showed she had no brain function. They did a life-skills test. Everyone left the room but her mother and I. We held hands and tried to will her into having some type of function. There was nothing. I am good at holding it together. Her mother did not need me to be a hot mess; instead, she needed my support. I was the rock for Kassie's mother, father and siblings that week.

Once I could leave the room, I headed for the chapel where I tried to bargain with God. I was screaming and crying in a manner that was the most painful of my life. The priest came out, because I was so loud. I would have given my own life for Kassie to survive. I screamed for forty-five minutes before my mother found me and said, "Get up now and stop this. You are not doing Kassie any good acting like this. She needs you to be strong and take care of everyone else. Get it together." I found my strength again. I stood up, dried my eyes and went back to make sure everyone else was okay. I never became hysterical in front of people again.

We went home and got the other children. We brought them to see Kassie before they took her off life support on Friday. Her eight-year-old step-sister just stood there holding her hand and cried. Her seven-year-old brother was just in shock, said nothing and just watched. Her five-year-old brother walked into the room like he ran the place. He wanted to know why she was naked, why the tubes where there and what was going on. Taking them up there to give them one last chance to see Kassie was the single hardest thing we have ever had to do.

On Friday morning, they again performed the life-skills test. Again, it was just her mother and I holding hands willing Kassie to have some response. There was none. The priest came in and gave Kassie last rites. Both families were there as the rites were given and we had our chance to say goodbye. When it was time to finally take her off life support it was just her mother, her father and I. Shortly after the machines were withdrawn, her father could not stay any longer and had to leave. I sat there with Kassie's mother, rocking her. I stroked Kassie's hair as her heart stopped beating. I left to allow her mother privacy with her and to find her father.

Kassie died April 21, 2000, on Good Friday.

On Saturday, April 22, we planned her funeral and celebrated her step-sister's ninth birthday.

We held Kassie's rosary on April 23 and her burial April 24.

Once Kassie was buried and that part of this terrible murder was over (because that is, I strongly believe, what it was), we started to deal with the fallout. For a couple of months the boys were not allowed to see their mom without supervision. Once that was over they began to get visits with her. The investigation went on. It was clear that Kassie's injuries were so bad that they occurred within ten to thirty minutes before she started having seizures. She had a six-and-a-half-inch skull fracture through a growth plate, retinal hemorrhages and subdural hematoma.

Michael was charged with first degree murder and was released on bond his family posted. A year later, we sat through a terrible trial. I attended every day except for the part where the autopsy photos were shown—I could not do that. I could not see her like that. The jury listened and found him guilty, but only of involuntary manslaughter. They just could not understand what made him so angry at a young child. Michael served twenty-two months (he was sentenced to thirty-six). He basically served a month for every month of her life. The unfairness in that is beyond overwhelming.

This event has completely changed the outcome of this family. The boys' mother no longer has any rights to them or any type of contact. For years they refused to see her. Years ago, they asked that I be allowed to adopt them. Their mother finally allowed it. She gave them that one last gift. For that, I will forever be grateful. They deserve peace. They deserve to move on in their lives from all of the traumatic events that the choices of adults brought into their world. Kassie's brutal death has done more damage than I can even begin to describe; to her mother, her father and to myself. But I focus on the kids, because they are the innocents in this. Please remember that one act can cause so many ripple effects.

There is not a day that goes by that I don't think of Kassie. Her pictures hang in our front room. We still visit her grave and have lunch with her. The kids love to take lunchables, as that is how I helped them grieve when they were young. I clean her grave when we go, which is the only way I can still care for her. Her father rarely goes—it is just too hard for him. Her stocking hangs empty at Christmas and every holiday she is missed. She would have been fifteen this year and a sophomore in high school. Her absence is felt every day.

—Tonya Harp

How can those who commit such crimes against the innocent be caught? How can one perpetrator be identified if an infant has multiple caregivers? What are some strategies for doing this? (i.e. statement analysis, timeline review, etc.)

What was the motive? Many times, investigators can discover the trigger for a shaking event by asking questions. How did the caregiver deal with crying? Was the child old enough to be toilet-trained? Was there a problem with that? Or it could be that a young child touched something he or she wasn't supposed to or spilled something. The motive for the shaking (the trigger event) is present; it just needs to be uncovered by the investigator.

What are prosecutors up against in cases of shaking? Some defense experts state that there is no such thing as SBS, especially since there have been no large studies that involve live infants; the syndrome can't be proven. Yet there are many cases which have been studied where researchers have looked at the outcome *after* an infant has been shaken. This helps us not only understand the syndrome better, but it also helps prosecute those responsible.

INVESTIGATION

In shaken baby cases, there needs to be a sound investigation, which is key in having a good criminal case against an alleged perpetrator. Every detail needs to be documented, wherever the injury took place. All witnesses need to be thoroughly interviewed, including other children in the home.

Each year, many infants' and children's deaths are diagnosed as accidental falls, congenital disorders, etc., yet are actually cases of murder by shaking. Autopsies may not be performed, no one is prosecuted and homes are not investigated. As the pathophysiology of SBS becomes more widely known, fewer such cases will be mismanaged. There will always be pockets of ignorance and irresponsibility, but a keen investigation from the start will help to bring justice to victims and families.

Death and injury from SBS and other forms of physical child abuse are seriously underestimated. When an infant or young child is shaken and injured, there are several issues on which to focus. The primary emphases should be the nature of the injuries to the child, when the injuries were inflicted and who inflicted them.

Awareness of these injuries and the way they are produced is not common knowledge among law enforcement investigators, pathologists, medical personnel and social workers. Cases will be missed and not completely investigated. The more training opportunities there are for the professionals, the better they will be at identifying SBS injuries and fatalities. Only then can more cases be prosecuted and more killers brought to justice.

Intraocular and intracranial bleeding and rapidly progressing edema caused by traumatic shaking will be preceded by the onset of symptoms appearing immediately or within minutes. Less severe shaking will produce less severe symptoms over a longer period of time. Perpetrators of shaking incidents can be identified more readily if investigators and medical personnel are aware of this principle. A symptomatic infant connected to a caregiver who offers an incomplete or skewed history of the child's injury may ultimately be identified as the perpetrator of the crime. Because of inadequacies in the reported history of injury, this person is more readily identified as the cause of the injury. It is important that investigators review statements given to all medical personnel (including emergency personnel) and other family members before an alleged perpetrator is questioned. These can support or negate the accuracy of injury details.

Investigations by law enforcement personnel are performed to determine the course of action appropriate for any criminal violation and to determine how victims can best be protected. All aspects of the family structure and quality of relationships should be documented. This includes the assessment of positive or negative interactions among family members, amount of time individuals spend at home and the type of emotional support that is received from extended family members.

Many initial assumptions about an infant's death are not what they seem. For example, Bass and associates found that further investigation into Sudden Infant Death Syndrome deaths led to the finding that several of the infants had been shaken to death.[1] They concluded that information obtained during the death-scene investigation should lead, when suspicious, to special examination of internal organs during autopsy. Even then, a trained eye should know what to look for and its possible cause.

Perpetrators of shaking crimes will offer stories that do not account for the severity of SBS injuries. A perpetrator identified for obviously inflicted injuries may give no explanation. He or she may say, "The baby was fine one minute and was twitching and breathing funny the next." Though SBS is typically a crime of seclusion, there may be witnesses. Other children in the house, other caregivers, etc., need to be interviewed completely away from the alleged perpetrator. Stories that do not match often reveal evidence and answers for investigators.

Shaking incidents may arise from single moments of violence where a caregiver lashes out in a rage at an infant. The perpetrator may or may not be a biological parent. No one can be absolved as a suspect until the investigation is complete and all persons connected with the crime have been interviewed. Shaking can be a single event or a part of a vicious cycle. A pattern of abuse will emerge and be verified with a physical and diagnostic examination of the child. If there is a history of prior domestic violence or child abuse, then investigators may not need to look too hard for potential suspects.

The police interview process is important to the whole of the investigation. Proper interviews will lead an investigator to the correct answers. In shaken infant deaths, investigators can interview at the crime scene or at the police station. The process is often aided by having the interview videotaped. The tape can be used in court at a later date and videotaping puts a potential perpetrator emotionally on edge.

Ideally, the reconstruction of the "accident" should be in the environment where the injury took place. Dolls should be used to make the reconstruction of the crime more real. If the story is of a short fall, then the caregiver should reconstruct the alleged fall with video that documents the individual showing what happened. He or she can push the doll off the same piece of furniture (bed, couch, table, etc.) from which the child allegedly fell. If the caregiver reports shaking the baby (either during a choking or apnea event) this needs to be demonstrated as well. Using these methods can make excuses for injuries more unreasonable.

Investigators should pose their inquiries this way: "The child could not have been injured [or died] as you described. Help me understand by showing me just what happened." Or, "I know you want to help me understand what happened to this child." Phrases such as these may invite the accused into conversation with the investigator. The self-esteem of such perpetrators is typically so immature in the first place that such a stance by the investigator can make the perpetrator believe he or she is really helping out. Building a rapport with the perpetrator can ultimately lead to a confession.

During an interview, if the investigator is aware of bruises on the infant or child, it should be brought up. For example, "I heard from the ER doctor that your baby had a strange bruise on its back [or leg, arm, head, etc.]. She said that the description is like a stippling mark or strike mark—can you tell me about that?" If no information is forthcoming, it would be important to access the house, look around and find out what the instrument could be that might have caused the marks on the baby. It could be a hairbrush or a cord or something different. Often in SBS cases, there is a multitude of other abusive acts that the baby experiences.

Videotaping a reconstruction with the suspect should occur prior to a formal police interview. The investigator and suspect then can look at the tape together and point out any inconsistencies. Juries will also benefit from videotaped reconstruction, because they typically find such evidence persuasive. If a confession is made, investigators should get the most out of the interview by asking the perpetrator about the number of shakes, the frequency of shaking incidents and the severity of the shakes. Having the perpetrator demonstrate on a doll while being videotaped can be an important addition to a prosecuting attorney's case in court.

Breaking investigations down into steps allows for more thorough work. There is usually only one chance to investigate a crime scene and few chances to investigate a crime victim. So, careful work must secure all necessary information at once.

When a child has been transported to a hospital, it's at this time that (after a suspicion of abuse is determined) police are called. At the hospital, there are various questions for the investigator to consider when reviewing the child's injuries. Findings can later be compared with information provided by an accused perpetrator, i.e. a story given in the hospital of an infant falling down a flight of stairs will be obviously conflicting if the investigator finds the home environment is a one-story dwelling. Here are some important questions for investigators to ask medical personnel:

Is there external bruising? If so, what type?

Depending on the age of the child, bruising may occur with normal activity. A bruise does not always equate with abuse. Infants who are beginning to crawl tend to bump into household objects. They have not figured out that a hard object can cause them pain. With toddlers, the instability of walking can cause frequent bruise marks. But it is important to note that such marks should be largely confined to areas where there is bone underlying the skin, such as the forehead, shins, etc. The child also needs to be examined for a pattern to the bruises, which will be discussed more in depth later.

Were seizures reported?

Marie Bourgeois and her researchers looked at 404 children hospitalized with Shaken Baby Syndrome over a period of several years and they saw that epileptic seizures were found 73 percent of the time.[2] Only 11 percent of the shaken children had a normal EEG initially upon admission. When investigators are reviewing medical records or obtaining any sort of statement from the hospital/doctor and "seizures on admission" is one of the findings coupled with a diagnosis of Shaken Baby Syndrome, then this is an important point to possibly be used later in court.

Does the child appear well-nourished?

Generally, is the child well-cared for and well-fed? This is only one part of the larger snapshot of an infant or child, but is important since it gives information about how the child is thriving in its environment.

Did the child vomit?

This is important to assess. Many head injuries can cause vomiting, including ones caused by shaking.

Was the child bleeding?

Head injuries can cause bleeding from the ears and nose. Though medical personnel may make this diagnosis, it is an important finding to be noted, especially if there was a delay in seeking treatment for the child.

Are there any areas of swelling on the child's body?

The fontanelles (or "soft spots") on a baby's head will typically swell or be firm and tense after a head injury. There may also be signs of swelling on other parts of the body from grip marks or impact that have not yet begun to bruise, but still swell in response to trauma.

Are there cutaneous marks present on the child's body?

Are there cutaneous (affecting the skin) cuts on the child or other marks, such as burns? What was the cause of such marks? What are the caregivers saying?

The physical surroundings should be the next target in the investigative process. This is very important, as careful observation and a detailed description are vital in obtaining a case for the prosecutor. The whole room where a shaking incident occurred must be properly examined.

Other items to examine are:

Condition of the Living Environment

How clean is the living space? While this is not a determinant of a crime, it does aid in profiling the care of a child. Haphazard living environments may point to substandard care of one's children.

Discarding of Infant Clothing or
Other Materials Used in a "Clean-up" Process

If there was a delay in seeking medical treatment for an injured child, there may be signs of this around the house. Any blood stains on rags or infant clothing? Any vomit cleaned up (without reporting that the child had vomited)? If found, these items should be collected and the caregivers questioned about them.

Height of Infant Sleeping Area

Investigators should always document the height of a child's crib/bed. This should be done with images and written documentation, complete with a measuring stick that shows height. One never knows the direction of an investigation or what an alleged perpetrator may report as the mechanism of injury. If there is a carpet on the floor of the bedroom, then the floor covering thickness should be measured and photographed as well. Considerable doubt can be raised regarding a perpetrator's story in the minds of a jury if there was a well-padded carpet versus a hard wooden floor.

Condition of Infant Sleeping Area

Are there signs of poor care in the sleeping area? For example, old food in the crib, multiple formula bottles, dirty linen, used diapers, etc.

Height of Infant Feeding Chair

Just like the height of the bed, an investigator should document where a child spends much of his or her time. If there is a feeding chair in the home, document with images, complete with a measuring stick, and a written description. As investigators are aware, reported histories of child abuse injuries change. Originally, the perpetrator of a shaking crime could focus on a bed fall as an excuse, but later may report the fall occurred while the child was in his or her high chair. So, the locale of an excuse used by a suspect may change, which is why broad scene documentation is key to a solid investigation.

Physical Evidence

If the alleged story of a child's injury is that he or she fell against a coffee table, is there any evidence—e.g., blood, skin or a mark on the coffee table? Even if this occurred, such evidence may not be present, but an investigator needs to match the story with the physical evidence in the home.

Overt Signs of Alcohol or Drug Use

This also points to the kind of environment a child lives in, e.g., beer bottles, a crack cocaine pipe, the smell of marijuana.

Finally, investigators will want to thoroughly document interviews with all caregivers within the last twenty-four hours. Much information can be garnered by simple observation on the part of the investigator or clinician. How do family members interact? Is there appropriate eye contact? How do family members react to the findings that the injuries to the child are abuse-related? Is there a willingness to cooperate? How do family members place themselves when sitting or standing? Specifically, investigators will want to note:

Body Language

During an interview, investigators want to watch the body language of family members. Even an EMT might report that the family was very nervous and they gave off strange vibes. So this information is important to gather. While most police interviews are videotaped, a body language expert can also comment on sensitive areas that are seen when certain questions are posed to the suspect. This person can be brought back for a second interview and asked those same questions again that made him or her react a certain way.

Who Called 911?

This is an important aspect of case investigation on multiple levels. Did the boyfriend drive the baby to the mother's work and she called 911? Or did the mother who was staying with the child all day at home call 911? What was said on the 911 call is very important as well and can be used very effectively during a police interview. A 911 call can also be reviewed using statement analysis for inconsistencies, hesitancies, emotional distance and so on.

Stories That Do Not Match the Gravity of the Crime

Seasoned investigators know that infants and young children can bounce back better than adults after minor trauma. So, if the initial story of a child's injury is a fall to the ground and the child is on a respirator in the hospital clinging to life, this should raise doubt in the mind of an investigator (as well as hospital staff). Though minor to professionals, falls from short heights may seem extreme in the minds of perpetrators, which is why the topic of falls is so common in stories of abuse.

Excited Utterances

Perpetrators of crimes often put themselves in the middle of the act even when they are trying to divert the truth. So when a caregiver suddenly says, "I didn't hurt that baby!" this is an expression that is important and needs to be not only questioned, but documented.

Differences in Successive Caregiver Accounts of the Same Event

What is left out of statements about a "routine" day? When one parent goes to work and leaves his or her child with the other, how is the day described? Perpetrators of shaking crimes will often call the working parent and give reports on the child and daily activities. How did the caregiver sound? Did the caregiver report any problems? Are there two different accounts shared with police investigators? Another example of this occurs when a parent drops off a child at day care and the child is awake and alert upon arrival, but when interviewed the daycare worker states that the child was asleep. This seemingly simple difference needs to be addressed.

Who were the caregivers of the child on the day of the injury?

Are there multiple caregivers or are there only two individuals (the parents)? The answer to that question will focus the attention on who was caring for the child at the time of injury. It may be that the child typically is cared for by his or her grandmother, but that day the father was off work and decided to be the caregiver.

When was the child last said to be well and acting normally?

This issue dovetails with the previous topic and should be part of a timeline of events. It is key to note when the victim was last healthy and acting normally. This allows the investigator to focus the subject list more tightly.

Are there expectations of the child that are not age-appropriate?

A caregiver may inject statements into the conversation that he or she was trying to get the baby to walk (even though the baby is seven or eight months old), or trying to potty train a one-year-old. These are examples of possible trigger events that may have led to the shaking event.

What sort of childcare experience has the person had? Is he or she comfortable with children? Is there any part of child care that the person doesn't like?

When did the incident occur?

This will tell investigators if a delay occurred between the incident and when help was sought. The caregiver may not offer this information freely and will most likely try to divert the truth. The problem with this tactic is that the perpetrator locks him or herself into a timeframe of when the infant or child was well.

Accounts from Other Children Present at the Time of the Incident

If there are siblings in the home or at a daycare center, did they witness anything? What was the tone of the caregiver throughout the day? Did the child cry a lot? What was reported to parents by the children?

The Demeanor of the Child Throughout the Day

When questioning a caregiver, it is important to ask questions about the infant or young child's emotional state. The investigator is searching for triggers. The caregiver may not give up this kind of information easily, trying to make it seem that the child was happy and then a tragic accident occurred. The caregiver can be thoroughly questioned, though, to see how he or she handles the behavior of a child when the child is not happy.

Recent Psychosocial Stressors
Affecting Any of the Infant's Caregivers

Has the caregiver recently lost a job? Is the caregiver having money problems? What are some of life's stressors that may cause a caregiver to abuse a child? Often, alleged perpetrators may freely open up to an investigator who appears generally interested in their well-being.

The Condition of Other Siblings within the Home

Sometimes, the child who has been shaken is the "target child." For some reason, other children do not affect the caregiver negatively, but the victim has been labeled as "bad." This is classic in infant and child starvation cases, where the other children in the home are well-fed and generally happy and the starved child is targeted by having food withheld.

What was the position or placement of the child when found?

If this can be ascertained, does the position of the child make sense? For example, if the child has died and the initial investigation (prior to autopsy) is pointing to SIDS, then ask the parent or caregiver what position the infant was found in. Could the baby turn over in his or her sleep? Do the parents know about "back to sleep?" If a diagnosis of SBS is confirmed, then the sleep position of the child may be a moot point. Also, did the caregiver move the child after calling 911? If so, what was the purpose of this?

STATEMENT ANALYSIS

When we communicate with other individuals, whether it is through written or verbal interaction, we choose the words and phrases that we want to in order to get our point across. There is a subtle psychological drive that subconsciously helps us to choose what words we want and how we should say them. Statement analysis is used by investigators and behavioral analysts to assess the true meaning of the words that subjects speak or write. This is an important tool when looking at individuals who may be perpetrators of a crime. Statement analysis is not an end-all method of solving a crime, but it helps expose inaccuracies.

There are many principles within statement analysis that are used to identify problem areas with wording. For example, if a person is asked to recount a certain day that he experienced, then he should include the words "I" and "my," since the person is a part of his own story. If he leaves these words out of the story, then it is identified as sensitive. When the pronoun "I" is missing from a statement, this is an indication the person is not totally committed to the facts in the statement. "On Saturday, I went to the store and bought milk. The store was busy, but the lines weren't long. I even ran into my friend, John. Afterward, I went home, slept for a few hours and then I got ready for work," is a straightforward account of someone's day. If the subject said, "On Saturday, I went to the store. After, went home, slept and went to work," then there are pieces missing in his account of his day, as well as the missing pronoun "I." This is problematic, especially if the subject was asked for an exact description of his timeline. There are some parts of his story that he doesn't want to share, so he glosses over them—it is not event-specific.

Other principles of statement analysis include verb tense changes (story recounting should be in the past tense, but often sensitive parts are changed to present tense), using equivocal words ("I think," failing to use specific words) and having a change of language should represent a change in the subject's reality ("car" becomes "vehicle" later in the statement).

In the 1994 Susan Smith case, her own words betrayed her when she was giving a dramatic interview on a television program, in which she pleaded to have her two children returned to her. She said, "my children needed me." But she should have said, "my children *need* me." She made a mistake and used the verb in the past tense, because she knew her children were already dead.[3]

TIMELINES

Timelines are meant to be written down, not simply explained. So, caregivers need to document on paper the days preceding the injury or death of the baby. For example, the baby's injury occurred on a Thursday, so the caregiver begins the timeline on Tuesday; the baby was fine. Wednesday? The baby was fine. On the morning of the injury, he was doing pretty well. What about the hours surrounding the injury? A timeline breaks down what's been going on with the baby. Other questions to examine include: "How was the baby feeding?" "Has the baby been on a routine sleep schedule?" "Have there been any recent pediatric visits to his doctor?" "How has behavior of the baby been?" "Is he colicky? Or happy-go-lucky?" and "What other caregivers are there?"

When an investigator reviews a timeline spanning the last few days prior to the injury and the day of the injury, it becomes a key piece of the inquiry into abuse. A timeline tells the condition of the child, who he or she was with and details the continuum of a well child to an injured child in an SBS investigation. A timeline establishes when the suspect was alone with the child. Within the context of the timeline, investigators not only look at all the possibilities for injuries, but also at who could have inflicted them.

Investigators also assess victimology in the timeline. How physically well was the baby? Was the baby behaving normally and feeling well? What was his or her normal daily routine? For example, if the shaking event occurred at home and the baby's father was the caregiver, then what time did the mother go to work? In another example, if the child had a babysitter, when was the baby dropped off? How long has the baby been going to this caregiver? This information is a vital piece of the investigation.

Using a timeline also determines the time of the last normal activity for the baby. So, when was the baby playing last? Was the baby sleeping when he or she got to the daycare center? Or when the babysitter started caring for the baby? Timeline information can also introduce other caregivers who may have been involved. Did other people come and visit the house? How many caregivers were in the daycare center? Which ones cared for the baby?

As discussed earlier, investigators should look at delays in seeking treatment as part of the timeline. The baby may have been symptomatic, but the caregiver called 911 or another caregiver three hours later. If the alleged perpetrator did make a call to 911, investigators want to match what was said on that call to what was reported in the hospital to medical professionals. If there is a discrepancy, it can be used later in court.

Finally, can the alleged perpetrator repeat the timeline backwards? This shouldn't be done on paper, but as the person is telling it. If it is made up, then the person will have a great deal of trouble describing the event backwards and will leave out or confuse key things. Someone who is telling the truth can repeat things in reverse order.

CASE EXAMPLE OF A TIMELINE

Police and EMTs knocked on the front door of the Eappen home in 1997 after nineteen-year-old au pair Louise Woodward called 911. Upon opening the door, Woodward was on the phone with a friend. The police asked, "Ma'am, where's the baby?" Woodward kept talking to her friend on the phone. The question was repeated, "Ma'am, where's the baby?" and they looked in the living room to see eight-month-old Matthew "Matty" Eappen on the floor, not moving. They rushed him to the hospital, where he died several days later. One really important step that one of the investigators performed was to open the refrigerator. This was key, because inside the investigator found a half-eaten jar of baby food and with that, investigators asked Woodward when Matty ate it. She replied that he ate it for lunch that day. So, since Woodward called 911 in the afternoon, it shows that the baby was acting normally at lunchtime. Her attorneys later tried to blame the injury on Matty's parents—who weren't home at the time of the injury or most of that fateful day.

Videotaping a Recreation of the Event

Investigators need to look at the important details of the injury event and have the perpetrator recreate what he or she thought happened. For example, "Okay, so you shook the baby to revive him after he stopped breathing. Let's see that on video." Using a video recording app on a smartphone is easy. This video can be used later in the courtroom and could be vital to the prosecutor's case. An investigator wants to see how hard the baby fell off of the couch. Many child abuse investigators have a doll on hand in their car, so it can be brought into the scene where the event occurred. It's crucial to have the potential perpetrators show what happened and to document it on video.

Does the Injury Make Sense?

Finally, for the investigator, when looking at the entire scenario and the child's injury, he or she should ask if it was an accident or abuse. For example, if the baby is at the top of the stairs in a walker and tumbles all the way downstairs, head over heels, does it make sense for the baby to have a subdural hematoma and a skull fracture? Yes, it does. Does it make sense for the baby to have multiple skull fractures in a short translational fall? No.

CRIMINAL INVESTIGATIONS

The American Academy of Pediatrics (AAP) has released three statements over the past fifteen years regarding their definition of SBS and their professional stance on the seriousness of the condition in a young child. In their most recent statement in 2009, they suggested that "Shaken Baby Syndrome" should be changed to the more comprehensive term "Abusive Head Trauma" (AHT).[4] This was changed partly due to the fact that many defense experts believe that there is no such thing as Shaken Baby Syndrome and have influenced juries into returning a "not guilty" verdict in many SBS trials. The term Abusive Head Trauma also incorporates head injuries where shaking may or may not be a direct cause, such as impact by fist, object, etc.

Types of Charges

The actual type of charge depends on three things. It depends on the gravity of the crime, the style of the prosecutor and the evidence. In terms of the gravity of the crime, a prosecutor may have a case of a child who has been moderately shaken and left with some residual physical deficits. Is this attempted murder? In some jurisdictions, an aggressive prosecutor might pursue this charge. Often, abuse charges are typically "felony child abuse," which is a watered-down version of attempted murder. But what if the child died? Would a prosecutor go for reckless homicide or first-degree murder? This all depends on the prosecutor, on the evidence and on how comfortable the subject of abusive head trauma has been in the region's courtrooms. Do the charges actually fit the crime? This is important to consider, because sometimes a prosecutor considers lesser initial charges, like reckless homicide, since such a charge is potentially easier to get a successful conviction, rather than a charge like first-degree murder. But a prosecutor must ask if this is justice for the infant or toddler who died. Since the violence that is required to shake a baby to death is so great, there should be appropriate charges; often there are not.

The prosecutor also needs to consider what the defense will be. Is there probable cause for this type of charge? There also needs to be the consideration of multiple charges. For example, did the child have old injuries? Are there witnesses in the abusive household? All these issues must be taken into account during the charging phase.

After an arrest is made and charges brought, there needs to be a focused prosecution. This means the State will prepare for an upcoming trial by thoroughly researching SBS and all its intricacies, securing expert witnesses who will benefit the case and utilizing visual aids that make sense to a jury. The prosecution also needs to be ready for what the defense will bring to the table and whom they plan on using as expert witnesses.

As a way of introducing the section on prosecution, let's first look at some history. There have been many previous child abuse and SBS cases that have set precedent over the years. Here are some that might be introduced in current shaken baby cases:

Estelle v. McGuire

This case went all the way to the United States Supreme Court and it was heard and decided in 1991. It was a Battered Child Syndrome appeal case and so can be applied to other child abuse cases, like SBS. The justices said that prior abuse evidence was not properly introduced during the trial, but it was still acceptable to present. The prosecuting attorneys said that the baby at the center of the trial was previously abused (they didn't know by whom), but they decided to make McGuire the defendant, based on his abusive history with the baby. The original trial judge agreed and this set the stage for the Supreme Court to ultimately hear the case. The Supreme Court felt that McGuire was clearly targeted, but felt that it was still acceptable. McGuire was denied his appeal.[5]

U.S. v. Gaskell

In this case a demonstration of shaking a mechanical doll was considered "inflammatory." The defense attorneys said that the act of shaking a doll by a doctor swayed the jurors to return a guilty verdict of involuntary manslaughter. The attorneys claimed that it was the construction of the doll (which needed more force to move the head than a live baby would need) and the oscillations of the head were under the doctor's control (he testified that he did not know how many oscillations were required for SBS injuries). So, because of these factors, it was not appropriate to use a doll to sway jurors. On appeal in 1993, this defense was successful as the judges reversed the guilty verdict. To avoid a *Gaskell* ruling in today's cases, many expert witnesses for the prosecution are using toy animals and limiting the demonstration to shaking them a few times with force. Others are verbally describing shaking forces based on their own knowledge and medical research. Still others are using videotaped evidence taken from police interviews with the defendant demonstrating the shaking (using a doll) and having an expert witness comment on the validity of the forces.[6]

State of Wisconsin v. Edmunds

This appeal case created a new controversy, as the defense claimed that SBS was "flawed science." The appellate judges were, in fact, swayed by the defense experts and said that the prosecution experts didn't present a united front on the topic of Shaken Baby Syndrome and agreed that it was flawed, so they sided with the defense—"significant and legitimate debate in the medical community has developed in the past ten years." In 2008, the judges decided to comment on the negative influence defense experts have had on the science of SBS, rather than looking at the facts for what they were.[7]

State of Ohio v. Edwards

Several years ago, defendant Edwards asked for an appeal of his eight-year SBS conviction, stating that he had an excessive sentence, he was painted prejudicially as being an abusive caregiver in the past and he didn't have a Daubert hearing (claiming insufficient data to support his conviction). The judges upheld the trial court decision and Edwards returned to prison to serve out his sentence. They felt that using differential diagnoses during the trial was very appropriate—"differential diagnosis is a standard scientific method for determining causation."[8]

Warden v. Grant

The appellate court in this Connecticut case actually agreed there was substantial research and science behind SBS and that it has been documented in hundreds of journal articles over many years. The defense attempted to use excuses such as lucid interval, impact of the four-month-old victim's head was necessary to cause harm, the victim died from DIC (disseminated intravascular coagulation) and other issues. The prosecution pointed out that the baby died from combined injuries only seen in SBS and referred back to the defendant's original changing history during the investigation. The court stated that there was a sound investigation and the State proved its case against the defendant in claiming that SBS was a real entity and well-researched. The appeal was rejected.[9]

When a case is gearing up to go to trial, there are several processes that typically occur prior to the actual courtroom experience:

PRE-TRIAL PROCESSES

These motions can significantly influence the outcome of an SBS case. The judge listens to arguments from both sides and will ultimately allow certain approaches promoting each side's cause. Of late, it is common for the defense to ask a judge to disallow testimony regarding SBS since they claim the diagnosis is not supported by reliable science. Next are components of the pre-trial process:

Discovery

Child Protective Services and medical records are part of a prosecutor's case and they don't need to be released, but the defense might ask that certain evidence not be released (or used in the trial), such as videotape evidence, allegedly inflammatory autopsy pictures, etc. Discovery is something that the prosecution can prepare for even at the point of charging a perpetrator for a shaking crime. Important documents include transcription of video statements made by the accused.

Bill of Particulars

This written document requested by the defendant targets specific information for the prosecutor to turn over. For example, it could involve the date of the abuse. A defendant may claim that he was caring for a baby on July 24, but other people say it was the 23rd. The defendant wants proof that others are claiming this, so he would request a bill of particulars from the prosecutor.

Change of Venue

Does the trial need to be moved to another county? Is there too much media focus on the case? How does media influence come into play with a shaken baby trial? In many communities, the influence of media coverage can affect the outcome of a trial. One benefit of the media is that they educate about the various aspects of SBS. On the other hand, the media will also report the controversial features of a trial, which ironically can perpetuate falsehoods. Media influence is very powerful and may necessitate a change of venue.

Daubert Hearings

This topic can be a sticking point in shaken baby cases. Can SBS be proven as scientific fact? First, some background on Daubert. In the early 1990s, the *Daubert v. Merrill-Dow Pharmaceuticals* case went all the way to the U.S. Supreme Court. The Court ruled that expert witnesses cannot bring "junk science" into the courtroom. It was Rule 702, with the following three basic concepts:

- Is the testimony based on sufficient facts or data?
- Is the testimony the product of reliable principles and methods?

- Has the expert witness applied these principles and methods reliably to the facts of the case?[10]

In terms of SBS and the first principle of sufficient facts or data—yes, there are decades of shaken baby cases that have been studied: those in medical journal articles, witness accounts, etc. With regard to the second concept about being the products of reliable principles, yes, these medical articles have had peer reviews and are not "junk," but well-researched. And as for part three, has the expert witness applied the principles to the facts of the case? What were the findings? The findings might be that there has been a fall, so the expert witnesses have applied physics to show the power of a fall or lack thereof.

The strength of Daubert was challenged in subsequent years. In 2009, the U.S. Supreme Court favored the power of cross-examination, rather than using a *Daubert* hearing. In *Melendez-Diaz v. Massachusetts*, an expert's opinion wasn't offered in the court trial; instead, the expert's documentation was provided. The Supreme Court felt that the defendant's Sixth Amendment right (the right of an accused to confront the witnesses against him) was violated.[11] For Daubert, though, physicians and professional expert witnesses need to review the wealth of evidence-based literature that there is on SBS, comment on the strengths and limitations of said research and report that the literature is reliable in the science of SBS.

Court Continuance

The evidence in a case may not be ready, or the prosecution or defense might need more time for witnesses to prepare for testimony.

Motions for Admittance of Evidence/Witness Exclusion

Either side can ask for exclusion of evidence or witnesses. For example, there might be a particular witness who is inappropriate for some reason or has a track record of lying on the stand. The prosecutor will want to exclude that witness. The appropriate time for asking for this exclusion is in a pre-trial motion.

Prior Child Protective Services (CPS) Involvement

The prosecutor is showing a propensity of the defendant toward abuse or neglect of a child. The alleged perpetrator may have a history of others calling CPS on him or her, so this would be a very appropriate pre-trial motion to seek.

Prior Acts of Abuse

These could be acts of abuse toward the victim or toward others. Is the defendant a hothead and is he beating up his wife or other children? Is there an arrest record that could be put forth as evidence?

Plea Deals

Sometimes it is easier to arrange a plea deal with a defendant versus going to trial, because there is currently a great deal of controversy in the news and juries can become confused. When both sides have experts testifying that their claim is the one to listen to and accept as truth, it can make for confusion all around. This is something that a prosecutor needs to weigh heavily. He or she should also speak separately with the victim's family if this is a decision to be made.

When considering a plea offer, a prosecutor should ask several questions: What evidence do they have? What has been the media's influence on the case? What is the defendant's criminal background? How might the accused present him or herself in a trial setting? These are all questions that will influence the decision to offer a plea bargain.

Plea Deal in Action

My son was shaken at the age of five months (April 20, 1997) by Shane Ellis, who was my boyfriend and not the father. Shane shook my son from a standing position and then dropped him on the floor (he confessed to this). He never called for medical help. He did call my sister, who took them both to the local hospital. My sister had to bounce him to keep him breathing on the way to the hospital. My baby was life-flighted to a bigger hospital that had more experience and specialists.

At the hospital he was given several different tests including a CT scan, an MRI and x-rays. They determined that he had retinal hemorrhages in both eyes and a subdural hematoma. I had taken him to the doctor a month before after my son stopped breathing for the first time while in Shane's care. The doctors had done an x-ray to rule out pneumonia. On that x-ray, he had a broken clavicle that the doctor who read the x-ray failed to put in his report to my doctor. We did not find that out until this second occurrence.

A couple days into his stay, the doctors discovered that my son had bruising at the back of his brain which was causing pressure in his skull. He then started having seizures. The doctors performed surgery to insert drainage tubes. A day later they did another surgery to insert a shunt. He was having daily CT scans and x-rays.

The first week at the hospital was horrible. I was not allowed in to see my son without someone supervising me. I was not allowed to hold him and at times different nurses would not let me touch him. The hospital, police and Child Protective Services had a meeting to discuss my son and me. I was later told that the doctors and nurses had stated that they were unsure of me because I did not react "appropriately" in the circumstances. I believe it was because I was in a state of shock, numb and trying to maintain my composure. After Shane's confession, I was then treated better at the hospital.

When he was released from the hospital, he was still having seizures and was placed on medication. When they increased the dose, his seizures increased too. Sometimes he had up to twenty-six seizures a day. Developmentally he was back to newborn stage. He is still way behind other kids his age. Mentally he is at around a first to second-grade level, but physically he is seventeen years old. His speech is sometimes hard to understand. He has problems with different letters and letter combinations. He also uses adaptive devices in gym class such as a bigger ball.

While I was upset with the hospital staff and doctors for their initial behavior, I also understand why they behaved that way. The remainder of our time there, the staff was amazing. My best experience was not with a medical worker, but with the volunteer who sat *outside the ICU waiting room handling questions and phone calls. She was there every day that we were there. She held me as I cried and listened to me as I vented about the unfairness of the situation.*

I handled the change by trying to keep my emotions undercover. I tried to stay strong. My mom cried a lot during this time. My dad is the silent type of guy. His way of coping was to keep busy by fixing my car, working, cleaning my house and theirs. My sister was pregnant at the time and doctors banned her from visiting after she started having pains.

We have an amazing support system that includes my family and many friends. My son is involved with Supported Community Living Services three times a week. He also works two afternoons a week at a center that caters to those with disabilities. He has formed a strong bond with several of the workers there as well as the staff. Several of my coworkers go out of their way to include us in different events/ get-togethers.

Shane was charged with two counts of child endangerment. The officer handling the investigation was wonderful and very supportive. Shane was offered a plea agreement where he would plead guilty to one charge and the other would be dropped. Shane took the plea. He served a little over four years before being released. The entire legal process was difficult and stressful. They waited almost eight months before arresting Shane and, being from a small town, we ran into each other several times.

Shane was a long-time friend of my brother-in-law. I had known Shane for about seven or eight years prior to the abuse. He was twenty-six at the time. He had no kids of his own, but I had seen him with my sister's kids and other kids. He claimed that he was tired and frustrated and that is why he shook my son.

The district attorney was very hard to get a hold of and did not return my calls. I found out about the plea bargain from someone at the grocery store. The DA did not register us as victims through the state so we were not notified of parole hearings. I filed that paperwork on my own. I was advised to get my own attorney, which I did, but we didn't get along and eventually I terminated his counsel.

—Michele Pickett

How Will the Prosecution Counter Defense Strategies?

What is the defense going to be? Is it going to be lucid interval? Was the baby injured a week prior to being in the care of a different caregiver, only to decline physically later? Is this a short-fall defense? A vaccination defense? A rebleed defense? Or even an "Adults just can't shake that hard" defense? It's very beneficial to know what the defense will propose as an alternate theory of injury, so the prosecution can attack it head-on.

VOIR DIRE

What should the prosecution ask potential jurors in SBS cases? Depending on the defense strategy for manner of injury or death to the child, here are some questions to ask:

Fall Defense

Have you ever had a child fall off of a bed or couch? Did the child get hurt in that fall? Did you ever know a child with a serious head injury from a fall to the ground (a two to three-foot fall)? The prosecution will get a sense of how people respond in terms of babies being fragile.

Vaccine Defense

One rare defense arising as a strategy for explaining injury to a child is the effect of vaccines. So the prosecution may ask questions like: Do you believe vaccines are generally safe? Did you have your children vaccinated? Have you read or heard anything in the news about infants having problems with vaccines?

Delayed Medical Treatment

This is more of a prosecution strategy if there was a known delayed response in getting the victim to the hospital. So a prosecutor might ask, "Have you ever had a child who became critically ill at home? What would you do?" The prosecutor will want to hear from the potential jury members, "I'd call

911 immediately." It would be important to put in the mind of potential jurors that if they had a baby who was severely injured at home, then they would need to get help and call 911 immediately, rather than sit around to wait for the baby to get better and then call the mother. The prosecutor will get a sense of how people respond to an emergency scenario.

Expert Witnesses

The prosecutor can ask, "As a juror, should you believe all expert witnesses just because they are doctors?" The defense will have witnesses who are MDs or PhDs and if jurors hear the word "doctor," they will be more likely to believe what he or she has to say. The prosecutor can also ask, "Are you someone who might get a second opinion if you don't agree with what your doctor says?" This is important for figuring out how each potential juror thinks about certain issues. Also, the prosecutor can educate jurors about certain types of witnesses: "There are defense experts all over the world trying to confuse juries and their focus is to get money, to get recognition for their names and so on, which is very unfortunate." Expert witnesses know that juries are ignorant of research and specialized knowledge, which is why they can easily make claims that will confuse jury members. This can be supported by testimony from others, like an ER nurse testifying for the defense on a certain medical symptom that she noted in the baby.

OPENING STATEMENTS

If the prosecutor is aware that there will be some challenging expert witnesses or the case is going to be tricky, then he or she should open by calling a spade a spade. The prosecution should tell the jury and everyone in attendance that there will be controversies in the case—"Do I believe them? No. Should you believe them? No. Do we know the exact measurements of how much force it takes for shaking to cause injury to a baby? What is the limit for shaking—light jostling, a little harder or a lot harder? So, yes, there is controversy, since we don't know the exact limitation." Prosecutors should avoid dealing with biomechanical data in opening statements or even in the heart of a trial (except in *Daubert* hearings), as the physics part of Shaken

Baby Syndrome could confuse a jury. Here are some things prosecutors can bring to the jury's attention during opening statements:

DNA

In shaken baby cases, DNA isn't applicable. The prosecutor can include this reminder in opening statements: "It's not like a sex crime where we might be able to get DNA or capture skin cells. DNA is not an issue here; it is a shaken baby case."

Bruising

One key defense strategy that is often used is that due to the fact that there were no visible bruises, cuts or scrapes on the victim, then it wasn't child abuse. The prosecutor can simply educate jurors that bruising is not always present, because the damage is on the inside of the body and only about 50 percent of shaken babies have external bruising.

Nanny Cams

Many times, jury members like visual proof of crimes having been committed. Prosecutors can inform jurors that, though shaking a baby is not only dangerous, but can kill, there have been no known fatal cases caught on home video cameras. There have been incidents of light to moderate shaking caught on "nanny cams" but none of the babies were injured.

CPR Defense

In such cases, the caregiver claims that the baby suddenly stopped breathing and he or she started CPR. The defense attorney later uses this story and states that this CPR event must have caused the retinal hemorrhages, because the blood in the chest was forced up to the brain and into the baby's eyes, which caused hemorrhages. What does research tell us about the facts of CPR and retinal hemorrhages? This is something that defense attorneys don't share with juries (or they may not know themselves). Juries hear that CPR can produce retinal hemorrhages, but what they don't know is that these hemorrhages look nothing like the ones seen in SBS. It takes a keen prosecutor to share the whole story and to explain to jurors that the defendant shook first and then, in a panic, tried CPR when the child stopped breathing. Retinal hemorrhages were already present. Then the prosecutor will have one or more of their experts explain the facts about CPR and retinal hemorrhages.

Different Levels of SBS

There are different results from different situations. There are moderate and fatal results. A diagnosis from slight shaking may never be made, because in order to have a diagnosis of SBS, the baby needs clinical findings—such as subdural and retinal bleeding.

Diagnoses Similar to SBS

Yes, there are similar diagnoses, but nothing looks exactly like Shaken Baby Syndrome. Even if a young child was in a car accident, the amount and type of retinal hemorrhaging is not the same as Shaken Baby Syndrome (there would also be evidence of the car accident, which would serve as proof). Even if the defense attempts to demonstrate an alternative reason for the bleeding on the brain of the victim, it doesn't account for the retinal hemorrhages.

In the opening statement, it is important for the prosecutor to focus on the violence of the act and the failure of the caregiver to get help for the injured infant or child that he or she shook. Jurors are going to be asked by the defense to suspend their belief that violence occurred to the child and accept a conclusion that is counter to decades of legitimate medical science.

Using Expert Witnesses

An expert witness for the prosecution needs to be very knowledgeable about Shaken Baby Syndrome and Abusive Head Trauma. These are professionals prosecutors want to use who will be composed under cross-examination and come across as experts in their field (they know what they are talking about). Prosecutors need to be aware of defense strategies and have an expert say that any demonstrations are for illustration only and not exactly what happened to the baby. So, if the expert witness shakes a baby doll, he or she could say, "We don't know how hard the baby was shaken. This doll might not be the same size as the baby, so this doll-shaking is for illustration only."

There are certain strategies that prosecutors can be successful in using to obtain guilty verdicts in SBS cases. Let's focus on some tactics that have worked:

Using Multiple Experts

Prosecutors should not have only one local doctor who simply concurs that the baby was shaken. He or she may not be aware of the intricacies of SBS and recently updated medical literature and may believe that even one tiny retinal hemorrhage is enough to make a diagnosis of SBS. If there are multiple experts who are knowledgeable about SBS, the jury can hear consistent expert testimony. Child abuse-trained ophthalmologists and pediatric neurosurgeons can be brought in to help the prosecution explain the specific injuries the child has experienced. Emergency room doctors, nurse practitioners, authors, child abuse consultants and others are more examples of professionals who can also be used as expert witnesses.

Challenging Inconsistent Statements to Witnesses

If, after the shaking event, the defendant made statements to an emergency medical technician, nurse, doctor, Child Protective Services worker, hospital social worker or others, prosecutors will make headway in their case if those statements are not only shared in court, but challenged. These are the types of professionals to put on the witness stand, beyond other expert witnesses. Juries will be able to hear firsthand from the people who encountered not only the victim, but the defendant as well. Often, the defendant's own words betray him or her, as slight variations have been told to different people. Such inconsistencies can be used very effectively against the defendant.

Delayed Treatment

This is an important issue that jury members take seriously. Even though this topic has been reviewed before, it's worth repeating as a prosecution presentation technique. By focusing on the delay in seeking help that occurred when the child was injured, the prosecutor does two things. First, he or she makes the point that a delay occurred and the defendant knew that the child was injured but hoped the child would recover. And it wasn't until the child began seizing, blood started coming from the nose or the child started turning purple that the defendant knew there was a big problem. The prosecutor might even play a video of the police interview, where the defendant was asked about the delay in getting help. Why did it take two or three hours (or more)? The second objective for using the "delay in seeking treatment" technique is to show that the child was last behaving and acting normally while in the care of the defendant. This may be used as evidence (i.e. daycare behavior sheets, police interview video, etc.). Since perpetrators of child abuse crimes are often egocentric, they want to be seen as competent caregivers and will tell investigators that a child was eating and playing as usual and then became ill later in the day. The person pins him or herself to the crime when he or she does this.

Use of Medical Information

Prosecutors need to be knowledgeable about the medical facts of SBS and to combine information in a baby's medical records with medical records of a child's injuries. By piecing together various aspects of the case and applying the baby's medical history to their clinical findings after a shaking event, prosecutors show there is nothing in the baby's past to point to *naturally* occurring intracranial or intraocular bleeding. It is a way of demonstrating that where there was once a healthy baby, there is one now permanently damaged by an abusive act. Within the medical information, there may be a record of the defendant having attended a hospital informational session at the time of the infant's birth that warned about the dangers of shaking. If this record is present and shows that the defendant took part in the education, then it shows that he or she knew it was wrong to shake a child.

Sound Prosecution

Prosecutors need to come across to a jury as being thorough, professional and sharing information in a very succinct way. Trials are not a place to call names, make fun of the defendant, etc. The prosecutor needs to be direct and professional. If the prosecutor proves the defendant guilty, he or she will make a connection with the jury that will help win the case. If the defendant is guilty, the jury will understand this and will reach an appropriate verdict when the prosecution presents a sound case.

CHALLENGING THE DEFENSE EXPERTS

Prosecutors will often need to confront experts about their opinions. The theories of certain defense experts are truly outlandish and a prosecutor can ask them about what proof they have to back up such theories. If a prosecutor uses sound, research-based data (such as statistics regarding falls in infants and young children), this is good information for juries. There are many questions that can be posed to defense witnesses to challenge their opinions of the reason for the medical findings:[12]

"Did you have the opportunity to actually examine the victim?"

This is a valid point to make, especially if the case is about an injured child who survived. Has the defense expert actually seen, in person, the damage that has been done to the child or is his or her testimony based on a simple review of medical records? The majority of witnesses for the defense have never laid eyes on the victim.

"What reputable research supports your claim?"

There have been decades of research and thousands of valid medical articles that have been soundly tested and peer reviewed. Some journals, however, are not considered reputable in the medical world, yet expert witnesses refer to them. When theories are either used or developed by expert defense witnesses, they may be missing many things. One must ask if these articles were published and peer reviewed. Who supports the defense expert's hypothesis? For example, does it make sense that a bed fall would cause death versus a three-story fall that rarely does? Does it make sense that an intracranial bleed is caused by a lack of vitamin C? These theories are short on logic and conflict with what generally occurs in children.

"Have you worked extensively as a pediatrician or in pediatrics?"

One pathologist often testifies as a defense expert witness at SBS cases and has performed hundreds of adult autopsies, but supposedly has only done a few on children. Such individuals do not have the experience in pediatrics that others do. Their expertise should be questioned.

"Why would a child die from a bed fall versus violent shaking?"

Even in cases of one or two outliers, why do they advance the concept of "killer beds" and "killer couches?"

"How has criticism by your peers made you a better witness?"

Initially, it was a lonely life for the one or two defense experts in the 1990s who were staunch about their unique positions on SBS. Since that time, many have banded together to strengthen their cause.

Addressing False Excuses With Medical Testimony

When defense attorneys attempt to present a "short-fall defense" to jury members in child abuse/homicide trials, they tend not to distinguish between two types of subdurals that may occur. The attorneys don't discount the presence of a subdural, but rather the action that caused it.

As addressed in the SBS physiology section of chapter 2, can a contact subdural be confused with an abusive subdural? Yes and no. SBS subdurals are typically bilateral and accompanied by severe retinal hemorrhages, and the stories that are offered do not relate to the intensity of the findings. Contact subdurals can occur in a short-fall situation, but these are exceedingly rare. In fact, children falling from large heights (several stories) are often found *not* to have subdural hematomas. Can an infant or child develop a contact subdural from being thrown against a wall or down to the floor? Yes, but there will often be bruising and other injuries present which are difficult for a perpetrator to explain.

To counter such a defense, an expert witness for the prosecution (such as a pediatric neurosurgeon) should be asked to address contact subdurals and how these are different from abusive subdurals. They should report that contact subdurals form from an impact to the head. Ask a question such as, "Can contact subdurals occur in short falls?" An appropriate answer would be, "Yes. If diagnosed, there is often a concomittant skull fracture. Contact subdurals swell over time and are surgical emergencies—similar to epidural hematomas." The prosecutor can then ask if these types of subdurals are commonly seen in short falls or are bilateral subdurals more commonly seen? This impresses upon the jury that SBS subdurals are significantly different from contact subdurals.

Visual Aids

If a prosecutor is using a timeline that chronicles the baby's health-to-injury, it should be projected on a wall or used as a poster on an easel. Also, if investigators have videotaped the perpetrator shaking a baby doll (as a demonstration of how hard he or she shook at the time of injury), then that should be shared as well. The more the prosecution can paint a true picture of the abuse that occurred (not necessarily graphic), the better the chance the jury will understand.

CLOSING ARGUMENTS

The prosecutor needs to make several key statements for the jury in order to reach a conclusion that makes sense to them. Closing arguments, prior to the jury deciding the fate of the defendant, need to be a synopsis of the case and its findings. This should be done thoroughly and simply to get the message of intent and culpability across to a jury. Below are some suggestions for effectively closing an SBS trial:

Reiterate the Violence of the Act

When the shaking occurred, it was not play and not light shaking—it was violent. Review what expert witnesses said about the extreme accelerations/decelerations that are needed in SBS injury development. Compare the injuries in other, similar violent acts, such as motor vehicle accidents, with those identified in the case. Often comparisons like this bring up memories of real-life tragedies for jury members.

Review Expert Testimony

Remind the jurors about what prosecution expert witnesses have said—that the diagnosis of SBS is not only well-known, but well-documented. For example, if the case was a short-fall defense, then repeat what one of the expert doctors had to say about the lack of clinical findings in short falls.

Emphasize the Defendant's Failure of Entrustment

The entire case relates back to the fact that the defendant was entrusted with the care of a child and he or she failed. The caregiver could have done the right thing and helped the baby through a period of crying (or whatever the trigger event was) and as a caregiver, he or she was unable to perform this simple act. Instead, he or she took his or her own problems out on the baby. This tactic can focus the jury members' minds toward the issue of responsibility—why they are there in the first place.

Does This Make Sense?

Even in closing arguments, prosecutors can use a doll (or stuffed toy) as a visual aid. For short-fall defenses, one concept that defense attorneys try to promote is that research has shown that adults can't shake a baby hard enough to kill. One of the things that attorney Brian Holmgren teaches in regard to countering defense strategies is to have an expert witness take a baby doll, explain that the shaking demonstration is for illustration only, shake it violently for ten to fifteen seconds as hard he or she can (the doll's head whipping back and forth) and then set the doll on the edge of a table, tap it off and watch it fall lightly to the ground.[13] At closing, a prosecutor can give a similar demonstration and then ask the jury, "Does this make sense? The defense is claiming that a short fall like this can kill the baby, but that an adult can't shake a baby hard enough for the same result?" It is quite a disparity and the true facts can make a huge visual impact on the jury.

What Has Been Lost?

What's been lost not only to the family, but in the life of the child? If this child survived, then 80 percent won't be able to carry on a normal life. If the child has died, then he or she is missing the rest of life and the defendant should be held responsible for that terrible loss.

The Jury's Statement

With a guilty verdict, the jury is making a statement not only to the defendant that he or she was culpable for his or her crime, but it makes a statement to the community. It is a statement that this group of people believes that SBS is real and that caregivers who shake infants and children should be held responsible.

SENTENCING

In Ohio, in 2011, a twenty-one-year-old woman was sentenced to fifteen years to life for the shaking death of an infant. In 2014, a Lansing, Michigan, man was given a life sentence after he shook and beat his three-month-old daughter. These are examples of strict sentencing based on the type of charge for which the defendant was found guilty.[14]

There may be factors in sentencing that prosecutors cannot control. For example, a judge might say that he believes the defendant didn't mean to shake a victim and sentence him or her to two years and time served (e.g., Louise Woodward). There also might be friends and family of the defendant who plead for mercy during sentencing. Ultimately, however, it will be the loss of the child and his or her potential that will affect the verdict.

Some things can be done to affect the outcome of the sentencing phase of a trial:

Making a Statement

After a guilty verdict is achieved and when the punishment is being decided, prosecutors need to make a statement. Prosecutors are showing the community that by achieving a conviction, the authorities don't take such crimes against children lightly.

Impassioned Family Statements

It is important for the judge and sentencing jury to hear what a family has lost. Families often describe to the court the milestones that the victim will lose—he or she will never be able to play like other children, will never go to the prom, will never hold a job and so on. It is also important for family members to face and talk directly to the defendant about their loss and ask the judge to render the maximum penalty in the name of justice. These statements give family members a sense of closure and a feeling that they have advocated for the victim.

Appeals

The Kentucky Court of Appeals decided two SBS cases in 2008 regarding the credibility of experts. The court sided with the Daubert analysis that there *are* reliable studies related to SBS and that the cross-examination in these particular trials was just and appropriate:

> *The Kentucky Court of Appeals held that the trial judge had impermissibly usurped the office of the jury by weighing the credibility of the experts. Under a Daubert analysis, the court is charged only with excluding unreliable or pseudoscientific testimony, while the jury determines the weight and credibility of admitted testimony. Although no Kentucky court had previously taken judicial notice of SBS, the state met its burden of production by showing that SBS is supported by numerous studies and that SBS testimony is accepted nationwide in both the legal and medical communities. The judge had based the exclusion in part by deciding that the scientific studies were more reliable than the clinical studies.*

> *The appellate court held that clinical studies are not inherently unreliable and are appropriate given the impossibility of employing the scientific method with infants in SBS studies. Furthermore, cross-examination is the appropriate means of attacking weaknesses in expert testimony, with the jury deciding the relative merits of the testimony. The appellate court's decision aligns Kentucky with virtually every other state in the nation in admitting SBS expert testimony.*[15]

EVALUATING PROSECUTION

After the trial and sentencing are over, prosecutors need to evaluate their performance. This can be measured on several issues: one, was the guilty party held accountable for his or her actions? Prosecutors should speak with jurors in any case as part of their own evaluation of the effectiveness of their presentation of the case. A jury member might speak up and say, "The defense was horrible and the experts were horrible and they weren't believed." That is the sort of feedback prosecutors want to hear. Did the prosecution present in a professional, succinct manner to the jury? Were the expert prosecution witnesses effective? Did their illustrations make sense and did they influence the jury? Even if the outcome was a not-guilty verdict, how did the prosecution feel about the expert witnesses? If these witnesses were professional and effective in their presentation, will they be used again in future cases? By taking the time to study the success (or limitations) of a prosecutorial presentation, future SBS case management will be that much better served.

Ready for an Appeal?

If there is a guilty verdict, there may or may not be an appeal. What does the prosecution need to do to prepare for the appeal? What are some key aspects of the trial that may be challenged? Will different expert witnesses need to be used to counter the defense arguments?

Prosecutor Resources

The National Center for Prosecution of Child Abuse has a prosecution and defense expert database of files on hundreds of SBS and child abuse cases. There are examples of when certain defense experts have been impeached or where they have succeeded.

Brian Holmgren, an Assistant District Attorney in Tennessee, is a great resource for vital information if a prosecutor needs guidance in presenting shaken baby cases.

CHAPTER 12

Prevention Efforts

MATTY EAPPEN

Eight-month-old Matthew Spellman Eappen was shaken and slammed on a hard, flat surface in his home by his caregiver, an au pair from Elton, England named Louise Woodward, on February 4, 1997. On February 9, he died. The entire world sat captive, watching the case, trial and sentencing unfold. Why would this particular story draw such attention and controversy? And why did this case become the groundbreaking one among the thousands of Shaken Baby Syndrome cases that have occurred throughout history?

The circumstances behind this tragedy are what proved controversial in the end. There was the eighteen-year-old au pair from a different country residing with a couple who were physicians and their two young children. Both boys were happy, playful and well nourished.

Debbie and Sunny Eappen sought an au pair to care for Matty, as they called him, when Debbie returned to her medical practice. Their modest home was in Newton, Massachusetts, and the Eappens had medical school loans to pay. Louise Woodward sought a career as an au pair to experience the thrill of life in the United States. Before the Eappens hired Woodward in November, they had briefly used two other au pairs for Matty. Woodward had been transferred to their home from another au pair placement. With this new family, Woodward was given regular instructions on caregiving expectations.

After some time, handling Woodward became increasingly challenging for the Eappens—countless trips into Boston to see plays, late nights out, long phone conversations with friends, etc. Her priority to care for the children soon diminished. One day, Sunny Eappen came home from work early and found his two boys alone in the family room as Woodward spent the next fifteen minutes down in the basement.

Sunny and Debbie both spoke with Woodward on January 30, 1997, about ways to improve her role as caregiver with the suggestion that she could leave if she was not happy with this particular assignment. She apologized and vowed to change; however, her behavior did not improve. The Eappens put Woodward on a curfew to help her focus on her caregiving responsibilities each morning. Little did the Eappens know that their au pair's pent-up anger and frustrations would soon change their lives forever.

The following sequence of events was never substantiated and is based only on reports Louise Woodward gave to investigators. Before she gave Matty his final bath, Woodward told investigators that the boy had been fussy and crying most of the morning. She reported that she dropped the boy onto a bed in the morning. In the early afternoon, Matty was bathed and Woodward told police that she shook him lightly afterward, as she was frustrated with his crying, then dropped him to the bathroom floor after placing a towel down, where he banged his head. According to Woodward, Matty became unconscious, vomited and stopped breathing. She then called 911. The dispatcher who took the call instructed the au pair several times to place the boy on his stomach after hearing the details of his condition.[1]

The first police officer responding called the home en route and found the phone line was busy. Upon arrival, the officer found that not only was the door to the house closed, but also that Woodward was on the phone. He asked the location of the injured boy. Woodward continued talking on the phone. She was asked again where Matty was. It was then that the officer saw the boy's feet in the living room, just as the emergency medical response team arrived. Matty was found on his back, not on his stomach as instructed, and he was in the first floor living room, not in the second floor bathroom. Woodward was still on the phone. Another officer removed the phone and escorted her into the living room to question her regarding what had happened to Matty. The boy was then rushed to the Children's Hospital in Boston in critical condition.

Debbie Eappen called Woodward from the hospital and asked for more details of the afternoon's incident, as doctors needed the information for Matty's treatment. It was soon afterward that Woodward was detained and questioned more thoroughly by police. The au pair was formally charged with assault the next day, February 5, 1997.

Matty Eappen never regained consciousness and his clinical status declined steadily after he was admitted to the hospital. He was found to have a subdural hematoma, progressive cerebral edema and retinal hemorrhaging. A two-and-a-half-inch occipital skull fracture would later be confirmed at autopsy. These features, in combination, were all consistent with Shaken Impact Syndrome. A wrist fracture, several weeks old, was also found showing previous abuse. Matty clung to life for five days, his family staying constantly at his bedside.

On February 9, 1997, the Eappens prayed, received communion, lit a candle belonging to Debbie's grandmother and held the child as he died. Meanwhile, the assault charge against Louise Woodward became a charge of murder.

Assistant District Attorney Lynn Rooney was assigned to the case and quickly requested that no bail be set for the au pair. Woodward pleaded not guilty to first-degree murder in Middlesex Superior Court on March 7, 1997. Debbie Eappen wore a button with a photograph of Matty's face pinned to her lapel. When bail was denied, the international controversy began. Supporters of Woodward contended that she was unaware of the U.S. court system and should not have been kept in the same correctional facility as other women who were "more dangerous."

Members of a local clergy association had written a letter of support for Woodward's bail and even the Newton mayor had placed his name on the list of signatures. This was a theme that would play continually throughout the trial and afterward—the poor, young foreigner being accused of a tragic crime by a middle/upper-class couple of doctors.

Medical examiners and child abuse professionals from the children's hospital stated that Matty's injuries were equivalent to that of a long fall. Andrew Good, Woodward's attorney, wanted to suppress statements Woodward had made to police: one to the responding officer after she called and a second statement to detectives who read her her rights before interviewing her.

Hiller Zobel was assigned as the judge in the case and originally set a July trial date. Woodward's team recruited Barry Scheck, a forensic attorney featured on the O.J. Simpson defense team, to help with their arguments. One of the first issues the defense tried to take on was the admissibility of a polygraph test that Woodward had taken—with guided questions such as "Did you ever hit or strike Matthew on the head?" Judge Zobel ruled that it was inadmissible, as independent evidence could not corroborate that polygraph tests were accepted within the scientific arena.

The defense gained a delay in the trial date. The defense team presented several clinical explanations for the injuries Matty sustained. First, the defense asked that DNA testing be performed to see if the boy had an underlying medical condition, which could have affected his bone strength and caused intracranial bleeding. This delayed the trial by three months and coincided with the pregnancy due date of prosecutor Lynn Rooney. When Rooney requested to take maternity leave, Judge Zobel would not extend the trial another three months, so attorney Gerry Leone replaced her.

Next, the defense focused their attention on Matty's two-year-old brother, as he was the only one in the house besides Woodward the day of the incident. The prosecution replied that no two-year-old could have inflicted such damage on an infant. Next, the defense proposed that Matty's retinal hemorrhaging from a sudden increase in intracranial pressure was induced by the rebleeding of a prior head injury, not by violent shaking.

In late September, the defense team asked to have the case dismissed after medical experts testified that sections of dura mater (brain lining) taken during Matty's autopsy were missing. The defense contended that these sections would have shown prior injury. Dr. Umberto De Girolami, the head of neuropathology for Brigham and Women's Hospital, examined the dura mater in question and it revealed no dark spots indicating a previous injury, which corroborated the findings of Dr. Gerald Feigin, the medical examiner who had performed Matty's autopsy.

Zobel denied the defense motion, noting that the dura sections could have been lost during Matty's surgery to remove his subdural hematoma soon after hospitalization and questioning why this was brought up two weeks short of the newly scheduled trial date.

When the trial finally began on October 6, 1997, both sides presented medical evidence as support for their arguments. The neurosurgeon who performed Matty's operation said there was no evidence that the hematoma was an old one that had begun to bleed again. An ophthalmologist offered key testimony on the retinal hemorrhages found in Matty, something the defense team could not counter. And Dr. Gerald Feigin, who performed the autopsy, testified that he saw no evidence of a prior head injury or bleeding within Matty's skull. He stated that the skull fracture was recent in appearance and the boy died from head trauma and subsequent brain swelling.

Police detective Byrne, who was on the scene after EMTs were called for Matty, testified that he interviewed Woodward and found her story to be feasible. It was not until he spoke with medical personnel at the hospital that he arrested the au pair the following day.

His report details what Woodward told him had happened on February 4, 1997. Woodward said that Matty was cranky, crying and fussing. She then carried the boy into the bedroom and supposedly "popped" him on the bed. Woodward stated she then went to the bathroom, placed a towel on the bathroom floor and then got Matty and dropped him on the floor as the child's crying had gotten to her. Later, she took the boy upstairs, changed his diaper, placed him in his crib and rested a musical toy on his chest. She soon returned to find Matty in distress: his eyes were rolled back in his head, he had shallow breathing and was unresponsive. She wiped vomit out of his mouth, breathed into his mouth several times and called 911. The fact that he had vomited was never substantiated.

Woodward took the stand in her own defense and was asked by the defense lawyer, "Did you slam Matthew Eappen? Did you do anything to hurt Matthew Eappen?" Woodward denied that she had ever told the police that she had "tossed" the baby on the bed before a bath and later "dropped" him onto the bathroom floor.

Three weeks later, when all testimony was finished and closing arguments made, the judge ruled that Woodward's jury could only consider two charges: first or second-degree murder. Her defense team had requested that a lesser charge of manslaughter be excluded from the jury's consideration as they hoped for an acquittal. The prosecution protested Zobel's ruling and appealed to the state's Supreme Judicial Court, only to have the appeal denied without a hearing.

The jury deliberated for several days and on October 30, 1997, nine women and three men found the British au pair guilty of murder in the second degree in the death of eight-month-old Matthew Eappen.

Woodward collapsed into the arms of her defense attorneys and screamed out, "Why did they do that to me? Why did they do that to me? I'm only nineteen. I didn't do anything. I didn't hurt Matty."

On November 10, 1997, Superior Court Judge Zobel reduced Woodward's second-degree murder conviction to manslaughter. The second-degree murder conviction carried a life sentence with the possibility of parole in fifteen years. Normally, judges do not exercise their judgment on jury verdicts, yet Zobel's rationale was that the au pair was confused and frustrated with Matty, which is why she had hurt him while he was in her care.

Even more dramatically, Zobel sentenced Woodward to time served (279 days since the original arrest). Zobel cited a state law known as Rule 25 when he lowered the verdict to manslaughter. The judge was to initially post this decision on the Internet, but computer problems altered that plan.

Supporters of Woodward in the United States and Britain cheered as the decision was announced. In fact, cameras directed on citizens in Elton, England, captured champagne bottles being popped with the news of Zobel's decision. Supporters of the Eappens, on the other hand, were left shocked and befuddled by what they believed was a breach of justice for the infant boy.

Woodward left the courtroom and went to the presidential suite at a Boston hotel with her parents. Prosecutor Gerry Leone did not anticipate the reduction of the sentence to manslaughter and was completely surprised by the announcement of "time served." Sunny and Debbie Eappen returned home with their three-year-old son and the constant tragic memory of another son they once had.

One of the initial legacies that Matthew Eappen provided was his heart. During his testimony, pathologist Gerald Feigin noted that two of Matty Eappen's heart valves had been removed when he was taken off life-support on February 9 and were donated to another child.

This was an act typical of the giving nature that the Eappens possessed as a family. The law was not as giving, as the battle of the appeal process began soon after Judge Zobel's decision. The prosecution hoped an appeal would return the manslaughter verdict to murder. The defense, on the other hand, hoped for an outright acquittal of Woodward.

Supreme Judicial Court Justice Ruth Abrams heard the arguments in December and she chose not to return Woodward to prison while awaiting the appellate hearing. The hearing was scheduled for March and seven justices then heard brief summaries and arguments from both sides. The decision would come in mid-June.

In the meantime, several changes began to occur throughout the United States and Britain in terms of childcare practices. In Britain, parents became hesitant about sending their daughters into au pair programs, haunted by the fears of another Woodward case. For some au pair agencies, the number of British women applying had fallen by half. Other aspects of the childcare system in the United States began to be more closely scrutinized. For example, in-home video monitoring sales skyrocketed after the Eappen/Woodward case broke. Some colleges offered nanny-training courses. Local and state legislatures launched efforts to prevent tragedies such as Matty's from ever happening again.[2]

One Massachusetts bill proposal put au pair agencies under the jurisdiction of the state's Office of Childcare Services, which regulates daycare centers. The bill was presented to improve the training that au pairs receive before and after going into homes. It also required that criminal and other background checks be performed.

One year after Matty Eappen's death, a children's playroom was dedicated in his name at the New England Eye Center's pediatric ophthalmology/ENT clinic. This center is a part of the larger New England Medical Center. The playroom offers games, toys and puzzles for pediatric patients and there is a plaque in Matty's honor.

On May 25, 1998, Debbie Eappen gave birth to another son, who weighed seven pounds, eight ounces. He was born one day after Matty would have turned two. He brought renewed happiness to the lives of Sunny and Debbie, who had endured great emotional pain for many months. The new baby's birth was another indicator that the Eappens were moving forward with their lives.

Shortly before the Supreme Judicial Court's decision was announced, the Eappens announced the formation of The Matty Eappen Foundation, based in Chicago. The thrust of the foundation is to educate the public about child abuse, specifically Shaken Baby Syndrome, provide support to families of child abuse victims and honor Matty's life.

On June 16, 1998, the Massachusetts Supreme Judicial Court upheld Judge Hiller Zobel's decision to reduce Louise Woodward's second-degree murder conviction to manslaughter. This was seen as a blessing and a blow. It meant that certain judges supported the idea that Woodward was responsible for the death of Matty, but I believe strongly it undercut juries, as it showed the court's ability to overrule verdicts.

Three members of the Court contended that Zobel had misused his authority and voted to keep the second-degree murder conviction, yet four others claimed Zobel's decision was within his legal power, though not necessarily right. Hence the verdict stood with a four–three vote. Woodward was allowed to return to England.

That afternoon, the Eappens filed a civil suit in federal court. The suit was filed for several reasons. First, Debbie and Sunny wanted to prohibit Woodward from receiving any financial gain from this tragedy. The couple was seeking compensatory and punitive damages for Matty's pain and suffering before his death and the hospital and funeral expenses they had paid.

In June, a federal judge made permanent an injunction that prevented Woodward from using any financial reward that she received regarding the case until the civil lawsuit was settled.

In July, Woodward failed to respond in U.S. court to the civil suit and hence defaulted. She claimed not to have the money to hire attorneys. The actual amount that Woodward had to pay would not be decided until January 1999. Woodward signed an agreement in the court settlement not to profit from her story. If she ever attempted to make money on the tragedy, she would donate any profits received to a charitable organization (UNICEF).

Debbie and Sunny Eappen joined 850 other professionals, parents and caregivers in September 1998 at the second National Conference on Shaken Baby Syndrome in Salt Lake City, Utah. Both the Eappens presented on the emotions of the ordeal and gave inspiration to attend-ees about their drive to fight child abuse. The family's three-year-old son accompanied the couple on this trip, which appeared to be a catharsis of sorts as they interacted with other parents who had suffered similarly. Their presence also brought about a feeling of completeness for hundreds of professionals working daily with child abuse and following the case so closely, as did people in many nations.

In December, *People* magazine wrote an update on the life of Louise Woodward since she went back to England. She had enrolled in law school. She claimed she wanted to help others so they wouldn't ex-perience a fate similar to what she had endured. In July 2002, Woodward graduated with honors from London South Bank University and began a training program with a law firm. The following year, however, she dropped out of the program in order to pursue a career as a dance teacher. In 2007, the Boston law magazine *Exhibit A* named Woodward the "most notorious criminal convicted in Massachusetts."

The Eappen case became the "talk of the town" for the media both before and after the trial. London Net set up a special page on their web-site in 1997 specifically devoted to Louise Woodward's guilt or inno-cence, asking questions like, "Do you think Louise Woodward did it? Has she had a fair trial?"[3] Those on the other side of the Atlantic had a par-ticular slant as to Woodward's culpability. Most British believed that the au pair was being railroaded as a victim in this "miscarriage of justice." In the States, the media also focused in on controversy. One man carried a banner outside the courthouse before Woodward's testimony which read, "Don't Blame the Nanny, Blame the Mother."[4] There were consistent news reports and specials on the case and Deborah Eappen was por-trayed many times as stoic and unemotional.[5] While Sunny wept on the stand during his trial testimony, Debbie was vilified as a working mother who should have been home caring for Matty (especially by the British press and public). Though she became outspoken about Woodward's act against her son, Debbie also became an advocate for SBS prevention in Matty's name—speaking openly at conferences and other public events and even orchestrating the forming of the Matthew Eappen Foundation.

In November 1997, a large team of U.S. child abuse physicians co-signed the letter "Shaken Baby Syndrome—a Forensic Pediatric Response," in which they addressed many fallacies that were advanced during Woodward's trial. This letter was widely published by the media and it appeared in most of the nation's major newspapers. It was also highlighted on television news shows. This was a positive response that helped educate the public about the signs and symptoms of SBS and pointed the finger of responsibility toward Woodward.

Finally, a Gallup poll queried the American public as to whether they approved or disapproved of Judge Zoebel's decision to reduce Woodward's second-degree murder conviction to involuntary manslaughter. Over half of the public approved and 10 percent had no opinion. But when asked if they approved or disapproved of the judge's decision to release Woodward with time served, the pubic had a reverse opinion, with 52 percent disapproving of the release.

Though the media had a strong influence on public opinion about the Eappen case, most people believed that an eighteen-year-old shouldn't be held to the standards of a murder conviction, but she shouldn't get off scot-free either. This case became a popularity contest, in my opinion, rather than a criminal action about the culpability of a caregiver.

In January 2014, Louise Woodward gave birth to a baby girl. At thirty-five and married, she began her new life as a mother. From a perpetrator profile point of view, I feel Woodward will go one of two ways with her role as new mom. She will either be very private, to not draw attention to herself, or she will be very outgoing to show what a good "mum" she is (as if to prove she can). Since Matty Eappen was allegedly shaken to death by her when he was a toddler, I also doubt that she will shake her daughter. For several reasons: her baby is not a male (statistics favor males to be shaken), her baby is her own flesh and blood (if Woodward is able to bond, it fares better for the baby) and she wouldn't take the risk of using shaking as a modus operandi (she'd lose again in court). But, I still feel that the toddler years will be a challenge for Woodward and that other forms of discipline (hopefully not severe) may be used.

The Matty Eappen Foundation has helped make SBS training mandatory for all au pairs employed by the company that hired Woodward. The Foundation is also advocating for criminal background checks on childcare personnel as well as providing general SBS information to parents and professionals.

PREVENTION EFFORTS NOW

Dr. Rachel Berger of the Children's Hospital of Pittsburgh published a study in the medical journal *Pediatrics* about the rise of Shaken Baby Syndrome during the recession years.[6] SBS has had its share of criticism over the past ten years, but prevention efforts have risen exponentially. We know a lot more about the condition than we did a decade ago. However, I believe dangerous statements have been made by defense experts who do not believe SBS exists. Does this back and forth affect the state of SBS? No. I doubt that an adult who shakes an infant stops to consider the legal outcome prior to a shaking event. But I do believe that most people are aware that violently shaking a child is dangerous. Is this due to prevention efforts or common sense?

Hospitals across the U.S. and in other countries are showing SBS prevention videos to new parents. Scores of prevention publications are in the hands of adult caregivers. So why the rise in abuse cases? Perhaps it is because some countries are continuing to suffer financial woes. With financial pressure comes negative attention toward those most vulnerable—the young. Is our society becoming more lenient toward those who abuse, which is counteracting the prevention efforts that local agencies are struggling to put forth? Are more "mother's boyfriends" coming out of the woodwork? Or those with no emotional bond with the children? These are the most tragic cases—those who could care less about the infants and children they watch while mom or dad is at the store or work. I'm not excusing the biological mothers and fathers who abuse too—I simply want to show the shift away from the traditional family that has been building over the years. When this happens, you have a distance in emotions. The bond is either very loose or nonexistent. Combine this with effects of the recession and you have a perfect storm, as Dr. Berger put it. Add to this problem the resistance of officials to prosecute and a laughable Casey Anthony trial outcome—this equals a rise in child abuse, no matter what agencies are putting forth.[7]

One of the key parts of SBS prevention and its positive effect in the community comes from history. In 1974, John Caffey's second discourse on "Whiplash Shaken Infant Syndrome" called for a nationwide educational campaign against shaking. Though this would not formally occur until 1989, it was important that Caffey brought the subject up in his plan. The number of infants killed and disabled as a result of SBS during that span of time without a national prevention program can only be presumed. For years it was ignored and poorly serviced by the medical and legislative communities. Prior to 1990, there were less than twenty articles and books that directly referred to SBS. It appeared as though abuse of children continued to hold a low priority.

Prevention of a syndrome can be a relatively straightforward process, especially SBS. But are prevention efforts successful? The concept that shaking infants is potentially fatal should be an ingrained part of society, similar to the prevention message of "Don't Drive Drunk." Dr. Carol Kandall, a physician in New Haven, Connecticut, wrote a letter in 1990 to the editors of the *American Journal of Diseases in Children*, imploring pediatricians and other medical personnel to listen to parents and other caregivers frustrated by the cries of their children.[8] She felt that, in some way, prevention efforts could reduce the wider incidence of SBS.

There are three types of prevention. Primary prevention, being the most direct, targets an entire community to prevent abuse before it starts. It sets in place community policies and programs to have a visible effect on parents and caregivers so abuse is less likely to occur. General public awareness campaigns are an example of primary prevention.

Secondary prevention comes in the form of intervention after there are early signs of abuse. Any "at-risk" parents or caregivers are the focus for intervention services to provide positive options and support. Problems are treated as they appear and efforts are strengthened. Regular clinic or home visits are examples of secondary prevention.

Tertiary prevention is treatment given after abuse has occurred. This type of prevention is aimed toward stopping further abuse. If successful, these efforts will halt the cycle of abuse from generation to generation. Group therapy, home visitation, crisis drop-off centers and foster care are examples of tertiary prevention.

Public education and sound intervention programs appear to be the best type of prevention. Such programming is very inexpensive compared to the cost of even one case of SBS (with the majority of the care costs being non-medical).[9]

Community-wide child abuse prevention programs work in theory but their overall effectiveness has not been measured. As a result, such prevention programs are infrequently accepted or supported. Suppose that in one county the number of infants shaken drops dramatically from the previous year. Such a result could be attributed to a SBS prevention program. It might also mean that more shaken infants were missed or not reported. Or it might mean that more perpetrators did not seek medical attention for the shaken children. Regardless of the statistics, few would deny that prevention programs are needed to protect children.

Successful prevention programs provide positive options to parents and other caregivers for dealing with the multitude of stressors associated with caring for an infant. These programs also save lives. It would be ideal for SBS prevention programs to be a part of every segment of the community, but this is typically not financially or logistically feasible. Instead, those most at-risk would need to be the focus of direct SBS prevention and education.

Next let's look at some possible settings for SBS prevention programs:

Babysitting and Parenting Classes

Caring for an infant brings a multitude of emotions and challenges. Many experiences can be frustrating and, in turn, cause feelings of anger. Individuals may even be left with the responsibility of *having to* care for a child when they want to be doing other activities. New parents and other caregivers need to be educated on properly caring for an infant to prevent shaking and abuse from ever happening.

Part of that education should cover the dangers of shaking infants. This can occur through a "ground zero" approach for prevention. Such an approach capitalizes on an audience of students (babysitting class, Lamaze class, new parents class, etc.) and includes SBS prevention within a curriculum. Childbirth education classes will typically include a section on newborn care and even a discussion on how to soothe a crying baby. This is a perfect opportunity to bring up the topic of SBS. It is also a good opportunity to briefly discuss the importance of knowing and trusting others who may care for a couple's baby. The couple can then be the ones to instruct babysitters, relatives and others to never shake the child and how to contact them for help.

In America there are national programs targeting at-risk parents that use specific interventions to enhance basic child care and assist in stress management such as Parent Effectiveness Training (PET) and Systematic Training for Effective Parenting (STEP). Programs like these have been proven to reduce the risk factors associated with physical child abuse. Parents Anonymous is one mutual support group that allows members to increase social contacts at the same time as assisting with child development strategies. There are many other types of programs that focus on support for parents who find themselves in similar circumstances.

There is a significant impact on students in babysitting classes who observe an egg broken into a small plastic container: dropped three feet, the yolk remains intact, but when the container is shaken, the yolk scrambles.

Unfortunately, not all new parents and caregivers will be reached. Many will not want to participate in SBS prevention instruction. I strongly feel it is the duty of all members of the community, professional and layperson alike, to set in place opportunities to learn rules and behaviors for prevention and education. There are untapped areas where a great deal of abuse happens. Anyone can become a community advocate for providing SBS information. This process may start by simply hearing about this information in a classroom setting. The word can then be spread to reach those who need it most.

Childcare Facilities and In-Home Care Services

SBS prevention efforts need to be on the same front line as other types of prevention that are emphasized at childcare facilities, such as injury prevention. Child abuse is one of those life issues that is not discussed within wide circles. Because of this, licensing requirements established to prevent child abuse injuries might be minimal at best in many states and countries.

Directors of childcare facilities may fall into the mental trap of "not in my backyard" when it comes to abuse happening in their facility. Adjusting this thinking can lead to the implementation of a plan that teaches safe childcare. Such a plan would require education about SBS and other acts of physical abuse for all providers. This plan would also have a requirement for a minimum number of hours of care experience for all employees. Directors would keep in the forefront of their programming ways to keep employees regularly trained on proper childcare techniques.

Parents and caregivers have a role in the prevention of abuse by a childcare provider. Examining materials about potential childcare providers could be an initial step in developing educated and informed childcare choices. Many communities have agency licensing files that may be perused. Childcare resource and referral agencies are also in place to provide guidance in the process of selecting reputable childcare facilities. Parents and caregivers should also interview directors of potential facilities to learn the training background requirements for workers. Directors of facilities should be asked about ongoing child abuse training offered to the staff. Finally, unannounced visits by parents and caregivers after a child begins attending a facility are reasonable and should be welcomed.

SBS and other acts of abuse can never be completely prevented within any type of childcare system. There will always be people who intentionally misuse their positions to hurt and control those under their watch. Parents and caregivers need to avoid blaming themselves if abuse does occur. These incidents are never expected and breach all aspects of trust.

A strong message was sent to au pair and nanny agencies throughout the world when Louise Woodward, the Boston-area au pair, was convicted of shaking eight-month-old Matty Eappen to death. The message called for greater safety of infants and children under the care of these specialized employees. Agency directors did not want the stigma nor liability of abused children, so screening criteria were improved at many companies and educational programs on proper care were increased.

Many parents with in-home services have made changes over the years, as the use of video surveillance units ("nanny cams") in homes has skyrocketed. Such provisions are a result of what our society has become. Sad though it may be, this is an example of actively preventing child abuse injuries in the home.

Training programs for au pairs and nannies that emphasize safety and choice need to be the foundation of any in-home service agency. SBS prevention information should be a basic part of this training.

Besides training, there are other provisions that can be taken to lessen the risk of hiring a potentially abusive caregiver. These include complete criminal background checks, quality references and a minimum number of hours of caregiving experience.

Hiring caregivers from licensed and insured agencies with good references should only be a starting point. Parents should also interview prospective au pairs or nannies about the types of care they provide, their knowledge of SBS, how they soothe crying babies, etc. These are ways parents can help protect their children.

Community Agencies

Professionals who are a part of the front line in working with children and families can provide methods for SBS prevention. Basic childhood injury prevention has been studied in depth for years. The tenets of such programs include defining the injury, targeting resources and people to carry out the program and determining which strategies and interventions will be used. Tools of these prevention programs include posters, brochures, billboards, TV public service announcements, giveaways, radio programs, newspaper articles and even text messages. The same structure can be used in SBS prevention.

Community agencies have a duty to provide crisis management for all families who have children at risk for being shaken and abused. One of the main reasons why a child is shaken is that the caregiver feels no support is available. Community agencies can solve this easily by putting services in place. Free crisis hotlines, low-cost crisis drop-off centers, experienced crisis babysitter services and crisis counseling should be available for families with such needs. Immediate support can save lives either over the phone or through in-person counseling and assistance.

Community agencies can obtain grants to offset the costs of such programming. Hundreds of national organizations have millions of dollars that are given away annually. Most grants need to be very specific, detailing both target audience and method of implementation. Upon completion of the grant, feedback on the program's outcome is typically required in order to fund future initiatives.

Many communities have developed neighborhood-based programs that provide counseling and support. Neighborhood centers can focus on heightening the involvement of parents and caregivers with their children on a more positive and consistent basis. These programs could also support efforts to improve community services, from housing to transportation. When individuals are given options, their sense of self-esteem increases, as does their sense of control. These positive efforts can influence families and may make them less likely to abuse their children.

Finally, representatives from community agencies need to come together on a regular basis to share ideas regarding SBS prevention. By discussing what is available and what is lacking in a community, opportunities can be created for new safeguards. Developing an SBS prevention task force requires both telephone calls and follow-up. Community agencies typically come together after a tragedy has already occurred. Enlisting help for primary, rather than tertiary, prevention is the path that makes most sense.

Home Visiting

Home visiting is a concept that was originated by C. Henry Kempe, the lead author of the trailblazing article, "The Battered Child Syndrome." Home visiting programs, performed by social service agencies and hospitals, have established over time a great rate of success in preventing abuse and neglect in at-risk families. Home visiting provides one-on-one guidance and care by a professional. Agencies utilize nurses, social workers and volunteers to provide these services. The visitors need to be adequately trained in order to provide thorough education and be positive role models.

The effectiveness of home visiting programs depends on several factors. The parents or caregivers who are the focus of the visits need to be accepting of the services that are presented to them. They also need to be consistently present in the lives of their children in order to learn appropriate caregiving from the home visitors. Finally, they need to have their basic emotional and physical needs met. Otherwise the services that are presented will not be effective.

Several communities have adopted a program for new parents whereby a physician recommends visits to a newborn's home by a perinatal coach for several weeks. The coach keys into many important issues with the new parents, especially coping mechanisms for frustrating situations, developing a support system and the importance of teamwork to maximize success in their parenting roles. The program is offered to mothers while the mother and newborn are still in the hospital and it is free of charge. This program is usually sponsored by a hospital or community social service agency.

Hospitals: Assessments and Programs

Medical providers have the chance to heavily influence parents and caregivers they feel are at risk for child abuse. As healthcare providers, by the nature of their work, they are on the front line of child abuse prevention. They can assess if a parent or caregiver is in need of support during an emergency room visit. They can involve child protective services if abuse is suspected. They can evaluate the siblings of injured children for abuse. They can openly discuss findings with parents and caregivers to foster communication. These are all avenues to protect a child from further harm.

It's imperative that healthcare providers maintain some semblance of suspicion in *all* cases of injuries to infants and children. Such vigilance can be one's greatest prevention tool. This requires both training and experience on the part of providers. Looking at issues, such as injuries without relevant explanation or caregivers seeking medical care at odd hours, as red flags is important in determining the etiology of a child's injuries.

All medical institutions can benefit from a child abuse team. Once a team is in place, there can be ongoing discussion about prevention services within the hospital. If medical providers within the hospital setting can stay abreast of the latest information on SBS, they will then be better equipped to identify and treat associated injuries more thoroughly.

Hospital administrators can do their part in the prevention of SBS through the sponsorship of prevention/education programs. Hospital-based prevention programs that provide the latest educational training for all medical personnel, specific to their areas of care, in addition to brochures, medical posters and more, are extremely beneficial. These programs also incorporate the use of a "contract" for new parents to sign that asserts their acknowledgment of the dangers of shaking an infant, as well as having an SBS prevention video to watch. Using this type of prevention program has been found successful in reducing the number of SBS cases in certain areas of the country. The "Period of Purple Crying" program from the National Center on Shaken Baby Syndrome uses DVDs, posters, brochures, training, etc. as the basis for their curriculum.

Obstetric (OB) Information Providers

OB offices can easily provide the basic information on SBS prevention which is important for early intervention processes to begin. For example, some agencies use "Preventing Shaken Baby Syndrome" brochures in OB offices to give expectant parents positive options and information in their new roles as primary caregivers. Posters and other prevention materials also communicate the dangers of shaking to expectant parents.

Medical providers can encourage psychological bonding between parents and the unborn child through methods that draw couples closer together. The expectant parents can develop a birth plan that lists their criteria for an optimum birth. They can be encouraged to make prenatal visits together. They can attend a childbirth education class together. The expectant father can attend a parenting workshop designed specifically for men, such as the nationally recognized *Boot Camp for New Dads*. If there are signs that the parents may be at greater risk for abuse, because of any triggers that the medical provider observes, they can be guided toward more extensive help, e.g., through a hospital or a community social worker.

Physicians Providing Education

Family practices and pediatric offices are good examples of places where there is an opportunity to educate parents and caregivers about SBS and what they should look for to identify symptoms after a shaking incident has occurred. There is typically a high volume of patients that medical providers see throughout the day. They often do not take the time to assess parenting skills or hear concerns about other caregivers.

Providing education about SBS should be a standard medical practice. This can be done in person by the medical provider or through prevention materials. At an initial visit, providers can talk with parents and caregivers about the physiology of an infant's head in relation to its neck and that it must be adequately supported. Warnings about shaking and symptoms that might be evident are basic topics that require minimal time but can save hundreds of lives annually. Some pediatric offices have been providing or endorsing specialty books to promote safe, effective caregiving during potentially stressful times in parents' lives. For example, East Bay Pediatrics in Berkeley, CA provides for free the reference book *Your Child's First Year* (American Academy of Pediatrics) for new parents.[10]

A belief held by many is that physicians should treat the parents of potentially abused children *first* to prevent problems from occurring. Such basic, primary prevention includes assessing parental stressors, identifying family social problems, offering social work services, home visitation or parenting classes and providing options which discourage negativity in the home environment.

School Information Programs

Many schools around the country are including SBS as an educational topic each April, which is Child Abuse Prevention Month. By considering SBS as not merely a problem of parents or childcare providers, school systems take a proactive approach.

Prevention programs such as the "Don't Shake the Baby" campaign have age-appropriate presentations for children as young as preschool-age which educate on the dangers of shaking an infant. Programs for older children, who may have the responsibility in their home of caring for infants or children, are provided with options that can be used for an inconsolable child under the student's care.

Some schools are developing their own SBS prevention campaigns. These innovative programs often receive positive media coverage and send important motivational messages to other students, parents and teachers.

As in any prevention program, the younger the age of the listener when the message is started and repeated over time, the more successful the outcome. Students learn that shaking and other types of abuse toward infants and children should not be tolerated.

Training Programs

Professionals from the realms of medicine and law enforcement may personally experience a case of SBS at some time in their careers. Because of this, there needs to be preparedness training. A standard curriculum can be developed, similar to CPR training classes, where professionals learn about the unique physiological and social aspects of SBS to help with aspects of investigation.

Annually, medical, legal and law enforcement personnel should receive information and updates on the physiology of all types of abusive head trauma, a study of local SBS cases and ways of improving prevention efforts. This will allow for more thorough evaluation of children who are suspected of being shaken, as well as more complete investigations leading to better consistency in prosecution.

One organization has already incorporated SBS prevention into its training programs. The American Red Cross has developed an activity on SBS that is included in their Babysitter's Training Instructor's Manual. The course instructor leads students through an activity that describes the scenario of an infant who will not stop crying. Students brainstorm how they would correctly handle the situation and then act out the scenario. Follow-up discussion educates participants about the dangers of shaking an infant. Students also learn positive ways to soothe infants in their care.[11] Similar training programs that are given across a range of disciplines can make SBS prevention a standard topic in areas where it is most needed.

Whenever an infant is shaken, anyone who potentially has an influence on prevention should pause and ask two questions, "Why did this happen?" and "What can I do to prevent other SBS cases from happening?" Anyone may find themselves at some point in a position to help save lives and save families.

Education of Professionals

Importantly, many states are now requiring SBS education for workers in the medical field. This is vital, because these professionals are out in the field with infants and families and they are being taught what to look for and how they can educate those in need. How does this fit with prevention efforts? Consider a nurse who goes out on a well-baby visit. While speaking with the mother and attending to the baby, the father yells out from another room, "Will you shut that kid up?" This becomes a teachable moment for the nurse, since she's recently been trained on the risk factors for shaking and how to calmly intervene and educate. This is a time for in-person prevention.

The state of Kentucky requires information about "pediatric abusive head trauma" for nurse relicensure.[12] They also make this training available to social workers, paramedics and emergency medical technicians. The objectives of the training are to:

- Identify the risk factors, clinical presentation and physical findings of pediatric abusive head trauma in children.

- Discuss the mechanism of injury of pediatric abusive head trauma and the diagnostic workup and prognosis.

- Describe how healthcare providers as a team can educate families, the public and other healthcare professionals about pediatric abusive head trauma to help reduce the incidence, morbidity and mortality.

SBS PREVENTION TODAY

What are some vital programs that are being run throughout the United States and in other countries on ways to prevent Shaken Baby Syndrome? There are many. Besides having a bi-annual interdisciplinary conference sponsored by the National Center on Shaken Baby Syndrome and a bi-annual medical professionals conference at Hershey Medical Center, there are many local meetings, fundraisers and community action boards dedicated to stopping the incidents of shaking that affect so many children. Next we'll discuss some important programs.

Hospital-Based Prevention Programs

From 1998 to 2004, Mark Dias, MD, and his colleagues implemented a hospital-based parent educational program at Kaleida Children's Hospital in Buffalo, New York, to teach new parents about the dangers of infant shaking. They utilized brochures, video training and in-person support for all new parents. Over this period, they saw a dramatic drop in the number of local SBS cases and attributed it to the prevention program. Many other hospitals across the world have begun using this program and have seen success. The University of New Mexico Hospital has an SBS prevention and education program. They use posters, videos and phone follow-ups as check-ins for new parents to assess whether they comprehend the materials. They then collect special hospital codes to track the incidence of SBS in their hospital.

Blank Children's Hospital in Des Moines, Iowa, is using the child development education approach that was created by the National Center on Shaken Baby Syndrome, "The Period of PURPLE Crying." This program helps parents and caregivers understand the features of crying in normal infants that can lead to shaking. One highlight of the program is a ten-minute DVD given to new parents to take home. The DVD teaches certain characteristics of crying, which can be shared with anyone else who will be caring for their new baby. It has been a very successful program for many other hospitals as well.[13]

Community-Based Prevention Programs

The Centers for Disease Control and Prevention (CDC) have produced a guide for community agencies, "Preventing Shaken Baby Syndrome: A Guide for Health Departments and Community-Based Organizations." The purpose of this guide is to help organizations identify their lead role to take action to protect infants from SBS. It outlines steps to implement evidence-based intervention strategies, to integrate specific education messages into existing programs for new parents, caregivers, professionals and the general public and to engage in activities that impact policy development that are effective in preventing SBS. This is a solid information provider for agencies that shows how to make changes quickly and efficiently.[14]

In Council Bluffs, Iowa, a group known as the Shaken Baby Task Force is comprised of twenty community agencies and businesses who work toward one goal: to prevent Shaken Baby Syndrome. Their focus is on education and the members use campaigns to increase awareness. Members of the Shaken Baby Task Force provide educational materials to parents at local hospitals. SBS education is also given at hospitals, doctor's offices, Lamaze classes, babysitting classes and in-home visits. The task force attends health fairs, provides community presentations and visits school programs from elementary to high school. Finally, the group arranges for media campaigns to increase public awareness about the issue of SBS through television and radio PSAs, billboards and print advertisements. For around-the-clock support, the group developed a twenty-four-hour hotline for frustrated caregivers and a helper website. This is a huge undertaking, but it shows what one community can do to make strides in preventing just one infant or child from being shaken.

LEGISLATIVE ACTIONS

Typically, parents are the driving forces behind any sort of legal action used to improve laws or make punishments more severe. If such laws had been in place prior to their son or daughter being shaken, then maybe the perpetrator would have thought twice about the abusive act. Such legislative actions can take years to enact. In fact, the U.S. Congress has yet to approve a Shaken Baby Syndrome Prevention Act, though it's been before legislators for years. Here are some of the main child abuse and SBS laws passed over the years:

Brendan's Law

Originally enacted in 1996 and later enhanced (2012) in Rhode Island, Brendan's Law includes Shaken Baby Syndrome as a form of child abuse in the first degree. This law carries penalties of ten years mandatory jail time for a first offense and twenty years for subsequent offenses. Parole is not allowed until the perpetrator serves at least eight years in prison.[15]

Cynthia's Law

In 2006, this law was enacted in New York, creating the new crime of felony reckless assault for causing serious physical injury to the brain of a child less than five years old by means of shaking, slamming or throwing. Cynthia's Law also required the New York State Department of Health to implement an ongoing Shaken Baby Public Information and Educational Campaign to inform the public about the dangers of shaking children. This law was introduced by Cynthia' father, Darryl Gibbs. Cynthia died when she was eight months old. Darryl also created the Cynthia Gibbs Foundation, which is an organization that focuses on the prevention of Shaken Baby Syndrome by raising public awareness, advocating for criminal justice and providing support to families of SBS and its victims.[16]

Claire's Law

Named after Claire Fishpaw, shaken by her babysitter in 2000, the law was enacted in Ohio in 2008. It comprehensively mandates SBS prevention materials be made available in childbirth education centers, hospitals and childcare centers. Also, the law mandates that public children services employees who are entering a report of an investigation of child abuse into the statewide automated child welfare information system make a notation on each case of child abuse that indicates whether the child abuse arose from an act that caused SBS. This will track the number of reported cases of SBS in the state of Ohio.[17]

Jared's Law

Jared's Law was passed by the Virginia state legislature in 2010. It requires "the Department of Social Services to make information about shaken baby syndrome, its effects, and resources for help and support for caregivers available in a printable format, and information about how to acquire such information in an audiovisual format, available on a website maintained by the Department, and to inform every child welfare program licensed by the Department about the available information." This bill also provides that information about Shaken Baby Syndrome "shall be made available to foster and adoptive parents, and staff of child day programs and children's residential facilities."[18] Jared was shaken by his father at six weeks of age and then lived for four years with major physical deficits, cared for by his grandparents. Jared's father was sentenced to seven years in prison and fourteen years probation.

Next let's focus on some state-based SBS prevention and education laws. Though this is not an all-inclusive list, we will show a sample of many of the states' initiatives for information on SBS:

Florida (Fla. Stat. § 411.233)

"Requires child care personnel to be trained in recognizing and preventing shaken baby syndrome, preventing sudden infant death syndrome, and understanding early childhood brain development."[19]

Massachusetts (Title XVI Public Health, Chapter 111, § 24K)

"Provides an act for prevention of shaken baby syndrome. Defines shaken baby syndrome. Requires the departments of public health to collaborate with the department of social services, the Massachusetts Children's Trust Fund, other state agencies, law enforcement personnel, healthcare providers, human service providers and child advocacy organizations to develop and implement a comprehensive, state-wide Shaken Baby Syndrome Prevention Initiative to reduce death and disability resulting from Shaken Baby Syndrome. Creates a surveillance and data collection program to measure the incidence of Shaken Baby Syndrome and traumatic brain injury. Provides for education and training programs to be disseminated to parents prior to discharge from a hospital or birthing center, and to healthcare providers and caregivers. Requires the programs to include information on the medical and physical effects of shaking infants and children, appropriate methods of handling infants and children, methods to prevent and reduce the risk of shaking infants and children and the availability of community-based resources and other resources to prevent shaken baby syndrome. Requires an annual evaluation and report to the governor of the initiative."[20]

Minnesota (Minn. Stat. § 245A.1445)

"Licensed child care and child foster care programs must document that before staff persons, caregivers, and helpers assist in the care of infants, they receive training on shaken baby syndrome."[21]

New York (NY Public Health Law 2803-J)

"Every hospital and birth center shall request that each maternity patient and father of a newborn child, if available, view a video presentation, approved by the commissioner, on the dangers of shaking infants and young children, and the symptoms of shaken baby syndrome. After viewing such a video presentation or upon refusal to view such a video presentation, the hospital or birth center shall request that such patient and/or father sign a form stating that they have viewed or refused to view such video presentation. All training materials and forms required to implement the provisions of this subdivision shall be provided by the commissioner."[22]

Ohio (OH Revised Code 3701.63 & 3701.64)

"Requires the Director of Health to establish the Shaken Baby Syndrome Education Program and materials. Requires the material to be distributed to parents and expectant parents by hospitals, pediatricians, birthing centers and 'Help Me Grow' programs."[23]

Oklahoma (HB 2920, Chapter 368)

"Creates the Oklahoma Maternal-Infant Quality Care Act. Creates a task force to identify evidence-based models for reducing the incidence of abusive head trauma of infants in the area of infant injury and death, and to develop a plan for implementing a model or models statewide and improve infant health outcomes."[24]

Rhode Island (R.I. Gen. Laws § 40-11-17)

"The department of health shall collaborate with the department of children, youth and families and other state agencies serving families and children, the medical community, law enforcement, human service providers, and child advocacy organizations to develop and implement a comprehensive, statewide initiative to reduce death and disability resulting from shaken baby syndrome."[25]

Texas (TX Health & Safety Code Title 2 Subtitle H Chapter 161 Subchapter T Sec. 161.501)

"Requires the inclusion of information on preventing shaken baby syndrome, including techniques for coping with anger caused by a crying baby; different methods for preventing a person from shaking a newborn, infant, or other young child; the dangerous effects of shaking a newborn, infant, or other young child; the symptoms of shaken baby syndrome and who to contact, as recommended by the American Academy of Pediatrics, if a parent suspects or knows that a baby has been shaken, in order to receive prompt medical treatment."[26]

Virginia (VA. Code Ann. § 32.1-134.01)

"Every licensed nurse midwife, licensed midwife, or hospital providing maternity care shall, prior to releasing each maternity patient, make available to such patient and, if present, to the father of the infant, other relevant family members or caregivers, information about the incidence of postpartum blues and perinatal depression and information to increase awareness of shaken baby syndrome and the dangers of shaking infants. This information shall be discussed with the maternity patient and the father of the infant, other relevant family members, or caregivers who are present at discharge."[27]

Internet mailing lists

More active interest is needed in shaken baby, child abuse, police investigation and even prosecution mailing lists and online forums—so people can communicate with each other about cases of SBS where an official needs to find out information about the case. For example, a prosecutor may have some problems with a certain defense theory. He or she can ask the list, "How can we overcome this?" There is already a very active group of child abuse physicians that addresses SBS and other abusive injuries, but we need to expand this to other disciplines as well, so incidents of Shaken Baby Syndrome can be stopped before tragedy occurs.

SIGCA-MD-L is the listserv of The Special Interest Group on Child Abuse for Medical Providers. The group is sponsored by LifeNet and the Child Abuse Prevention Network out of Cornell University. The listserv is for physicians and those involved in the clinical issues surrounding child abuse—physical and sexual. Another listserv that focuses on child abuse is The International Society For The Prevention Of Child Abuse And Neglect (IPSCAN). The American Professional Society on the Abuse of Children (APSCA) is the leading national organization supporting professionals who serve children and families affected by child maltreatment and violence. They publish a quarterly newsletter, *The APSCA Advisor*, that covers the latest news in practice, research, legislation, publication and events in the field of child maltreatment.

CHAPTER 13

Soothing Crying Babies

There are many reasons why babies fuss and over one hundred ways to soothe a crying baby. Shaking is not one of them. First, let's look at possible sources of a baby's discomfort and then focus on some important strategies that parents and caregivers can use that will help calm a baby. After reading these tips from my book, *101 Ways to Soothe a Crying Baby*, if you know of someone who might benefit from one or more of the suggestions, please share them:

Expressing Discomfort

Babies cry mainly because they are uncomfortable. Such discomfort can be for any number of basic reasons—hunger, temperature, stomach gas, diaper rash, etc. Babies cry to communicate to an adult that they need something. The first strategy is to pick a baby up. Often, attention is the only thing a baby needs to help stop crying.

Seeking Comfort

A baby's needs are simple. Most needs focus on basic comfort. Babies enjoy happy things and people in their environment. Select certain times for stimulation and other times for quiet and comforting physical contact. Some things that can provide comfort to a baby are lukewarm baths, massages, skin-to-skin contact, cuddling, pacifiers and forehead strokes.

Utilize Music and Sound

A baby's hearing is functioning by the third month in utero. Because of this, a baby is used to certain sounds, some more comforting than others. Discover which noises and sounds a baby likes best and use these to your benefit when you need them most. Here are some suggestions: reassure with quiet words, sing softly, play quiet music, hum in low tones or use a music box.

Employ Motion

Motion is one of the best ways to calm a crying baby. It doesn't matter if the baby is moving or the outside world is moving—motion is always an intriguing experience. What works well? Try rocking the baby side to side, taking a drive in a car, using a wind-up swing, doing slight knee bends while holding the baby, gently swinging a baby in a car seat or walking in large circles while holding the baby.

Make Use of Rhythm

Babies respond to rhythmic sounds, patterns and movements. The repetition becomes soothing as well as distracting for them. Parents can create easy rhythms any time. Here are some simple, soothing rhythmic patterns that can be used: gently tap a baby's back, have the baby look at a lighted mobile, have the baby listen to a ticking clock or read rhymes to the baby.

Create a Soothing Environment

Look at the home living environment. Is it chaotic or mellow? What is the best kind of environment for a baby? Does a home's arrangement have an effect on the frequency of a baby's crying? Here are suggestions for creating a more calming environment: lower the lights during a crying episode, have the baby look out a window, hold the baby up to a mirror or play on the carpet with the baby.

Care for the Caregiver

You can do certain things for yourself that will directly help soothe a baby. Parenting and caregiving can be fulfilling and frustrating at the same time. Make sure you are okay before you try to help the baby. Some ways to do this are to relax yourself, meditate for a few minutes, take turns soothing the baby with another person, look for a crying pattern and prepare for it, avoid conflict in the home, treat yourself kindly and keep your mood upbeat. Crying that is hard to console is the primary trigger for a shaking event. Some caregivers are highly sensitive to such crying and can become anxious very quickly, especially when they are alone in the home with the baby. The longer the crying goes, the higher the level of frustration and anger. Even though babies are communicating a need through crying, many adults don't understand this.

Research has shown that crying increases at about two to three weeks of age and peaks around six to eight weeks. It is the negative reaction to crying that complicates the interaction between caregiver and child. The more tension and anger present, the more crying escalates.

New parents and caregivers who are not familiar or bonded with a baby can find themselves unprepared when placed in the role of caring for the baby. If the adult has additional issues in his or her life (job stress, financial problems, addiction issues), then the mix can become potentially lethal.

What can a parent or caregiver do in cases where there is stress when caring for a crying baby? The strategy seems to be multifaceted. First of all, the adult needs to calm down. It is not a situation that is impossible to handle and it is not an emergency situation either. There is a crying baby and when the adult can center him or herself, he or she can center the child. Sometimes the centering doesn't start with the adult. So, a person should use the multiple suggestions listed in this chapter. The key word is "multiple." One or two are not good enough, because the caregiver might not be honing in on what is causing the crying. For example, the baby might be hungry and the adult simply offers a pacifier or talks quietly to the baby. By going through a mental checklist, the caregiver can possibly get to the core of the crying problem. Using a checklist, such as fed, changed, temperature, over-stimulated, tired or scared can help stop the crying. Finally, the adult can try some of the favorite motions that the baby may enjoy—rocking, swinging, walking in circles, deep knee bends, etc.

What if all else fails and the caregiver can't take the stress anymore? Then comes the "adult timeout." Babies don't die from crying alone. Usually babies become exhausted and cry themselves to sleep.

An inconsolable baby should be put in a crib on his or her back, should be checked for safety and the adult should leave the room and close the door. The caregiver should then call another adult for support. The baby can be checked on every five to ten minutes. No parent will become angry if the caregiver says that the baby was inconsolable and was put to bed because the stress was too much.

Finally, any parent who has another person care for his or her baby needs to tell that person about the dangers of shaking. The parent also needs to stress to the caregiver to call him or her if there is a problem with behavior or crying. Usually either issue can be solved easily. Parents also need to speak up to another person if they need a break from caregiving. Most times, the mother is the primary caregiver for a baby. If she becomes overly stressed, she needs to ask the father (or another family member) to take over for her.

Crying is normal and it is short-lived. Parents need to care for themselves and keep their baby safe by using a variety of creative methods when dealing with crying.

Conclusion

When you began this journey, you learned about Patience Gill, an innocent who lost her life after being shaken to death. By learning about her injuries, her victimology and the perpetrator, you found that she was a "classic" shaken baby case. But she is not just a statistic. She was a small person who was communicating a need. She was not out to get anyone. She didn't hold a grudge. She was simply communicating. For that, she was punished. If her father had had some previous parenting intervention, then Patience may not have died so tragically. That is what was missing in her case—the prevention aspect prior to shaking (which is so easily prevented). It is my hope that we learn from Patience's case. Her tragedy is the same as when John David Stewart came home after work one evening in 1905 and shook and slammed his ten-month-old daughter for not being quiet. Nothing has changed. We've only learned more.

After the Eappen case in 1997, a progression of studies occurred and thousands of reports were made in medical literature. Because of these, society now understands SBS more completely. Even in light of this understanding, hundreds to thousands of infants are being shaken each year. Prevention initiatives are ongoing in every section of our nation, but so far only limited change has been achieved. For example, not every state requires hospitals to educate new parents on the dangers of shaking and ways to effectively soothe crying babies. As of 2014, only eighteen out of the fifty states mandate hospital-based SBS prevention. Eight states require employees of licensed childcare centers to receive specialized SBS training. And twelve states have legislation that offers statewide public awareness for

SBS prevention. The state of New York should be commended for having five different pieces of legislation that relate to getting the message about the dangers of shaking out to the community—including schools and correctional facilities. No other state has this number of law-backed SBS education programs for its citizens.

HOW HAS THE MEDIA HANDLED THIS HORRIFIC SUBJECT?

Over the past decade, numerous high-profile media sources (*The New York Times, Washington Post, Discover Magazine*, etc.) have provided coverage about SBS, but their approach has been toward doubt and the prosecution of the wrong. A much more favorable and objective account of SBS would be for a reporter to cover a case from the hospital admission of a shaken child to the conclusion of a jury's verdict—all in real time, not look-back reporting. Then the reporter could speak firsthand with medical personnel, EMS, victim's family members, the accused perpetrator, police investigators and finally prosecutors to tell the story of what goes on over the life of an SBS criminal case. This would be a process that would not only educate the public, but provide accurate reporting of a now controversial and sensitive topic.

WHAT IS HAPPENING IN OUR COURTROOMS?

Even when the identities of the perpetrators of shaking crimes are well-established, their prosecution is difficult, largely due to lack of knowledge on the part of juries and judges, both of whom can be convinced by the strategies of defense teams. It doesn't help the progress of the work that has been done thus far on the validity of the diagnosis of Shaken Baby Syndrome when so many books, articles, newspaper accounts and television programs are produced whose sole purpose is to chip away at the wall that science and medicine have built. SBS has been stripped down by bad press and a growing sense among the American public (this is happening in Britain as well) that SBS is a fallacy. Look at any Internet news blog account of any recent shaken baby case. Nearly half of the comments claim that SBS is a figment of the medical community destined to join the ranks of 1950s UFO sightings. These comments are made by everyday people who have either read accounts, seen programs or heard from neighbors that SBS has been "proven" to be false. What are juries and judges to think with all the lies being circulated? No wonder there has been an increasing number of acquittals of SBS perpetrators.

WHAT CAN BE DONE PRIOR TO THE COURTROOM?

Scene investigations and autopsy protocols surrounding SBS cases are currently not standard and up to par in many jurisdictions of the country. Training and other educational efforts seem to be important vehicles that can only heighten the understanding of SBS among a variety of professionals. Once you have a strong case (which includes all the suggestions that have been mentioned in previous sections of this book), then a prosecutor can proceed with more confidence in his or her ability to secure a conviction. In the courtroom, a team of expert witnesses, timeline documents and defendant statements provide you with a baseline for a solid case.

HOW ARE HOSPITALS TREATING SBS?

Medical schools are beginning to incorporate into their curricula the process of identifying the signs and symptoms of physical child abuse. Yet cases are still being misdiagnosed. When a child presents with lethargy and no outward signs of abuse, then physicians may not jump to order a head CT, since lethargy is a common symptom in flu and other child maladies. But does the physician truly listen to the presenting stories? As previously suggested, amid the words of a presenting history lies the truth. Interwoven might be words like "fall," "crying," "I didn't know" and so on. Though not part and parcel of a child abuse confession, these words and others offer glimpses of a larger story for those who wish to hear. If a physician in the ER would ask, "Who else was at home with the baby when he got sick?" then there would be an opening for a conversation about the stresses of caregiving, versus the more general question, "When did the baby start to show signs of being sick?" Another question that could be asked is, "Does the baby cry often?" and

"How do you handle this?" In the ER and the pediatrician's office, the medical professional should always consider child abuse as a differential to certain signs and symptoms of illness. This might spur further testing, such as blood studies, head CT scans, etc., which might ultimately save the life of a child.

WHAT OCCURS AT VICTIMS' HOMES?

There are parents and caregivers who still believe that shaking is an acceptable way to calm or manage a crying child, even though prevention efforts against shaking have been in place for years. National efforts should go beyond the "don't shake" and soothing crying prevention strategies. They should also include messages of "call for help" (a hotline or another family member) and "adult timeout" (leaving the baby or child in a room alone so the caregiver can cool off from the stresses that crying can present).

Prevention of SBS can reach the general population but agencies need to target those caregivers who are most at risk—young, male, lower income and so on. Each agency should study shaken babies in their own locale over the past five years to look at the reasons for victimology as well as perpetrators. Are there areas of the community that are being missed?

Families of shaken children are often left to fend for themselves. There are no nationally recognized support groups specific to SBS, but thanks to the Internet, there are many social sites, such as Facebook, where families can go to ask questions and get support from each other. The process of the long-term effects of the syndrome becomes emotionally oppressive as families are going through uncharted territory without a guide. They are unsure of the medical, legal and social questions to ask. Having a support group (in person or online) can be a huge aid for families.

Often, the experience of SBS is new to the professionals who handle their cases, for example, the small sheriff's department which has never had a shaken child and is unsure what questions may benefit their case. Or awareness that a timeline could mean the difference in a successful prosecution. Having a supportive forum to go to for help could mean a great deal to law enforcement or social work professionals.

Some recent provisions of support have been set up for both families and professionals. Until 1997, there had been no national front to collectively explore the various aspects of SBS. In the fall of 1997, the mother of an SBS survivor began an Internet mailing list devoted to the families of shaken children and the professionals who worked with them. It quickly became an oasis for many people who had experienced directly the tragedy of such violence. On a computer screen, they could share stories, advice and care. Physicians also developed a child abuse forum which is still going strong. This group presents cases for hundreds of child abuse professionals from around the world to offer opinions and suggestions. This has made a difference in numerous non-definitive cases of abuse.

In 1998, the first national group made up of families of shaken children was established. The Shaken Baby Alliance assists families who have experienced shaking incidents on all levels, be it treatment issues, education or courtroom support. There are several chapters of the Alliance around the United States to offer support and information to anyone in need—family and professional alike. You can visit their website at **www.shakenbaby.com**.

Every two years, Hershey Medical Center and the National Center on Shaken Baby Syndrome alternately host their own conferences on Abusive Head Trauma/Shaken Baby Syndrome. The Hershey program, begun by Dr. Mark Dias, brings in professionals from a clinical and forensic realm to hear presentations that are scientific, peer-reviewed and medically based. At the National Center on Shaken Baby Syndrome-sponsored conference, hundreds of individuals attend to hear state-of-the-art research, programming and family stories. At both conferences, speakers openly address the controversies that are present in the media about the reality of SBS. The more individuals learn and talk about this tragedy, the better prevention and treatment of children and families will be.

CHAMPIONS OF SBS

Though SBS faces many obstacles in the media, in the courtroom and even on the medical examination table, there are also many people who are advocates for SBS education and awareness.

Dr. Betty Spivack is a well-known and well-versed child abuse pediatrician. Besides working in pediatric intensive care units, she is the only pediatrician to have worked in the Office of the Chief Medical Examiner in Kentucky. Currently, Dr. Spivack is a private child abuse consultant, accepting cases for review from prosecutors, defense lawyers, family lawyers, hospital lawyers, municipalities and private entities. She is known to tell the truth as she sees it and does not modify her opinions to benefit either side.

Dr. Mark Dias is professor and vice chair of Neurosurgery as well as director of Pediatric Neurosurgery at Penn State Hershey Medical Center. Dr. Dias is best known for beginning the first hospital-based SBS prevention program, which received national media attention and was subsequently replicated in dozens of hospitals across the U.S. He also is one of the founders of the biannual Abusive Head Trauma conference for professionals and researchers.

Dr. Randell Alexander is chief of the division of Child Protection and Forensic Pediatrics and program director of the Pediatric Child Abuse fellowship at University of Florida College of Medicine in Jacksonville. He is well known in the child abuse arena and has written numerous books and articles on SBS. He also testifies at SBS-related trials across the U.S. He is on the International Advisory Board at the National Center on Shaken Baby Syndrome.

Dr. Christopher Greeley is a pediatrician in Texas and is a member of the American Academy of Pediatrics (AAP) Section on Child Abuse and Neglect Executive Committee. Dr. Greeley is a main researcher on all types of child abuse and has a plethora of information on the many aspects of SBS.

Dr. Robert Block is a past president of the American Academy of Pediatrics (AAP). Dr. Block is also a professor of pediatrics at the University of Oklahoma. Dr. Block was appointed Oklahoma's first Chief Child Abuse Examiner in 1989, and he served in that capacity until October 2011. Dr. Block has authored several papers and a textbook and has delivered over two thousand public presentations.

Dr. Mary Case is the chief medical examiner of St. Louis County and has special interest and expertise in the areas of head injury in both children and adults and in child abuse. She has written and lectured widely in these areas and has consulted with many police agencies, prosecutors, other attorneys and families on cases of child head injury.

Dr. Alex Levin is chief of the Wills Eye Pediatric Ophthalmology and Ocular Genetics Service. He is widely published and is frequently invited to speak at national and international conferences. He is also on the International Advisory Board at the National Center on Shaken Baby Syndrome.

Dr. David Chadwick is the previous director emeritus of Rady Children's Hospital in San Diego. Dr. Chadwick is best-known in the child abuse arena for his research on falls by children. The Chadwick Center at Rady Children's Hospital is named after him. It is one of the largest hospital-based child advocacy and trauma treatment centers in the nation. Dr. Chadwick is also on the International Advisory Board at the National Center on Shaken Baby Syndrome.

Brian Holmgren, JD, is an assistant district attorney general with the Davidson County District Attorney General's Office in Nashville, Tennessee. He is the team leader of the child abuse unit. Holmgren is best known for his manuscripts on SBS in the courtroom. He is one of the best resources in the U.S. for prosecutors needing assistance with difficult SBS cases.

I make the following recommendations in an effort to encourage others to develop strategies to keep children safer; to help treat and ultimately prevent this terrible form of child abuse.

RECOMMENDATIONS

- Social network and search engine support of SBS awareness and prevention campaigns.
- Continued studies on diagnosing SBS through imaging and blood chemistry evaluation.
- Mandated education on child abuse injuries, diagnosis and treatment in medical schools.
- Continued studies on the timing and forces involved in SBS.
- Broadening of the CDC's national tracking of cases identified as SBS.

- Improved childcare and monitoring statutes.
- Changing of state criminal statues for physical child abuse injuries and death.
- Mandated SBS prevention/education in hospitals and schools across all states via a Federal bill.
- Standardize a system within hospitals for identifying, reporting and discussing cases of suspected child abuse.
- Federal or state financial support for families of shaken infants and children.
- Increased education on SBS for law enforcement personnel, prosecuting attorneys and judges.
- Increased education on statement analysis of perpetrators of child abuse for law enforcement personnel.
- Broadening the national support group network for families of shaken infants and children.
- Continued coordinated multi-center hospital studies of SBS processes, including presentation, lab findings and treatment.
- Development of a computerized tool for hospitals to use to help identify likely perpetrators of SBS when presented with an abused infant or child.
- Screening to reduce irresponsible testimony by expert witnesses at SBS trials.
- County reviews of closed cases of past infant deaths to assess if the cause might now be changed to non-accidental and their perpetrators brought to justice.

I end this book on a note of hope. In the midst of all the rhetoric being bandied about there is something that can be done by anyone who is affected by SBS: believe it has occurred.

If you are a medical professional who has been involved with or treated a shaken baby, then be willing to testify in court about the damage that you've witnessed firsthand and what shaking does to the young body. If you are a social worker, get to know the family members of the child—what do they have to say about the shaking incident? Use your interviewing skills to get potentially vital information to help the larger investigation. Document what you hear and notice. Use your peer contacts to help you gain more information about SBS and the sticky areas that are often present.

If you are a law enforcement professional, take your investigation to the next level and work on multiple levels, as previously suggested, to not only identify a subject but make the case solid. Use timelines, statement analysis, polygraphy, scene investigation, video and essential interviewing to close the door on fabricated stories. If you are a prosecutor, don't settle because of media influence. There are many resources available of successfully prosecuted SBS cases. Also, there are key players in the child abuse field whom you can use for consultation and/or as expert witnesses. If you are a judge sentencing a guilty defendant, make the term fair for the life of a child and the toll that has been taken on a family. Make a statement during sentencing that rings out against such abusive acts and the perpetrators who cause the damage. This may be the only shaken baby case over which you preside in your career and sentencing is the time to state your opinion about this violence.

If you are a legislator, please sponsor bills that help curb the scope of SBS and push for their passage. If you are a child welfare agency coordinator, what are some different strategies that your team can use to combat SBS in your community? Are your prevention approaches effective? Do they reach out to the right people in the most efficient ways? Are you working with local hospitals and schools to give alternatives to shaking as a means of dealing with a stressful childcare experience?

If you are a parent, how do you best care for your infant or child? One of the greatest means of keeping your child safe is to know who is caring for him or her. While you can't predict a violent act, you can educate by saying, "Here is what to do if he cries too much or becomes upset. Please call me if you are having trouble controlling him and I can tell you how to calm him down. Please don't do something like shake him, because that can really hurt or even kill a child. Just call me."

Finally, if you are in the media, please be responsible and use common sense and decades of SBS research to drive your words about the evil of SBS, which are very influential to the larger community.

SBS is preventable. While there are pockets in society that will be missed, this deadly form of child abuse can be reduced in terms of the number of occurrences from year to year. Nothing has changed and everything has changed. Let's make change happen in favor of the child in danger who can be saved.

NOTES

Introduction

1. Spaide RF. et al. "Shaken baby syndrome." Am Fam Physician.1990 Apr; 41(4):114–2.

Chapter 1

1. *South Bend Tribune,* AREABriefs, http://community.fortunecity.ws/emachines/e9/209/.

1. *Denver Tribune,* February 4, 1909, Denver, Indiana.

2. *Syracuse Herald,* February 17, 1937, Syracuse, New York.

3. *Charleston Daily Mail,* May 18, 1938, Charleston, West Virginia.

4. Guthkelch, AN. "Infantile Subdural Hematoma and its Relationship to Whiplash Injuries." BMJ 1971; 2: 43–31.

5. Ommaya AK. et al. "Whiplash Injury and Brain Damage. An Experimental Study." JAMA 1968; 204: 285–289.

6. Caffey, J. "Multiple Fractures in Long Bones of Infants Suffering from Chronic Subdural Hematoma." Am J Roentgenol 1946; 56: 16–73.

7. Kempe, CH. et al. "The Battered Child Syndrome." JAMA 1962; 181: 10–12.

8. Caffey, J. "The parent-infant traumatic stress syndrome." Am J Roentgenol 1972 114(2):21–9.

9. Caffey, J. "On the Theory and Practice of Shaking Infants." Am J Dis Child 1972; 124: 16–69.

10. Caffey, J. "The Whiplash-Shaken Infant Syndrome: Manual Shaking by the Extremities with Whiplash-Induced Intracranial and Intraocular Bleedings, Linked with Residual Permanent Brain Damage and Mental Retardation." Pediatrics 1974; 54: 39–03.

11. Peinkofer, J. *Lilacs in the Rain: The Shocking Story of Connecticut's Shaken-Baby Serial Killer.* Rooftop Publishing, 2007.

CHAPTER 3

1. Case, ME, "The Autopsy in AHT." Presented at the NYC AHT/SBS Training Conference Sept. 22, 2011.

2. Cohen, RA; et al. "Cranial Computed Tomography in the Abused Child with Head Injury." AJR 1986; 146: 9–02.

3. Duhaime, AC, et al. "The 'Big Black Brain': Radiographic Changes after Severe Inflicted Injury in Infancy." J Neurotrauma 1993; 10: abstract 1: s59.

4. Jenny, C. et al. "Analysis of Missed Cases of Abusive Head Trauma." JAMA, 1999; 281: 62–26.

5. Zimmerman, RA, et al. "Interhemispheric Acute Subdural Hematoma: a Computed Tomographic Manifestation of Child Abuse by Shaking." Neuroradiology 1978; 16: 3–0.

CHAPTER 4

1. Levin, AV. "Retinal hemorrhage in abusive head trauma." Pediatrics (originally published online) October 4, 2010; DOI: 10.1542/peds.201–220.

2. Levin, AV. "Retinal Hemorrhages of Crush Head Injury: Learning From Outliers" Arch Ophthalmol. 2006; 124 (12):177–774.

3. Lantz, PE, et al. "Perimacular retinal folds from childhood head trauma." BMJ, 2004 Mar 27; 328 (7442):75–.

4. Lueder, GT. et al. "Perimacular retinal folds simulating nonaccidental injury in an infant." Arch Ophthalmol. 2006 Dec; 124 (12):178–.

5. Reddie, IC et al. "Bilateral retinoschisis in a 2-year-old following a three-storey fall." Eye (2010) 24, 1426–1427.

6. Levin, AV. "Retinal hemorrhages: Advances in Understanding." Pediatr Clin North Am. 2009 Apr; 56 (2):33–4.

7. Togioka, BM. et al. "Retinal hemorrhages and shaken baby syndrome: an evidence-based review." J Emerg Med. 2009 Jul; 37 (1):9–06.

8. Laghmari, M. et al. "Birth-related retinal hemorrhages in the newborn: Incidence and relationship with maternal, obstetric and neonatal factors. Prospective study of 2,031 cases." J Fr Ophtalmol. 2014 Feb 24. pii: S0181-5512(14)00012-6.

9. Spivack, B. Commonwealth of KY v Raymond Martin, Appellee; Commonwealth of KY v Christopher A. Davis, Appellee; Nos. 2006-CA-002236, 2006-CA-002237-MR – June 13, 2008, Court of Appeals of Kentucky.

10. Kivlin, JD, et al. "Retinal Hemorrhages in Children Following Fatal Motor Vehicle Crashes: A Case Series."; Arch Ophthalmol. 2008; 126(6):800-804.

11. Trenchs, V. et al. "Retinal haemorrhages in head trauma resulting from falls: differential diagnosis with non-accidental trauma in patients younger than 2 years of age." Childs Nerv Syst 2008 Jul;24(7):81–0.

12. Vinchon, M. et al., "Confessed Abuse Versus Witnessed Accidents in Infants: Comparison of Clinical, Radiological, and Ophthalmological Data in Corroborated Cases," 26 Childs Nerv Syst. 637, 638–39 (2010).

13. Vinchon, M. et al., "Confessed Abuse Versus Witnessed Accidents in Infants: Comparison of Clinical, Radiological, and Ophthalmological Data in Corroborated Cases," 26 Childs Nerv Syst. 637, 638–39 (2010).

14. Bhardwaj G, et al. "A systematic review of the diagnostic accuracy of ocular signs in pediatric abusive head trauma." Ophthalmology. 2010 May; 117(5):983-992.e17.

15. Wygnanski-Jaffe, T, et al. "Postmortem orbital findings in shaken baby syndrome."; Am J Ophthalmol. 2006 Aug; 142(2):233-40.

16. Jenny, C. for the Committee on Child Abuse and Neglect; "Evaluating Infants and Young Children With Multiple Fractures"; www.pediatrics.org/cgi/doi/10.1542/ peds.2006-1795.

CHAPTER 7

1. Barr, R. "What is All That Crying About?" Bulletin of the Centre of Excellence for Early Childhood Development; Volume 6, No 2-September 2007.

2. Brenner, SL, et al. "Race and the shaken baby syndrome: experience at one hospital" J Natl Med Assoc. 1989 February; 81(2): 183–184.

3. Sinal, SH. "Is race or ethnicity a predictive factor in Shaken Baby Syndrome?" Child Abuse Negl. 2000 Sep; 24(9):1241-6.

4. Esernio-Jenssen, D., et al. "Abusive head trauma in children: a comparison of male and female perpetrators." Pediatrics. 2011 Apr; 127(4):64–7.

CHAPTER 8

1. Adelson, L. "The Battering Child," *JAMA*. 1972; 222(2):15–61.

2. Starling, SP and Holden, JR. "Perpetrators of Abusive Head Trauma: a Comparison of Two Geographic Populations." South Med J 2000; 93: 46–65.

3. Berger, RP. "Abusive head trauma during a time of increased unemployment: a multicenter analysis." Pediatrics. 2011 Oct; 128(4):63–3.

4. American Academy of Pediatrics Committee on Child Abuse and Neglect, "Shaken Baby Syndrome: Inflicted Cerebral Trauma." Pediatrics Vol. 92 No. 6 December 1, 1993, 872–875.

5. Schnitzer, PG. & Ewigman, BG., "Child Deaths Resulting From Inflicted Injuries: Household Risk Factors and Perpetrator Characteristics Child Deaths Resulting From Inflicted Injuries: Household Risk Factors and Perpetrator Characteristics." Pediatrics .2005; 116:5 e687e693.

6. Carbaugh, S.F. "Understanding Shaken Baby Syndrome." Adv. Neonatal Care, 2004; 4(2): 105–117.

7. Overpeck, MD et al. "Risk factors for infant homicide in the United States."; New England Journal of Medicine. 1998 Oct 22;339(17):1211-6.

8. Maguire, S. et al., "What Clinical Features Distinguish Inflicted from Non-Inflicted Brain Injury?A Systematic Review." Arch Dis Child 94 860 (2009).

9. Alexander, R. et al. "Serial abuse in children who are shaken." Am J Dis Child. 1990 Jan; 144 (1): 5–0.

10. Adamsbaugh, C. et al. "Abusive Head Trauma: Judicial Admissions Highlight Violent and Repetitive Shaking" Pediatrics Vol. 126 No. 3, September 1, 2010 pp. 546–555.

11. Bergman, AB. et al. "Changing spectrum of serious child abuse." Pediatrics. 1986; 77: 113–116.

12. Gessner, RR. &. Runyan, DK. "The Shaken Infant: A Military Connection?" Arch Pediatr Adolesc Med. 1995; 149 (4): 46–69.

13. Gumbs, GR. et al. "Infant abusive head trauma in a military cohort." Pediatrics. 2013 Oct; 132 (4): 66–6.

14. Brenner, SL. et al. "Race and the Shaken Baby Syndrome: Experience at One Hospital." J. National Med Assoc, 1989; 81: 18–84.

15. Parks, SE, et al. "Characteristics of fatal abusive head trauma among children in the USA: 200–007: an application of the CDC operational case definition to national vital statistics data." Inj Prev. 2012 Jun; 18 (3): 19–.

16. Starling, SP. et al. "Abusive head trauma: the relationship of perpetrators to their victims." Pediatrics 95: 26–62, 1995.

17. Starling, SP and Holden, JR. "Perpetrators of Abusive Head Trauma: a Comparison of Two Geographic Populations." South Med J 2000; 93: 46–65.

18. Starling, SP. et al. "Analysis of perpetrator admissions to inflicted traumatic brain injury in children," Arch Ped Adoles Med. 2004; 158: 45–58.

19. Theodore, AD. et al., "Epidemiologic Features of the Physical and Sexual Maltreatment of Children in the Carolinas." Pediatrics Vol. 115 No. 3, March 1, 2005 pp. e331–e337.

20. Adamsbaugh, C. et al. "Abusive Head Trauma: Judicial Admissions Highlight Violent and Repetitive Shaking" Pediatrics Vol. 126 No. 3, September 1, 2010 pp. 546–555.

21. Esernio-Jenssen, D. et al. "Abusive head trauma in children: a comparison of male and female perpetrators." Pediatrics. 2011 Apr; 127 (4): 64–7.

22. Gumbs, GR. et al. "Infant abusive head trauma in a military cohort." Pediatrics. 2013 Oct; 132 (4): 66–6.

23. http://www.foxnews.com/us/2011/04/30/pa-girl-10-charged-murder-death-baby-547626361/.

24. Breen, D. "Amanda Brumfield: Billy Bob Thornton's daughter gets 20 years for child's death" *Orlando Sentinel*; October 6, 2011; http://articles.orlandosentinel.com/2011-10-06/entertainment/os-amanda-brumfield-sentencing-20111006_1_amanda-brumfield-olivia-madison-garcia-friend.

25. Smith, SR. Petitioner-Appellant, v. Gwendolyn MITCHELL, Warden, Respondent-Appellee.

26. Ibid.

27. Anuto, J. "Dad Gets Max Sentence for Shaken Baby Death." Community Newspaper Group, March 10, 2013; http://www.timesledger.com/stories/2013/10/shakenbabysentence_ne_2013_03_08_q.html.

28. Jenkins, J. "Father Pleads Guilty to Son's Death; Released from Prison." MetroNews, WV; Aug 12, 2013; http://wvmetronews.com/2013/08/12/father-pleads-guilty-to-sons-death-released-from-prison.

CHAPTER 9

1. Bisaro, A. "Monkey Business: Some researchers of landmark shaken-baby syndrome studies question the diagnosis" The Medill Justice ProjectPublished: Dec. 12, 2013; http://www.medilljusticeproject.org/2013/12/12/monkey-business/

2. Personal communication with A.N. Guthkelch, MD 2/03/2014.

3. Carpenter, SL. et al. "Evaluating for Suspected Child Abuse: Conditions That Predispose to Bleeding." Pediatrics Vol. 131 No. 4 April 1, 2013 pp. e1357–e1373

4. Narang, SK, et al. "A *Daubert* Analysis of Abusive Head Trauma/Shaken Baby Syndrome—Part II: An Examination of the Differential Diagnosis." Houston J Health Law & Policy (pending publication).

5. Fackler, JC. "Retinal hemorrhages in newborn piglets following cardiopulmonary resuscitation." Am J Dis Child. 1992 Nov; 146 (11):129–.

6. Levin, AV. "Retinal Haemorrhages and Child Abuse," in David, TJ. ed., *Recent Advances inPaediatrics*, 2000; Churchill Livingstone.

7. Goetting, M and Sowa, B. "Retinal haemorrhage after cardiopulmonary resuscitation in children: an etiologic evaluation." Pediatrics.1990;85(4): 585–588; Gilliland M, Luckenbach M. "Are retinal hemorrhages found after resuscitation attempts? A study of the eyes of 169 children." Am J Forensic Med Pathol. 1993;14(3):187–192.

8. American Academy of Pediatrics Committee on Infectious Diseases. "The relationship between pertussis vaccine and central nervous system sequelae: continuing assessment." Pediatrics. 1996 Feb; 97(2):27–1.

9. Narang, SK, et al. "A *Daubert* Analysis of Abusive Head Trauma/Shaken Baby Syndrome—Part II: An Examination of the Differential Diagnosis." Houston J Health Law & Policy (pending publication).

10. Anderst, J. et al. "Evaluation for Bleeding Disorders in Suspected Child Abuse" Neoreviews Vol. 131 No. 4 April 1, 2013 pp. e1314–e1322.

11. Duhaime, AC et al., "The Shaken Baby Syndrome: A Clinical, Pathological, and Biomechanical Study," 66 J. Neurosurgery 409, 409 (1987).

12. Ibid.

13. Cory, CZ & Jones, MD. "Can Shaking Alone Cause Fatal Brain Injury? A Biomechanical Assessment of the Duhaime Shaken Baby Syndrome Model," 43 Med. Sci. & Law 317, (2003).

14. Wolfson, DR, et al. "Rigid-Body Modeling of Shaken Baby Syndrome." 219 Proc. Inst. Mechanical Engineering (Part H: J. Engineering Med.) 63, 66 (2005).

15. Chadwick, DL. "Shaken Baby Syndrome: Fact, Fiction and Controversy." Presentation at the second National Conference on SBS, September 1998.

16. Brown, JK, and Minns, RA. "Non-Accidental Head Injury, with Particular Reference to Whiplash Shaking Injury and Medico-Legal Aspects." Ped Ann; 1989; 18-:482-494.

17. Bandak, FA. "Shaken Baby Syndrome: A Biomechanical Analysis of Injury Mechanisms," 151 Forensic Sci. Int'L 71, 7–9 (2005).

18. Rooks, VJ et al. "Prevalence and Evolution of Intracranial Hemorrhage in Asymptomatic Term Infants." AJNR June 2008 29: 108–089.

19. Geddes, JF et al. "Neuropathology of Inflicted Head Injury in Children I. Patterns of Brain Damage," 124 Brain 1290 (2001); Geddes, JF et al. "Neuropathology of Inflicted Head Injury in Children II. Microscopic Brain Injury in Infants," 124 Brain 1299 (2001); Geddes, JF et al. "Dural Haemorrhage in Non-Traumatic Infant Deaths: Does it Explain the Bleeding in Shaken Baby Syndrome'?"29 Neuropathology & Applied Neurobiology 14, 1–9 (2003).

20. Punt, J, et al. "The 'unified hypothesis' of Geddes et al is not supported by the data." Pediatric Rehabilitation 2004. 7, 173–184.

21. Binenbaum, Gil, et al. "Retinal hemorrhage and brain injury patterns on diffusion-weighted magnetic resonance imaging in children with head trauma."; Journal of American Association for Pediatric Ophthalmology and Strabismus; Vol. 17, Issue 6, Dec. 2013, 603–608.

22. Chadwick, DL et al. "Annual Risk of Death Resulting From Short Falls Among Young Children: Less Than 1 in 1 Million", 121 Pediatrics 1213, (2008).

23. Barlow, B, et al. "Ten years of experience with falls from height in children." J Pediatr Surg 1983; 18:509–11.

24. Warrington, SA et al. "Accidents and Resulting Injuries in Premobile Infants: Data from the ALSPAC Study", Arch. Dis. Child. 104, (2001).

25. Haney, SB. et al. "Characteristics of Falls and Risk of Injury in Children Younger Than 2 Years.", 26 Pediatric Emergency Care 914, 915 (2010).

26. Thompson, AK et al. "Pediatric Short-Distance Household Falls: Biomechanics and Associated Injury Severity,"43 Accident Analysis Prevention 143, (2011).

27. Spivak, B. "Falls from height, physical findings in children." In: Payne-James J, Byard R, Corey T, Henderson C, eds. Encyclopedia of Forensic and Legal Medicine. Oxford, England: Elsevier Academic Press; 2005:30–10.

28. Gardner, HA. "A Witnessed Short Fall Mimicking Presumed Shaken Baby Syndrome (Inflicted Childhood Neurotrauma)," Pediatric Neurosurg 2007; 43(5):43–.

29. Thibault, K. testimony; State of AZ vs. West & West 2 CA-CR 2008-0342 7; NO. CR-20063310; July 25, 2008.

30. Anderson, M. "Does Shaken Baby Syndrome Really Exist?" *Discover* magazine; http://discovermagazine.com/2008/dec/02-does-shaken-baby-syndrome-really-exist.

31. Barnes, PD et al. "Infant Acute Life-Threatening Event-Dysphagic Choking Versus Nonaccidental Trauma," 17 Seminars In Pediatric Neurology 7, –0 (2010).

32. Ibid.

33. Morad, Y, et al. "Correlation between retinal abnormalities and intracranial abnormalities in the shaken baby syndrome." Am J Ophthalmol 2002; 134:354–9; Schloff S, et al. "Retinal findings in children with intracranial hemorrhage." Ophthalmology 2002; 109 (8):1472–6.

34. Donohoe, M. "Evidence-Based Medicine and Shaken Baby Syndrome Part 1: Literature Review." 24 Am. J. of Med. Pathology 239, 24–1 (2003).

35. Bazelon, E. "Shaken-Baby Syndrome Faces New Questions in Court." New York Times Magazine; Feb. 2, 2011.

36. Plunkett, J. "Fatal Pediatric Head Injuries Caused by Short Distance Falls,"22 Am. J. Forensic Med. Pathology 1, 10 (2001).

37. Plunkett, J. testimony State v. Carr, 2010 Ohio 2764, 28 Ohio Ct. App., Hamilton County June 18, 2010.

38. Leetsma, J. "Shaken Baby Syndrome: Do Confessions by Alleged Perpetrators Validate the Concept?" J Am Phys Surg 2006 Vol.2, No. 1; 1–6.

39. Uscinski, R. Testimony at 21, State v. Cutro (South Carolina 1999).

40. Holmgren, B. "Damage Control in Abusive Head Trauma (AHT) Cases – A Legal Perspective." http://www.idcartf.org/ckfinder/userfiles/files/holmgren _Legal%20Damage%20Control%20in%20AHT%20Cases%20Fatalities%20 Conf%202009%20revised%201-17-11.pdf.

41. Scheibner, V. "Shaken Baby Syndrome- The Vaccination Link," *Nexus Magazine*, August-September 1998.

42. Innis, M. "Vaccines, Apparent Life-Threatening Events, Barlow's Disease, and Questions about Shaken Baby Syndrome." J Am Phys Surg 2006 Vol.2, No. 1; 1–6

43. Innis, M. Letter, electronic BMJ; April 27, 2004.

44. Narang, SK, et al. "A *Daubert* Analysis of Abusive Head Trauma/Shaken Baby Syndrome—Part II: An Examination of the Differential Diagnosis." Houston J Health Law & Policy (pending publication).

CHAPTER 10

1. Struthers, M. "The Evidence Base for Shaken Baby Syndrome." BMJ Online; 7 Sept. 2004; http://www.bmj.com/rapid-response/2011/10/30/%E2%80%9Cshaken -baby%E2%80%9D-conviction-overturned-case-alan-yurko.

CHAPTER 11

1. Bass, M. "Death-scene investigation in sudden infant death." New England Journal of Medicine,1986 Jul 10;315(2):10.

2. Bourgeois, M, et al. "Epilepsy associated with shaken baby syndrome"; Child's Nervous System, February 2008, Volume 24, Issue 2, 16–72.

3. S.H. Adams, "Statement Analysis: What Do Suspects' Words Really Reveal?" FBI Law Enforcement Bulletin, October 1996.

4. Christian, CW, Block, R and the Committee on Child Abuse and Neglect. "Abusive Head Trauma in Infants and Children." Pediatrics Vol. 123 No. 5 May 1, 2009 pp. 1409–1411.

5. Estelle v. McGuire, 502 U.S. 62 (1991) 112 S.Ct. 475.

6. U.S. v. Gaskell, 985 F.2d 1056 (11th Cir. 1993).

7. State of Wisconsin v. Edmunds, 746 N.W.2d 590 (Wis. Ct. App. 2008).

8. State v. Edwards, 2011-Ohio-1752.

9. Grant v. Warden, 2008-Conn.- 1402.

10. Holmgren, B. "Damage Control in Abusive Head Trauma Cases – A Legal Perspective." http://www.idcartf.org/ckfinder/userfiles/files/holmgren _Legal%20Damage%20Control%20in%20AHT%20Cases%20Fatalities%20 Conf%202009%20revised%201-17-11.pdf.

11. Melendez-Diaz v. Massachusetts, 557 U.S. 305 (2009).

12. Holmgren, B. "Evaluating Abusive Head Trauma Cases – Medical, Investigative & Prosecutorial Perspectives." http://www.idcartf.org/ckfinder/ userfiles/files/holmgren_Evaluating%20AHT%20Cases%20Medical%20%20 Legal%20Investigative%20Perspectives%202008%20(revised%2011-2-10).pdf.

13. Ibid.

14. State v. Calise, 2012-Ohio-4797; http://detroit.cbslocal.com/2014/01/18/man -gets-life-in-prison-in-death-of-3-month-old-daughter/.

15. Commonwealth v. Martin, Commonwealth v. Davis, 2008 KY.

CHAPTER 12

1. Peinkofer, J. *Silenced Angels: the Medical, Legal and Social Aspects of Shaken Baby Syndrome.* (2002) Auburn House Publishing p. 20–09.

2. Ibid.

3. http://www.londonnet.co.uk/ln/talk/news/louise_woodward_notguilty.html.

4. Karlin, M. "Damned If She Does, Damned If She Doesn't: De-Legitimization of Women's Agency in Commonwealth V. Woodward." Columbia Journal of Gender and Law, Vol. 18, No. 1.

5. Carlin, J. "Profile: The Eappens; A Dream Lies Shattered." Independent Voices, 11/9/97. http://www.independent.co.uk/voices/profile-the-eappens- a-dream-lies-shattered-1292932.html.

6. Berger, RP, et al. "Abusive Head Trauma During a Time of Increased Unemployment: A Multicenter Analysis." Pediatrics, published online. http:// pediatrics.aappublications.org/content/early/2011/09/15/peds.2010-2185. abstract?sid=580cab9e-faea-4092-b588-84671da67b97.

7. Peinkofer, J. http://childabuseconsulting.blogspot.com, 2012.

8.   Kandall, C. "Education Concerning Whiplash Shaken Infant Syndrome: An Unmet Need." (letter). Amer J Dis Child, 1990; 144:1180.

9.   Hunchak, C. "The Upstate New York Shaken Baby Syndrome (SBS) Education Program" In Volpe, R and Lewko, J Preventing Neurotrauma: A Casebook of Evidence Based Practices (2006) http://legacy.oise.utoronto.ca/research/ONF -SBSPrevention/Background/SBS%20Case%20Study-Hunchak-revised%2006.pdf

10. http://www.eastbaypediatrics.com/expecting.php.

11. http://editiondigital.net/publication/?i=55877.

12. http://ce.nurse.com/course/ce657/pediatric-abusive-head-trauma/.

13. https://www.unitypoint.org/blankchildrens/shaken-baby-prevention.aspx.

14. http://www.cdc.gov/concussion/pdf/preventing_sbs_508-a.pdf.

15. http://www.preventchildabuse-ri.org/parents/shakenbabysyndrome.html.

16. http://www.criminaljustice.ny.gov/legalservices/ch110_cynthiaslaw.htm.

17. http://www.odh.ohio.gov/~/media/ODH/ASSETS/Files/cfhs/shaken%20 baby%20syndrome/claireslaw.ashx.

18. http://www.shakenbabyva.org/information/presentations/.

19. http://www.ncsl.org/research/human-services/shaken-baby-syndrome- prevention-legislation.aspx.

20. Ibid.

21. Ibid.

22. http://www.health.ny.gov/facilities/hospital/maternity/public_health_law_ section_2803-j.htm.

23. http://www.ncsl.org/research/human-services/shaken-baby-syndrome- prevention-legislation.aspx.

24. Ibid.

25. http://webserver.rilin.state.ri.us/Statutes/TITLE40/40-11/40-11-17.HTM.

26. http://www.ncsl.org/research/human-services/shaken-baby-syndrome- prevention-legislation.aspx.

27. http://leg1.state.va.us/cgi-bin/legp504.exe?000+cod+32.1-134.01.